SPANISH MOROCCO

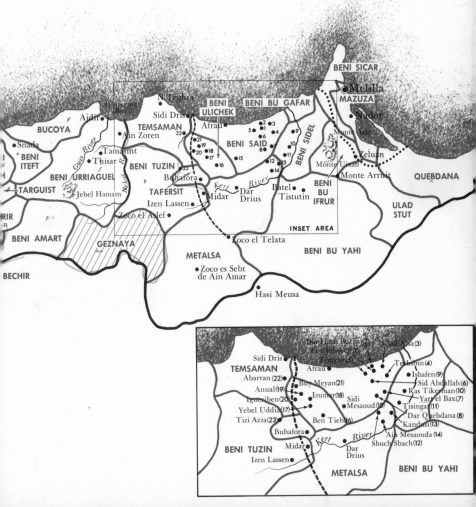

Rebels in the Rif

Rebels

Stanford University Press

in the Rif

ABD EL KRIM AND THE RIF REBELLION

David S. Woolman

Stanford, California   1968

Stanford University Press
Stanford, California
London: Oxford University Press

Printed in the United States of America

L.C. 68-12333

For JOHN HARLAN WOOLMAN
and MARIE BOLLES MOHLER

PREFACE

Whereas European imperialism in Morocco has been well documented, the history of the Spanish Protectorate in Morocco, and the Rif Rebellion in particular, have received little attention in works written in English. The Englishmen Walter Harris, in 1927, C. V. Usborne, in 1936, and Rupert Furneaux, in 1967, have written interesting but incomplete accounts of this era, and the American correspondents Vincent Sheean, in 1925, and Webb Miller, in 1936, published their impressions after brief interviews with some of the rebellion's leading personalities and quick visits to some of the battle sites. The best concise account of the Spanish Moroccan Protectorate and the Rif Rebellion is given by Stanley Payne in his *Politics and the Military in Modern Spain,* 1967. However, to the best of my knowledge, no writer before me has considered in as much detail the problems Spain encountered in the attempt to establish her Moroccan Protectorate.

In *Lawrence of Arabia,* Richard Aldington writes that "the difficulties of a biographer's trying to discover the facts are baffling, discouraging, and at times insuperable." I will vouch for the truth of this statement. In assembling the materials for this book, I found that the best sources of detailed information about Spanish Morocco are the books written by Spanish and French army officers and civilian administrators who fought against or worked with the tribesmen, and who knew them as well as anybody did. However, many of these books are hard to come by, and they vary considerably in quality and importance.

Rebels in the Rif is written largely from a European point of view, if only because European documentation outweighs Moroccan sources. Nevertheless, I have a very real sympathy for Abd el

Krim, for the Rifians, and indeed for all Moroccans, in whose country I have lived on and off for the past sixteen years.

My book begins with a discussion of twentieth-century European rivalry for control of Morocco, the political condition of that country in the early 1900's, the eventual triumph of France over her various rivals, and the subordinate role assigned to Spain in the Moroccan scheme of things. It goes on to describe the mountainous area of northern Morocco, over which Spain had long exercised a certain degree of peripheral control, and the tribes, particularly the Rifians, who live there—their economy, their way of life, and their relationship to the Moroccan Sultanate. Subsequent chapters are devoted to Spanish interests in Morocco during the fifty years preceding the establishment of the Protectorate in 1912, to the attempted occupation of the Spanish Zone by its new masters, and to the advent of Abd el Krim's rebellion in 1921. The tremendous rout of the Spanish Army at Anual is detailed, including its political effects in both Spain and Morocco, which culminated in the Spanish withdrawal from Chaouen.

An account of France's involvement in the Rif Rebellion, the military cooperation between France and Spain, and the ultimate defeat of the Rifian rebels concludes this history of the Protectorate, and brings the reader to the summer of 1927, when Spanish Morocco was at long last occupied and governed as a single unit. A final chapter traces briefly the subsequent careers of the leaders on both sides of the rebellion, shows how the uprisings were related to the Moroccan nationalist liberation movement of the middle 1950's, and describes the setting up of the modern Moroccan state and its present relation to the Rif.

The problems encountered in attempting a transliteration from Arabic or from *thamazighth* (the Berber language of the Rif) into English are considerable. When one considers that the name for the mountain town near Tetuan is variously spelled Chaouen, Shawan, Chauen, Xauen, Chefchaouene and Chechaouene, and that the most common Arabic name, Mohamed, is also spelled Mohammed, Muhamed, Mohamet, and various other ways, one has some idea of the difficulties involved. In general, the French have been more successful at such transliteration than the Spanish. My own solution has been to use names and places as I have encountered them in source material—Spanish terms for the Spanish Zone and French terms for the French Zone—but even here I have had to be inconsistent.

I owe an enormous debt to the American social anthropologist David Hart for sharing with me his expert analyses of the politico-social structure of the Rifian tribes, and for commenting on many other aspects of northern Moroccan tribal life. I am grateful too for the friendliness and good humor with which he endured my frequently obtuse interpretations of anthropological data. I wish to thank James F. Herriott for his help in researching material; Daphne Whitmarsh for her assistance with maps; Curt Day for his firsthand information about the Escadrille Chérifienne; and Carmen Griffin and Ricardo Saavedra of the United States Information Service library of Tangier for their many kindnesses. I am also indebted to Father Enrique López de Toro of the Biblioteca Nacional in Madrid, Francisco Vélez of the Biblioteca Española in Tangier, A. J. Sindall of the library of the British Embassy at Rabat, and E. F. E. Ryan of the Garrison Library at Gibraltar for their friendly cooperation. Abdeslam ben Thami ould Hadj assisted me with Arabic translations and acted as my guide on tours of the Rif.

Thanks are also due to Mohamed Azerkan, George Greaves, Ian Moxon, Marie Black, Eric Gifford, Merle Edelman, Donald Angus, Len Cowley, John Koon, Burnett Bolloten, Lic. Alfonso Quintana y Pena, George Hills, and John Wall, all of whom contributed to the book's production in various ways; and to Jess Bell and Gene Tanke of Stanford University Press, as well as to Stanley Payne of the University of California at Los Angeles, who supplied invaluable assistance and direction.

Tangier, 1968   D.S.W.

CONTENTS

MAPS

Rebels in the Rif

1. THE BACKGROUND

WHEREAS the relations between Spaniards and Moroccans cover several hundred years, the origins of the Spanish Protectorate in northern Morocco are to be found in modern European imperialism. Although it was the corner of the African continent closest to Europe (only eight miles separate Gibraltar from Ceuta across the Straits), Morocco at the dawn of the twentieth century was largely unknown to the Western world. In fact, the very name of the country—"Morocco" in English, "Maroc" in French, and "Marruecos" in Spanish—derives from a Western mispronunciation of the word "Marraksh" (Marrakech), the name of a red-walled city at the southern border of the Atlantic coastal plain that in 1900 was one of Morocco's three national capitals.* The Moroccans themselves called their country "Maghrib al Aqsa"—"the Farthest West."

The Phoenicians and the Carthaginians explored and settled the northern Moroccan seacoast in ancient times. The ubiquitous Romans, after founding Tingis, near the site of modern Tangier, eventually went on to settle as far south as the Sebu River: to found Tamuda, in the mountains near Tetuan; Lixus, outside modern Larache; Banasa, near Souk el Arba del Rharb; and Volubilis, north of Meknes. But these alien peoples either had been absorbed into the native Berber population through intermarriage or had been swept away altogether when the first Arab conquerors overran the northwestern corner of Africa in the seventh and eighth centuries after Christ.

The Arabs did not conquer Morocco with a sword in one hand

---

* In 1900, the three capitals were Marraksh in the south and Fez and Meknes in the north.

and the Koran in the other; their religion alone was sufficient. It appealed to the Berbers because it was simple and practical, worldly and tolerant, with moral force and a coherent doctrine.[1] The cultured Arab officials who settled in the cities and intermarried were an impressive lot, and the Moroccan people sought to emulate them. According to Roger le Tourneau, the cult of Islam gained such widespread and easy acceptance that by the end of the reign of Sultan Mulay Idris II in the ninth century, virtually the entire population of Morocco professed the Islamic religion and spoke the Arabic tongue.[2]

Until the first years of the twentieth century, no European nation had been successful in establishing more than isolated trading posts on Moroccan territory. Though many attempts had been made by Portuguese, Englishmen, and others to penetrate the interior of the country, they had failed. By 1900 Portugal and England had withdrawn entirely from Morocco, and only Spain, with her Mediterranean presidios of Ceuta and Melilla, actually possessed territory in Morocco. (Tangier, which was to be internationalized in 1925, was held over the years by a series of rulers including the Sultan, the Portuguese, the Berbers, the Spanish, and the English.)

It was ultimately the imperialistic scramble for Africa that brought the European powers to Morocco in full force. By the turn of the century, England, France, Portugal, and Belgium had already staked out vast claims in Africa; and now two new contenders, Germany and Italy, demanded to be allowed to enter the field. France, because she had built the Suez Canal and thus had influence in Egypt, held the advantage in this competition. She had occupied Morocco's neighbor Algeria in the 1830's, and had taken over Tunisia as a protectorate in 1881. Now she looked hungrily at Morocco. But both Spain and Germany were anxious to prevent further French aggrandizement, and England, ever conscious of the proximity of Morocco to the English fortress of Gibraltar, was determined to make Gibraltar safe by demanding that Tangier be internationalized.[3] On the eve of the twentieth century, Morocco was surrounded by powers determined to plunder her and to secure their own future on the African continent at her expense.

A land of barren mountains and deserts, rarely unified or paci-

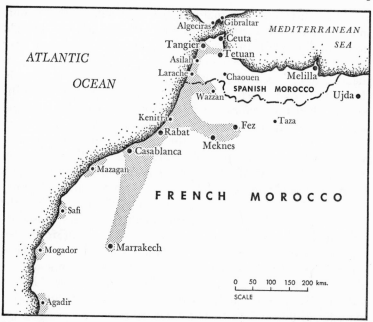

Map 1. Morocco in 1900. The extent of the Blad l-Makhzen is shown by the shaded area.

fied, chronically misruled, inhabited by a fanatically xenophobic population made up largely of primitive Muslim tribesmen, Morocco presented a challenge to the colonizer. Theoretically the land was ruled by a Sultan, who was allowed by custom to designate his successor; but in practice, this nomination was subject to ratification by the *ulema*—councils of wise men and religious leaders at Fez and Marrakech. Their announcement of ratification was usually the signal for a bloody revolt somewhere in the land, for there was sure to be more than one claimant to the throne. Each new Sultan was forced to gather an army and defend his claim among the tribes scattered throughout the country, then travel about enforcing his demands for taxes. To European observers used to less chaotic means of government, Morocco appeared to be in a state of constant anarchy, but the true picture was somewhat different. There was no lack of central authority in Morocco. The Sultan was acknowledged by all to be the spiritual head of state; but he was acknowledged as political head of state only in those areas he or his men had actually visited and pacified—that is, only in those areas that the royal army and tax collectors actually held under their control. In 1900, the Sultan's control extended over two rough triangles: one bounded by Tangier in the north, Fez in the east, and Rabat in the south; the other running from Rabat in the north to Marrakech in the east to Mogador (Essaouira) in the south.[4] These two regions, which contained all the chief cities and most of the easily accessible coastal plain, comprised no more than 20 per cent of the total area of the country, and were inhabited mainly by Arabs and Arabicized Berbers. Together the two regions comprised the Blad l-Makhzen (the land held by the government). All the rest of Morocco, most of which was mountainous country populated by Berber tribes, was known as the Blad s-Siba (the land of dissidence). The boundaries of the two areas constantly fluctuated as the royal forces withdrew or advanced. (More often than not, Carleton Coon says, the Sultan's men were unable to collect taxes directly; but the very threat of their presence was often sufficient to bring about submission, since it was well known that they lived off the land in whatever area they were attempting to pacify, killing and stealing as it pleased them.)

Only one Sultan, Mulay Ismail, who ruled from 1672 to 1727, proved capable of bringing most of the country under control. He maintained order by being demonstrably tougher than any of his opponents: reputedly sadistic, he is said to have killed more than twenty thousand persons with his own hands. At all events, Mulay Ismail virtually freed the country of bandits and rebels. This was an exceptional feat, for few Sultans were capable of operating effectively for the good of the people under the prevailing elastic system of governmental control.

In 1900, Morocco came under the rule of a twenty-year-old Sultan, Abd el Aziz. An intelligent, charming, well-intentioned young man, Abd el Aziz had grown up under the regency of the remarkable Ba Ahmed, the son of a Negro slave, who through a combination of intrigue and ability had become Court Chamberlain under Abd el Aziz's father, Mulay Hassan. Ba Ahmed had carefully encouraged the young prince to forgo the cares of state and to indulge himself in luxuries. When Mulay Hassan died in 1894, Ba Ahmed seized power and ruled Morocco virtually singlehanded until his death in 1900. According to Walter Harris, Ba Ahmed saw to it that Abd el Aziz was diverted from state matters as much as possible. Abd el Aziz's palaces were filled with mechanical toys, gold knicknacks, and other costly frivolities. He even possessed a miniature golden train, in which he traveled back and forth between his various palaces at Fez.[5] To support the reckless extravagances of Abd el Aziz and the corrupt government of Ba Ahmed, the Sultan's *mehallas* (troops) ranged everywhere, attempting to expand the boundaries of the Blad l-Makhzen. Opposition to the Sultan grew. The Bu Hamara Revolt broke out in the northwest in 1902, and all the land between the Algerian border and Fez, with the exception of the Rif, fell to the rebels. In the Jibala, the mountainous area of the northwest, Raisuli, a Sherif famous for his rapacity, terrorized the people. Abd el Aziz was totally unable to deal with either Bu Hamara or Raisuli, and anarchy seemed imminent. It soon became clear to all interested European powers that the Sherifian Empire was a fiction, and that Morocco was an unstable agglomeration of tribes.*

At this time the Sultanate was accustomed to depending heavily upon England's friendly support, locally interpreted since the 1850's by English diplomats like Sir John Drummond-Hay and William Kirby Green, as well as by such freelance gentlemen of affairs as Caid Maclean and Walter B. Harris.† Moroccans were horrified at the Western affectations of their Sultan, who attempted to ape his British mentors in many ways, and when English engineers were called in to survey the Meknes-Fez railroad bed, the local populace was convinced that the young Sultan intended to sell the land to infidels. A much more damaging incident

---

* The Sultan was always chosen from among the Sherifs—noble families who traced their lineage directly to the Prophet Mohamed.

† Sir Harry Maclean, one of the many colorful characters of this era, was a Scotsman who at one time had been a subaltern in the 69th Foot posted to the British garrison at Gibraltar. According to the British community at Tangier, Maclean ran off with his colonel's wife and set himself up as a merchant in Tangier. Somehow he managed to meet and become friendly with Sultan Mulay Hassan, who made him Inspector General of the Royal Army. (See Landau, p. 55, and Maxwell, p. 66.) Walter Harris, another English friend of three successive Sultans, was a wealthy aristocrat who came to Morocco in the 1880's, was captivated by the country, and stayed on for the rest of his life. An author with a flamboyant style, a traveler, a raconteur par excellence, Harris was Moroccan correspondent for the *London Times*, an intimate member of the Sultan's Court, and an unofficial agent of the British Government.

took place in October 1902, when the Moroccan fanatic who had assassinated Dr. Cooper, an English missionary at Fez, took sanctuary in a *zawia,* or place of pilgrimage (and a refuge for criminals), at the holy village of Mulay Idris, north of Meknes.[6] The Sultan ordered him dragged out and killed—a deed without precedent.

As the most important power in Morocco by virtue of her years of support of the Sultanate, England faced a dilemma. Though she wished heartily to strengthen the Sultanate and thus prevent France from encroaching upon the Moroccan preserve, she had to face the fact that in her recent struggle with the Boers she had lost face with the rest of the world as a military power. The new, dynamic, militaristic Germany was a very real threat to British hopes in Europe. Above all, England hoped for a prolonged period of peace and reorganization in order to build up her strength. Fortunately, the policy of Edward VII, newly come to the British throne upon the death of his mother, Queen Victoria, was one of magnanimity and good will toward all nations.[7] This policy applied particularly to France, where Edward had spent many delightful vacations as a young man, and where he enjoyed genuine popularity. In need of allies as a buttress against the German threat, England turned to her neighbor across the channel; and in casting about for some diplomatic cord with which to bind France to her support, she decided to utilize the situation in Morocco.

The French Foreign Minister at this time was Théophile Delcassé, an energetic diplomat who believed in the greatness of France.[8] It was his firm conviction that only territorial expansion could make and keep France a world power, and that because England was the world's leading maritime nation, France, as a colonial power, should cooperate with her. From the point of view of the French, anything that would help consolidate their North African empire while at the same time thwarting Germany would be a desirable move. Germany's smashing defeat of France in the Franco-Prussian War had been a terrible national humiliation, and the French needed to reassure themselves. It was imperative that France reestablish her reputation: it was in this spirit that she contemplated the conquest of Morocco. As Jean Jaurès said in 1906, "The occupation of Morocco . . . was a mission of glory."[9]

An Anglo-French agreement, signed in April 1904, permitted England liberty of action to further her aims and interests in Egypt, and granted identical leeway to France in Morocco. The British Government agreed that France would be responsible for the security of Morocco, and would take care of that country's administrative, economic, and military needs as well. In the light of subsequent developments, it is interesting to note that in Article 2 of this agreement, the French Government declares that "it is not its intention to change the political status of Morocco," but, "as a Power coterminous with Morocco to a vast extent" (a reference to French-controlled Algeria), to see to it that "the tranquillity of the country is preserved." No fortifications were to be allowed along the coasts between the Atlantic Ocean and the Spanish presidio of Melilla, situated on the Mediterranean far to the northeast, but Spain was to be allowed to hold whatever fortresses she already possessed in those areas. Furthermore, England and France agreed that Spain, because of her geographical position and her possessions on the Mediterranean littoral, was to be given special consideration.[10] This last agreement was a perfect example of the way in which British foreign policy functioned during this era: give generously, but make sure the gift, if it does not actually strengthen the British position, at least does not menace it. England preferred that the comparatively weak Spanish hold Morocco's northern margins if the French were to occupy the bulk of the country. France was to negotiate with the Spanish about this territorial arrangement and to inform the British of the result. A secret treaty signed at the same time by the British and French reconfirmed France as the sole arbiter and judge of any arrangement with Spain.

France had quietly taken the initiative early with regard to Spanish interests in Morocco. In 1902, Foreign Minister Delcassé had secretly proposed to Madrid a division of Morocco, promising Spain all the land north of the Sebu River, including the major cities of Fez and Taza as well as the Atlantic port of Agadir, and all the land below the Sous River far to the south.[11] But Spain feared British reaction if this scheme were discovered, and therefore rejected France's offer. Meanwhile the French were courting Italy, and by an agreement reached in 1903, France pledged herself to uphold Italian priority in Libya in exchange for a similar

French priority in Morocco. As for Spain, after the Anglo-French Agreement of 1904 providing for Spanish rights in Morocco had been signed, she found the necessary courage to complete an accord with France, in October 1904.[12] The public treaty briefly stated that France and Spain had agreed on the extent of their respective rights in Morocco; but a secret treaty, signed at the same time, was more explicit. This time the French were substantially less generous than they had been two years earlier, arguing that since they had been forced to give away certain rights in Libya, they should be given more land in Morocco as compensation. For this reason Spain was to receive only that portion of northern Morocco from the Muluya River on the east to the Atlantic Ocean on the west, and from the Mediterranean Sea on the north to a meandering line on the south running roughly east to west some twenty-five miles north of the Wergha River above Fez, plus a small desert area on the Atlantic coast far to the south of French Morocco. To help the Sultan keep order, Spain would furnish police officers at Tetuan and Larache, and France would furnish some at Rabat and Casablanca. Spain promised not to exercise her right of action in Morocco unless she had first obtained the consent of France. (In all these schemes, Tangier and its immediate environs on the northwest brow of the country were treated as a special international entity.) In order not to arouse international jealousies, the accord was kept secret until 1911, when France and Spain were already partially installed in Morocco. What the Moroccans might have thought of this arrogant division of their territory seems to have been considered unimportant, if it was considered at all.

The Anglo-French Agreement was to last for thirty years, and to be renewable at five-year intervals thereafter. There can be no doubt that this treaty and its adjuncts represented a triumph for France. The British, it can be argued, gave away an area—Morocco—in which their prestige and influence were paramount, in return for nothing more than the right to go ahead in another area—Egypt—where they already held effective military control. Spain thought she was getting something at a bargain price; Italy had been sidetracked; Germany had been effectively ignored; and in addition to a recognized claim to her new territory, France had acquired Britain as her ally against the day when Germany might provoke trouble in Europe.

For Spain, the decision to share in the partitioning of Morocco was a fateful one. The Spanish could not resist what appeared to be a bargain at the time; and yet Spain had no specific colonial policy nor any concrete plans for the territory that was to be hers. Raymond Carr believes that Spain accepted the Moroccan Protectorate out of pride, since she could not afford to appear to be a minor power incapable of taking part in the colonial scramble.[13] In any event, by the end of 1904, France had eliminated most of her rivals, and the fate of Morocco was all but sealed. As the historian E. D. Morel expressed it: "A secret sentence of doom had ... been pronounced against Morocco. France was to play the role of executioner, Spain that of interested assistant, and Britain that of interested witness."[14] There remained only one difficulty for France to surmount, and that was the problem of Germany, who refused to be ignored.

The Germans had been in Morocco as traders for many years,[15] and Oskar Lenz and Friedrich Rohlfs, German explorers, had been among the very first Europeans to travel extensively in the country during the latter half of the nineteenth century. By 1885, German shipping along the Moroccan coast was third in importance, behind that of England and France. By 1913, no fewer than twenty German steamers, each with a displacement of 1,500 to 2,000 tons, were servicing Moroccan ports. These firms invested in Morocco without guns or massacres, and there were nine German consulates in Morocco as well as German merchants in all the larger towns. Germans owned more land in Morocco, paid for in cash, than all other nationals combined; and, according to Morel, German post offices were the most numerous and best equipped.[16] German commercial endeavors were spread from Melilla all the way down the Atlantic coast to Agadir, and extended inland as far as Taroudant, forty miles from Agadir in the southern mountains, and even farther along the valley of the Sous River. Thorough, intelligent, and industrious, the Germans mastered Arabic and Berber dialects, then sent experts back into the mountains to copy native utensils and patterns, which were produced in iron and enamelware in Germany for sale on the Moroccan market. Credit terms were easy to obtain from the Germans, and in general they attended carefully and honestly to any complaints that arose. For these reasons, and because they were able to produce goods inexpensively, the Germans far outdid the French and

British in their economic dealings in Morocco. Walter Harris has made the telling point that Britain sold at comparatively high prices the goods that she felt the Moroccans *ought* to buy; whereas the Germans produced goods that the Moroccans actually wanted, and priced them within the reach of all.

Germany twice attempted to wedge her way into Moroccan political affairs. Even though Kaiser Wilhelm had told both Edward VII of England and Alfonso XIII of Spain that he had absolutely no interest in Morocco, diplomatic intrigue changed the picture.[17] The German Chancellor, Von Bülow, thought he could get rid of the Germanophobe Delcassé if he could persuade the Kaiser to take time off from his annual Mediterranean spring cruise to make a surprise landing at Tangier and announce his support of the Sultanate. The Kaiser agreed. In spite of a rough landing and a stallion that nearly threw him as he rode through the medina, the Kaiser paid a dramatic visit to Tangier at the end of March 1905.[18] He made a bombastic speech, claiming that Germany had valuable business interests in Morocco and that she would protect Moroccan sovereignty by lending financial assistance to the Sultan if need be. This bold statement frightened Germany's rivals, for it sounded as though Germany was prepared to enter the Moroccan fray in earnest. The Germans finally saw themselves rid of Delcassé: many of the leaders of the French Government feared that he was too defiantly anti-German, and forced him to resign. Nevertheless, his policy of isolating Germany and creating an Anglo-French alliance was to triumph eventually.

When the Kaiser persuaded Sultan Abd el Aziz to call a conference of all powers interested in Morocco, most of Europe, anxious to avert a general war, attended. This conference was held in 1906 at the Spanish port of Algeciras, westward around the bay from Gibraltar and diagonally across the Straits from Tangier.[19] In addition to Germany and Morocco, England, France, Spain, Italy, the United States, Austria-Hungary, Belgium, Holland, Portugal, Denmark, Russia, and even tiny Luxembourg were represented. The various accords and treaties that France had previously made with England, Spain, and Italy now stood her in good stead; and both the Kaiser's Tangier landing and his calling of the Algeciras Conference had brought France and England closer together. The result of the Act of Algeciras was to strengthen the French position in Morocco and to weaken that of Germany. Specifically, the signatory powers promised to uphold the sovereignty of the Sultan but at the same time to award one another equal commercial rights in Morocco. There was to be a new Moroccan State Bank set up for the Sherifian Empire, with one share for each of the participating nations except the United States and France; however, because of France's previous heavy loans to the Moroccan Government, she was to be allowed to form a syndicate that would hold two shares.* A very important practical result of the Act of Algeciras was the creation of a special police force to help the Sultan keep order. While this force was to be made up of native Moroccan troops, it was to be instructed by French and Spanish officers, thus ensuring that France and Spain would have on-the-spot influence. The Act of Algeciras, like all the accords pertaining to Morocco, was remarkable in that the Sultan himself was not consulted about his wishes for the defense and future development of his country.

The Germans did not give up without blustering. In the summer of 1911 they again aroused Europe by sending a gunboat, the *Panther,* to Agadir to "protect" German commercial interests in that area. Since there were no Germans at Agadir at that time, and since Agadir was a closed port where no foreign power could legally exercise any sort of supervision, the incident was a deliberate violation designed to blackmail France into giving Germany a heavy bribe to get out of Morocco for good. The *Panther* was only a one-thousand-ton warship armed with two small cannon and six machine guns, and Agadir was a relatively unimportant port, but the significance of the German attempt to interfere in the French sphere was strongly felt by France. She adroitly parried the German thrust by initiating two treaties, which Germany signed in November 1911. In these, Germany recognized the Anglo-French Agreement of 1904 and acknowledged the French right to a Moroccan protectorate so long as the commercial claims of the other powers, as set forth in the Act of Algeciras, were not abrogated. France made German acceptance of these treaties more palatable by giving Germany 275,000 square miles of land in the French

---

* In 1904, Delcassé had forced a loan of twelve and a half million dollars on Abd el Aziz; and the French bankers had so manipulated the sum that the Sultan actually received less than ten million. (See Morel, p. 41.)

Congo,* about two hundred miles south of Lake Chad.²⁰ Meanwhile, the Germans were legally entitled to pursue their commercial ventures in Morocco, and it was not until their defeat in World War I that they were driven completely from the Moroccan scene.

Thus the sole remaining obstacle in the way of French control of Morocco was the matter of coming to terms with the Sultanate, and that was hardly any obstacle at all. The internal affairs of the country had worsened considerably since Abd el Aziz had come to the throne. The Bu Hamara revolt in the east was still progressing, and Raisuli laughed at authority in the northwest. The Sultan's mediocre administration was almost powerless to keep order, much less to enforce obedience, even in the Blad l-Makhzen.²¹ The French, meanwhile, were using every pretext to invade the area they dominated on paper. Back in 1903 Abd el Aziz had promised to cooperate with the French in restoring order along the Algerian frontier north of Ujda, where the unruly Beni Snassen tribe was showing fight. Either he did not try to make good his promise or he could not; in any event, the French acted at once and without him. Colonel Hubert Lyautey, commander of all the French forces in the neighboring Oran Department of Algeria, marched over the border and quelled the Beni Snassen. After this had been done, the French simply remained at Ujda, on the Moroccan side of the border. The Sultan was powerless to put them out. When Dr. Mauchamps, a noted French scholar, was stabbed to death by a fanatic in Marrakech in 1906,† French troops marched inland from Casablanca and occupied Marrakech.²² In 1907, French troops again landed at Casablanca— this time to protect the European colony, which was menaced by a local uprising.

In January 1908, the *ulema,* a body of tribal chiefs and local notables, convened at the mosque of Mulay Idris in Fez to name a successor to Abd el Aziz, who had become intolerable to many Moroccans. His brother, Hafid, was elected on the assumption that he would make a holy war against France, denounce the Act of Algeciras, and keep foreigners out of the interior of the country.²³

---

* The French got it all back again after World War I.
† Mauchamps' book on Moroccan magic is a classic; he was almost surely killed as the result of his open opposition to local sorcerers.

Thus 1908 found the French and Abd el Aziz engaged in fighting local insurrections on the one hand and Mulay Hafid and his supporters on the other. At the same time the tribes of the Taza-Melilla area, where Bu Hamara was in control, and the tribes of the Tangier-Tetuan-Wazzan region in the northwest, where Raisuli ruled, acknowledged neither the warring sultans, nor the French, nor one another.

Matters reached a climax when Abd el Aziz, acting independently of the French, set out from the Atlantic coast to attack Marrakech in August 1908. Betrayed by a tribe he had counted on to support him, he was forced to retreat to the coast.[24] Realizing that he had lost all popular support, Abd el Aziz abdicated in favor of Mulay Hafid in November. This change in the Sultanate accomplished very little in checking either the native revolts or the influence of the French. The Germans were doing all they could to thwart French plans by secretly selling guns to dissident tribesmen, and the wretched Hafid was caught in the impossible position of trying to guarantee European rights while simultaneously backing the idea of an independent Morocco cleared of Europeans.[25] The harried Sultan, deprived of British support and overwhelmed with debts (the French had seen to it that Morocco owed them more than $33 million by 1910), took refuge in drugs.[26] Finally, in March 1911, Hafid called for French assistance in maintaining his empire. A year later, on March 30, 1912, under heavy pressure from the French, he sadly fixed his name to the Treaty of Fez—thereby signing away his country's independence and giving France a legal protectorate over Morocco.[27] This treaty, the final link in the triumphant chain of French diplomacy in North Africa, awarded France perpetual right to the Sherifian Empire. The distinguished colonial administrator Hubert Lyautey was named the first Resident-General in April 1912. When the treaty was announced, the people of Fez went on a rampage and attempted to kill every foreigner they could find in the city; but the French forces took over quickly, and order was reestablished in a matter of days.

According to the terms of the Treaty of Fez, the new French régime would be set up by French judges as soon as it could be usefully introduced into Morocco.[28] The Muslim religion and the traditional prestige of the Sultan were to be safeguarded. As in the past, Spain was to be consulted by France with relation to the governing of northern Morocco, and Tangier was to retain international standing. France was to proceed with military occupation and to police Moroccan land and waters. In return, she promised to support the Moroccan Sultan and his heirs. Article 5 provided that the French Government was to be represented in Morocco by a Resident-General, who would be the sole intermediary between the Sultan and all foreign representatives. Moroccan citizens abroad would be protected and represented by French diplomatic agents. Finally, the Sultan was enjoined from concluding any act of an international character without the previous agreement of the French Government; he became a puppet whose only function was to act as intermediary between the French and his people. In other words, by means of the Treaty of Fez, Morocco was reduced to vassal status and placed wholly at the mercy of France, while the Sultan, a ruler with nothing to rule, became a mouthpiece for French colonial policy.

The proof of Moroccan resentment of the French intrusion was borne out by the persistence with which the tribes—the Berbers in particular—fought France throughout much of the time she held her Moroccan Protectorate. Complete pacification was not achieved in Morocco until 1934; and had it not been for the leadership of Lyautey during the early years of occupation, the problems of conquest would have been a great deal more difficult than they were. General Guillaume, Resident-General of Morocco in 1953, stated: "No tribe came to us spontaneously. None gave in without fighting, and some of them not until they had exhausted every means of resistance. The formulae dear to Marshal Lyautey —'Show force in order to avoid the use of it,' and 'A gantry is worth more than a battalion'—could not be applied to a population desperate to defend their independence to the last."[29] In the light of current history, one might say that Morocco was never truly conquered by Europeans, but was only temporarily subdued.

On July 17, 1912, Mulay Hafid, signer of the Fez treaty, abdicated the Moroccan throne in favor of his younger brother Yussef. In November, France signed an *entente* with Spain at Madrid, and their respective spheres of authority in Morocco were publicly defined.[30] The new Spanish Protectorate was to be modeled on the French. The Sultan was guaranteed retention of his civil

and religious authority over the Moroccan peoples of the Spanish
Zone, but the actual administration was to be delegated to a Khalifa, who would be the Sultan's representative in Spanish Morocco.
However, just as the Sultan himself was only a figurehead under
French rule, so the Khalifa was only a figurehead under the Spanish High Commissioner. The Sultan was free to choose the Khalifa
—if one can call it "free" choice when the list of candidates submitted to him by the Spanish Government consisted of two names.
Finally, Spain accepted the provisions of the Treaty of Fez, which
stated that Morocco's foreign relations were to be the sole province of the French Resident-General at Rabat, who by this recognition became in effect the Minister of Foreign Affairs for both
Protectorates.

The Madrid treaty was not concluded without some bitter
wrangling among the delegates. The Spanish were convinced that
the French were selling arms to the tribes of the northern zone—
guns that the French must have realized would be used against the
Spanish. The French were more concerned about land, and they
stuck to their thesis that since it had been France who had disposed of Italian and German influence in Morocco at the price of
territorial losses elsewhere, France should now have a larger slice
of Morocco; and that Spain's share of the prize should be less than
that offered in 1904. In the end, France got her way by threatening Spain with higher tariff walls if she refused the French demands. As the Basque historian Azpeitua put it, the "rich meat of
Taza, the fertile fields of the Wergha, and the potentially valuable
plains of the Rharb were taken away by successive treaties with
France, and Spain was left with the bone of the Jibala and the
spine of the Rif."[31] Other clauses in the Madrid treaty related to
the Tangier boundary, to restrictions on Spanish fortifications
along the Mediterranean coast, to banking, taxation, and railroad
matters, and to safeguards for the protection of the native population. Here it is interesting to note that no sooner had Spain
signed this treaty than she began operating her own protectorate
quite independently of France, notwithstanding the statement in
the Fez treaty to the effect that France would handle the foreign
affairs of both Protectorates. France could do little about this. The
Franco-Spanish arrangement remained flexible to an amazing degree, for neither nation was prepared to come to blows over the

provisions of the Treaty of Fez, and the Moroccans were powerless to protest in any way at all. It must be emphasized that Morocco gave Spain nothing; the powers awarded to Spain were delegated by France.

As subsequent events proved, Spain and France had erred greatly
in attempting to set up protectorate governments without first consulting the Sultan, his advisers, and the tribal leaders. Another serious error was the failure to respect tribal boundaries. The arbitrary frontier between the French and Spanish Protectorates was
defined in vague terms in the Fez treaty. Spanish Morocco was to
extend from the lower Muluya River in the east to the Lukus
River and latitude 35° in the west. This frontier between the two
zones cut through mountainous country almost wholly unexplored
by Europeans. Occasionally, as in the cases of the Beni Bu Yahi,
Metalsa, and Geznaya tribes in the east, the boundary split tribal
areas, so that occupants of the northern sections fell under Spanish
administration, whereas those to the south were nominally under
French supervision. At all events, the boundary lines existed solely
on paper, and had no meaning whatever for the tribesmen, who
were unaware that a treaty even existed. They conducted their
affairs as they always had, oblivious to boundaries and regulations.
The blunder was apparent, however, to men like Gabriel Maura,
the son of one of Spain's leading politicians, who predicted that
these badly settled questions would produce conflict in the future.[32]
As it turned out, these unresolved details greatly hindered Spain
when she attempted to occupy her new protectorate, eventually
contributed to France's involvement in the Rif Rebellion, and
cost both Spain and France dearly in lives and money.

The status of Tangier presented special problems to the signers
of the Treaty of Fez. Britain was determined that there should
be no rival to Gibraltar, but France and Spain were equally determined not to allow Britain to dominate the government of
Tangier. Neither Britain nor France wanted Spain to have the
district, since Spain might conceivably ally herself later on with
Germany, who would thus be in a position to blockade the Atlantic gateway to the Mediterranean. A solution to the problem of
Tangier was finally found in the fact that for almost a hundred
years the city had been the residence of foreign diplomats accred-
ited to the Sultanate, and had thus come to acquire an informal

international status.* In view of this, Britain pressed for the formal internationalization of Tangier and its environs. Its status was to have been decided at a conference called in Madrid in 1913, but because of the First World War this conference was interrupted before any agreement could be arrived at. Tangier, still without specific legal status, simply remained separate from the other zones until 1925, when it was declared an international, duty-free zone.

In summary, by 1912, Morocco as a whole—the small enclave of Tangier, the long narrow Spanish Zone around and beyond it, and the far larger French Zone to the south—presented a strange pattern of overlapping spheres of influence. It was against this background that the Rif Rebellion was to run its violent course.

* The American Consulate at Tangier, for example, was established in 1791. Its premises, deep in the medina, represent the oldest parcel of American Government-owned property abroad (Hoffmann, p. 175). Tangier owed its international character to the fact that most of the Sherifian Sultans had been inimical to strangers and to Western culture, and had therefore deliberately confined foreigners to the periphery of the country. With the passage of time, the foreign representatives at Tangier had requested the Sultan's permission to regulate local matters of health and sanitation themselves, and the Sultan had gladly acceded. Cooperating on these and other aspects of local government, the representatives of the major powers had in effect provided Tangier with an efficient municipal administration—first through the so-called Sanitary Council and later through the Hygiene Commission (Stuart, p. 33). Since the foreign inhabitants of Tangier with diplomatic status enjoyed extraterritoriality, it was an easy step to extend this dispensation to the city itself.

2. SPANISH MOROCCO

THE Franco-Spanish Treaty of November 1912 had given Spain
dominion over a jagged rectangle of land stretching from the
Atlantic Ocean to the west to the Muluya River close to the border
of Algeria on the east, and from the Mediterranean Sea on the
north to an irregular line about twenty-five miles north of the
Wergha River on the south. Spanish Morocco extended approximately 225 miles west to east, and about thirty to fifty miles north
to south, with a total area of slightly under 7,700 square miles—
an area about the size of Massachusetts. (By comparison, French
Morocco was 154,054 miles square—or almost twenty times as
large.) This land is composed for the most part of mountains that
rise abruptly from the Mediterranean and fall away into a series
of peaks and valleys to the south, in the area that once was French
Morocco. The western portion of Spanish Morocco reminds one
of the Colorado Rockies; along the valley of the Beni Hassan that
leads from Tetuan up to Chaouen it resembles the dramatic escarpments and sharp crenellations of the Bernese Oberland or the Aus-
trian Tyrol. Here and there in the western and central regions the
mountains are patched with small forests, and in the Gomara and
Ketama sectors there are magnificent stands of cedars. To the east,
timber becomes scarce and the heights are almost bald; it is difficult to assess whether this barrenness has been caused by wood-
cutting without subsequent reforestation, by flocks of hungry
goats, by the Rifian practice of burning the houses and trees of
murderers, or by a combination of all three. Just south of the
mountains that enclose Melilla, the coastal Plain of Garet widens
and becomes a rocky funnel of desert about sixteen miles wide
and forty miles long, its narrow end pointing inland from the sea,
surrounded on three sides by barren mountains that grow higher

toward the west. The aridity of this country is extreme, though a few small rivers run between the rocky slopes.

Most of the valleys of the old Spanish Zone, however narrow they may be, are carefully cultivated. In many places the slopes and ravines are so sheer that cultivation is limited or impossible. The highest peak in the zone, Tidiguin, near Ketama, is 7,600 feet high, and is covered with snow during four or five months of the year. (Legend says that Noah's Ark rested there; and at Bu Hmid in the Gomara there is another peak called Jebel Sidna Nuh or Noah's Mountain.) Many mountains in this area reach 5,000 feet or more. Rainfall is heavy here during the winter, and the rivers and streams, fed by the rains, the melting snow, and the low sea clouds, rush from the heights down to the sea at a torrential pace. This abundance is seasonal, however, and water is a precious commodity that must be zealously husbanded. As a result, irrigation techniques are ingenious, and the distribution of water is correspondingly complex. The climate runs to harsh extremes: summer is a season of glaring heat, with hardly any precipitation; winter a time of rains and freezing temperatures.

This part of Morocco was an uncharted country when the Spanish assumed their protectorate in 1912. There were only three points of superficial penetration by Europeans: Larache, a small town on the Atlantic, unsuitable as a major port because of ripping winds and dangerous sandbars; Ceuta, on the Mediterranean at the northern tip of the Anjera Peninsula; and Melilla, far to the northeast, on the Mediterranean. Though Ceuta is about 135 miles west of Melilla, there was not a single road or formal land link between these two presidios, or between Ceuta and Larache, when the Spaniards took over. There were perilous trails, to be sure, but only a goat or a Rifian mountaineer would dare to follow them. Spanish communications were conducted by sea. The interior of the zone was an unexplored mystery. Villagers in Spain or Gibraltar, travelers aboard ship in the Mediterranean, and residents at Tangier or the presidios could easily see the Moroccan mountains only a few miles distant, and yet few knew anything about the tribes who lived among them.

At the time that the establishment of the new protectorate was announced, the native population was estimated at 760,000.[1] In this hard land of complicated ethnic background, the population was an all-important factor. The residents of these mountains are Berbers—a word that is a linguistic rather than a racial designation—white tribesmen who speak a language belonging to the Hamitic branch of the Hamito-Semitic language family. Berbers on the north coast are primarily descended from Mouillian hunters, a people whose origins go back to 10,000 B.C., and secondarily from sedentary, agricultural neolithic peoples dating from 7000 B.C. Modern Berbers appear to be a genetic blend of these two earlier population strata. The Mouillians may have come from either the Near East or the Iberian Peninsula, but there is no question that the neolithic peoples from the Near East introduced the cultivation of plants and the domestication of animals, and later the working of metals. In spite of the victories of Arab invaders from the late seventh century onward, the Berbers of the central Rif—the mountainous country of Morocco bordering the Mediterranean—remain, to an appreciable extent, racially unmixed.* Charles Gallagher points out that the original Arab invaders, themselves of mixed blood, and a second, much larger wave that followed in about A.D. 1050, together totaled no more than 300,000 persons. Since not all of them got as far as Morocco, it seems probable that modern Moroccans have little Arab blood in them, and that the Berbers of the Rif have even less. (In general, Arab influence in Morocco has been aesthetic and philosophical rather than genetic.)[2]

The Berbers are organized into tribes, and each tribe is named either for a common male ancestor or for the supposed place of tribal origin.[3] The words *beni* and *ulad* are Arabic for "sons of" and "children of," and the word *ait* or *aith* is Berber for "people of." Thus the tribal name Beni Selman means "the sons of Selman," and Aith Waryaghar, "the people of Waryaghar." The terms "Spanish Morocco" and "the Rif Mountains" are generally used synonymously by Europeans, and consequently the Spanish Protectorate and the Rif were often mistakenly considered to be the same thing or the same place. Such a definition is not precise enough for our purpose, and we shall therefore employ the names of the geographical *territorios* set up by the Spanish. It should be pointed out that the Spaniards did not adopt the *territorio* system

---

* "Rif" (pronounced *reef*) is an Arabic word meaning "edge."

until after they had subjugated the entire Protectorate; we use the
term here simply as a convenience.

The five *territorios* into which the Spanish divided their Pro-
tectorate were as follows: the *Jibala,* inhabited by the Anjera, El
Hauz, Wad Ras, Beni Musaur, Jebel Habib, Beni Ider, Beni Aros,
Beni Lait, Beni Hassan, and Beni Hozmar tribes; the *Lukus,*
where lived the Garbia, El Sahel, El Khlot, El Khlot-Tilig, Beni
Gorfet, Ahl Serif, Sumata, Beni Isef, and Beni Sakkar tribes; the
Gomara, home of the Beni Said, Beni Ziat, Beni Zeyel, Al Ahmas,
Gezawa, Beni Yahmed, Beni Kalid, Beni Erzin, Metiua, Beni
Smih, Beni Guerir, Beni Buzra, Beni Selman, Beni Mansur, and
Beni Zerwal tribes; the *Rif,* with its Mestasa, Beni Gmil, Beni Bu
Frah, Targuist, Ketama, Beni Amart, Beni Urriaguel, Bucoya,
Beni Iteft, Beni Tuzin, and Geznaya, as well as a group of small
tribes near Mt. Tidiguin known collectively as Senhadja; and the
Kert, in which lived the Temsaman, Beni Ulichek, Tafersit, Me-
talsa, Beni Said, Beni Bu Gafar, Beni Sicar, Mazuza, Beni Bu Ifrur,
Beni Sidel, Beni Bu Yahi, Ulad Stut, and Quebdana. In all, sixty-
six tribes inhabited the land that became the Spanish Zone of
Morocco.

According to David Hart, the greatest concentration of Berbers
in Spanish Morocco—genetically, linguistically, and institution-
ally speaking—is to be found among the Beni Urriaguel (Aith
Waryaghar), Beni Amart, and Geznaya tribes of the central Rif.[4]
These three tribes, the tribes of the Kert, the Bucoya, and the Beni
Tuzin all speak thamazighth. The tribes of the Lukus and the Jibala are much more Arabicized, especially linguistically; while the
Senhadja group, who live in both the French and Spanish zones
near the frontier, speak both Arabic and a Berber language related
to Rifian thamazighth, but not fully understood by Rifians of the
central Rif. A Berber dialect is spoken in parts of Beni Buzra and
Beni Mansur in the Gomara, but it is different from both senhadji
and thamazighth.

In discussing the complex tribal structure of the Rif, we will necessarily be brief. Most tribes in Morocco, whether Berber or Arab,
were segmentary; that is, they were organized in a descending series of ever-smaller agnatic units. The tribe was the largest segment
—the maximum grouping of related people in a given area. It was
subdivided into clans, the clans into subclans, the subclans into

lineages, and so on, down to the basic family unit made up of
father, mother, and unmarried children. Order was maintained
through a balance of power between numerically matched groups
at all these segmentary levels, and *liff* (intratribal) alliances reinforced the balance along other lines. The concept of balance largely prevented any single authority from gaining power in the tribe
because it minimized political specialization. Before the advent of
Abd el Krim in the early 1920's, the Sultans of Morocco nominated
Caids to rule each tribe. But the Sultan's commission meant little
or nothing, since most of northern Morocco was habitually in the
dissident Blad s-Siba, and tribal authority rested in the hands of
councilors. These councilors, known as *imgharen,* were the natural leaders among the tribesmen. Rifians, like all Berbers, are in-
tensely egalitarian; to them one man is as good as another. Only
power—relatives and friends who will fight for one—marks the
difference between peers. For this reason, it is true even today that
"in the Rif, where everyone is a strong personality, only a mass
policy, and not one oriented toward individuals, can be effective."[5]
   Of all the tribes in this rugged land, those of the Rif have always
been the most important and the strongest, and among the Rifians,
the Beni Urriaguel have long been the most numerous (between
35,000 and 40,000 in the 1920's) and the most belligerent.* They
have tenaciously resisted alien interference, and have played the
dominant role among northern Moroccan tribes throughout the
country's history. A Rifian proverb says that "the rest of the tribes
dance to the sound of the Waryaghli [Beni Urriaguel] drum."[6]
Few would dispute this. Outsiders knew scarcely anything of these
people, and as a result, most Europeans agreed with the Spanish
Minister at Tangier who said despairingly during the Rif Rebellion, "No one could rule these tribes. They are the most intrac-
table people on earth."[7] Even to this day, says David Hart, if you
ask an Arab in Tetuan or Tangier what he thinks of Rifians and
of the Beni Urriaguel in particular, he will probably tell you that
they are ferocious and treacherous, and that for a peseta any one
of them would cut your throat.[8]
   The typical Rifian is of medium stature, with dark hair, brown
or hazel eyes, and a strong, solid physique. At least a quarter of

* The official Moroccan census of 1960—the only one ever taken in the Rif—
listed the Beni Urriaguel population at 75,895.

them have green or blue eyes, light hair or red hair, and freckles, so that they resemble nothing so much as Iowa farm boys in turbans. The men often shave their heads entirely, and the older ones wear heavy beards; but in the days before Abd el Krim, Rifians often wore their hair in a long scalp lock. Although most Rifians are too poor to eat meat more than once a week, they are physically strong, thanks to the clear mountain air and their simple but well-balanced diet. The hard conditions of their life make them exceedingly independent and self-reliant.

The standard costume for Rifian men is the wool *jellaba,* a knee-length garment of dark brown homespun with voluminous arms and a cowl, which they usually wear in all seasons. Cotton *jellabas* are sometimes worn in summer. A rough white cotton turban, a heavy woolen shirt, baggy trousers called *serwal,* and hand-woven sandals of tough *esparto* grass complete the male attire. Rifian women wear long cotton or silk shirts that reach the knee, and baggy trousers that extend to a point between knee and ankle. A cotton shawl around the head and a wide, heavy belt of red wool at the waist to serve as a pocket or catchall complete the outfit. Rifian women often walk barefoot, whereas the women of the Jibala generally wrap homemade leather puttees around their legs to protect them from cactus spines and sharp rocks. Jibala women are commonly swathed in layers of red and white striped cotton toweling, and wear picturesque straw hats of enormous size reminiscent of Mexican sombreros. Though most of the women in the Moroccan cities go about wearing veils, few country women wear them; but Rifian women always cover their faces when outsiders and Rifian men of lineages other than their own approach.

Rifian "villages" (which David Hart prefers to call "local communities," since they are not compact centers in the Western sense) are dispersed collections of houses, each separated from its neighbor by perhaps 350 yards of land and a protective hedge of thorny cactus. Each house may shelter as many as two dozen people as well as various animals. One finds these local communities strung out along mountainsides. At one time, each house had its own pillbox, built just outside the main building, which was used for spying out or fighting off enemies; in 1922, Abd el Krim ordered that these structures be destroyed. A Rifian house is customarily a rectangular structure made of mud and stone, constructed around a courtyard, with an earthen roof supported by wooden beams. A room seldom has more than one small vertically rectangular window, which is meant to serve as a loophole when the house is under attack. The average Rifian house is simply furnished; its walls are whitewashed, and the guest room in particular is scrupulously clean. Beyond the house is the vegetable garden, a small field of grain, and generally a few fruit trees. The tribesmen raise a large variety of food products—wheat, corn, rye, barley, figs, grapes, apricots, pomegranates, olives, and almonds. Each family has a cow or two, a mule or a donkey, and some chickens or goats. Sheep are rare, except on the plains; and only the easternmost tribes, who live largely on flat land, have horses. The diet in the mountains consists mainly of dried figs, raisins, other dried fruits, almonds, bread, curdled milk, thick soup, and an oily stew called *tajine*. Rifian marjoram honey is a superior product: David Hart says that General Franco used to have two liters of it shipped to him at Madrid each week.

In spite of the variety of produce raised in the Rif, the amounts were never adequate for the needs of the people, since the population is denser there than in any other rural area in Morocco. The combination of primitive farming methods, poor land, insecurity, and fierce competition with their neighbors for the necessities of life are major problems for the Rifians. They have traditionally faced these problems in two ways: they have emigrated temporarily to look for work; and they have engaged in blood feuds. Thousands of Rifians would leave their homes every year to seek employment in the larger cities such as Tangier, Tetuan, Ceuta, Melilla, Casablanca, and in particular on the French farms of neighboring Algeria after the *colons* had opened up the country. This exodus was always accomplished with the tacit consent of the French Algerian authorities, who knew that the Rifians were excellent workers—far better than the native Algerians. But these journeys away from the Rif were almost always temporary, for the Rifian sooner or later returns to his native mountains, about which he has ambivalent but violent feelings. As David Hart says, the Rifian knows his land is poor and unproductive, but he does not want anybody else to have it.

Rifian education is entirely practical, based upon the hard facts of a hard life. Children are brought up to assume adult roles as

fast as they can fit into the pattern. If one is strong, one is "good";
if one is weak, one is "bad." One must be brave but careful. Personal power is the goal to be achieved, through force or trickery if
necessary. This opportunism is sanctioned by Rifian moral standards.[9]

Education in the mountains still centers around the teachings
of the Koran. Very young boys learn the verses of the Koran by
rote until they have mastered them. At that point they begin to
study Koranic commentary and *hadith,* the collected sayings of the
Prophet that are not included in the Koran. For girls, there is no
formal education. The Rifian world is overwhelmingly a man's
world, for every Rifian believes the Koran's statement that men
are superior to women. Male values are given religious validation,
and the men act accordingly. Women have little choice of whom
they will marry; they have no voice in government; and they are
absolutely forbidden to divorce their husbands. They work far
harder and longer than their men, yet they can inherit—if they
inherit at all—only half of any given estate. On the other hand, a
man can easily divorce his wife, and he is allowed to have as many
as four wives at a time. (Actually, divorce is less common than
might be expected; and most men are monogamous, for extra
wives mean extra expense and trouble.)

The most important enduring legacy left to the tribesmen by
the original Arab invaders is their Muslim religion. Over the years,
however, the Koran has incorporated and sanctioned beliefs in
dreams, omens, charms, the evil eye, spirits, ghosts, and demons
that were part of the preexisting religious systems of the early
Berbers. Most spirits are thought to be of the kind known as *jinns*
—supernatural creatures fashioned by God before men appeared
on earth.[10] *Jinns* are generally malign beings, both masculine and
feminine, with racial and even sectarian characteristics (Negro and
Christian *jinns* are held to be especially evil). Moreover, they are
invisible, and can travel anywhere. However, *jinns* are thought to
be powerless to hurt anyone carrying metal, so Rifian men, laden
with rifles and cartridges, feel safe from them.

Much more pertinent to the problems considered in this book
is the widespread Muslim belief in saints, which seems to have
begun in the thirteenth century. If *jinns* represent the forces of
evil, then saints represent the forces of good. Saints are of two

kinds: Sherifs, that is, descendants of the Prophet Mohamed through his daughter Fatima and her husband Ali, and *murabitin,* or *marabouts,* who have won their sainthood not by genealogical inheritance, as Sherifs do, but by the working of miracles and faith healing. At the time of the Protectorate, the holiest of the *marabouts* were held in great esteem, and acted as political mediators— sometimes interrupting feuds or calling truces so that a harvest could be gathered, for example. They received presents and gifts of money from their devotees, and some among them, playing roles in both the profane and the sacred spheres, became politically powerful. We will discuss the actions of Mulay Ahmed er Raisuli and the Darkawi Sherif, both politically powerful saints, later on.

At the time of the Spanish invasion, children of the Rif were brought up to hate those whom the family or the lineage hated, and to hate all traditional enemies, including Spaniards and Christians, as well. Violence and bloodshed were everyday matters, and every boy had learned to use knife and gun effectively by the time he reached adolescence. Given the Rifian's volatile temper, it is little wonder that the blood feud was common, especially in a land so infertile, where ownership of agricultural property, of animals, and of water rights was overwhelmingly important. Ernest Gellner illustrates the conditions that prevailed by quoting an Arab saying: "I against my brother; my brothers and I against our cousins; my brothers, my cousins, and I against [others]," and so on.[11] In the Rif, blood feuds could develop over the slightest incident involving two individuals, and could grow to such proportions that families, clans, and even whole tribes would become involved. These feuds were ruthlessly pursued, and provided a murderous pastime when there were no major wars to be fought or serious invasions to repel. Treachery and cruelty were common, with no quarter asked, expected, or given. Many a mountain tribe boasted that hardly a man among them lived to attain middle age. A male Rifian who had not taken a life before he was married was not considered a man.[12] When a young man had killed for the first time, he went out on the following market day, dressed in his best clothes and wearing a new bag on his right side instead of his left to indicate what he had done. Even when the customary law under which the Rifians lived provided a way out of further killing by the payment of blood money to the injured party, the latter usually preferred to refuse the money and continue the feud. David Hart reports the following examples of a blood feud, which forms a central theme in a book he is writing on the sociopolitical system of the Aith Waryaghar (Beni Urriaguel): "I have been informed that in the Aith Bu Ayyash—the political division of Aith Waryaghar which has the greatest fighting reputation—feuding assumed such proportions that, to take one example, the village of Aith Bu Khrif knew hardly any peace at all until the Spanish occupation. In another instance on record . . . the shooting began after the murder of a dog which belonged to a guest of a headman of Iburasen, the murderers having refused to pay the blood money claimed. Twelve men were killed in combat the first day; each side collected its allies, and soon the feud spread [through all the area]. In the following years, forty men died on one side, sixty-two on the other, in pitched battles alone. This does not take into account the number of those shot down in ambush or poisoned with arsenic sold by merchants at Alhucemas. The conquered group eventually decided to leave the country; almost no one was left but old men, women, and children, who sought refuge on the sacred mountain of Zerhoun after having sold all their property in order to hire a man who would avenge their dead [Jebel Zerhoun, just north of Meknes in French Morocco, upon whose southern flanks lies the Arab holy city of Mulay Idris]. The vengeance plan was carefully worked out . . . but in any event, the hired killer was found the next day . . . with a bullet through his own head, due as probably as not to the accurate marksmanship of a small boy hidden in a lentiscus bush."[13] Walter Harris commented on the prevalence of blood feuds in which there was no pardon and no mercy, but only hate and treachery, citing the butchery the Duas and Deylan families of the Anjera inflicted upon each other.[14] And Carleton Coon, writing about a feud in Beni Urriaguel, reports that one group shot a hydrocephalic boy merely in order to be able to see what his brain looked like.[15]

In view of the prevalence of blood feuds, it is easy to understand the necessity for the Berber institution called the *liff*.[16] A *liff* was a political alliance between any of the various segments of a tribe, some on one side, and some on the other. If the members of one side found themselves in desperate straits during a feud, they would lead a bull to the mosque of some neutral community whose assistance they hoped to obtain. The bull would be killed on the steps of the mosque, so that its blood spurted over the threshold. According to custom, the neutrals—whether they wished it or not —were then expected to join those who had killed the bull. Rifians, almost without exception, are impoverished vegetarians, and in thus killing a bull, the feuding group was destroying the most costly, useful animal it owned in order to shame the neutral group into joining it. It was almost unthinkable that the neutrals would not join those already involved after the slaughter of the bull, but should a rare group refuse a *liff* alliance, it would suffer a complete loss of social prestige. Until the reign of the warrior-statesman Abd el Krim, the *liff* alliance was standard procedure in the Rif. Each tribe was split into two fairly well-balanced but hostile halves, and these halves together formed the combined front the tribe presented to the world. Sometimes *liff* systems coincided with tribal segmentary systems: one subclan would have a *liff* alliance with another subclan, one family with another family, and so on. Each tribe in the Rif had its own *liff* system, internal to a given tribe—intratribal rather than intertribal—so that the clans of a given tribe were pitted against one another in almost equally balanced alliances. At a lower level, within each clan there was a similar set of alliances on a smaller scale. The Beni Urriaguel, which produced Abd el Krim, were too large and powerful to need formal alliances with other tribes, and their only allies on the sole occasion in modern times when they needed any, during the war against Bu Hamara in 1908, were the Beni Amart, who lived just south of them. A common boast among the Beni Urriaguel even today is, "We could still go out alone and beat Temsaman or Beni Tuzin [neighboring tribes to the east] any day of the week."[17] The *liff* was the best guarantee of survival, since it permitted smaller groups and tribes to exist while surrounded by much stronger opponents.[18] Life may or may not have been sweet in the Rif, but it was likely to be short, given the blood-feud version of the Golden Rule, which might be summed up as "Do unto others quickly, before they do unto you."

The customary law of the Berbers was called the *'urf*. As applied in the mountains of northern Morocco, it was a harsh code. Although the Koran prescribes a fine as punishment for bloodletting between two Muslims, the tribesmen usually preferred to invoke another teaching of the Koran: "Life for life, eye for eye, nose for nose, ear for ear, tooth for tooth." In the Rif there were feuds and fines, but no imprisonment or corporal punishment. However, in the Jibala (where, incidentally, the *liff* system seems not to have been used often), known criminals were often mutilated. A document of the Wad Ras tribe, dated 1863–64, reads: "Whoever is convicted of theft will have his eyes put out with a red hot iron, or will have his right hand cut off."[19] In the Rif, various fines were imposed for crimes large and small. Among the Beni Urriaguel, if a murder was committed on a path leading to a marketplace, the murderer was fined 1,000 duros (about $700); if he killed a man in the marketplace itself, his fine was doubled.[20] This was because the weekly market was not merely a place to buy and sell goods, but also a place of peace and social intercourse. The tribal council usually met in or near the market to debate issues, to see that peace was kept, and to impose fines as necessary. Of course the fines for murder were fantastically high. If the murderer was unable to pay, the tribal council would drive him and his family out of their home, burn the house and all the crops and trees, and confiscate his animals.*

The peoples of the Rif and the Jibala, the two most important tribal groups in what was Spanish Morocco, are quite dissimilar. In general, the Rifians are more Spartan, poorer, more sober, more austere, more direct, and mentally quicker, with higher moral standards. The Jiblis are good-natured, excitable, and somewhat credulous. They think of themselves as more sophisticated than their Rifian cousins, since they count the only three cities in the mountains—Tetuan and Chaouen in Spanish Morocco, and Wazzan, in the former French Zone—as part of their territory. A story related by Walter Harris gives an insight into the Jibala character: "A tribesman from the Jibala who was visiting the plains bought a sheep, determined to start his own flock, since in his mountain district there were only goats. Already in his mind he saw the slopes of his native hills white with the fleece of snowy lambs. And so when he returned home, he gave a great feast for all his friends

---

* The *qanun* (law) of the Aith Khattab of the Beni Urriaguel lowlands states that the fine for shooting a man and missing him was double the fine for wounding him. Presumably Rifians pride themselves on their marksmanship. (Hart, "Emilio Blanco Izaga," p. 199.)

in celebration of his new and rare acquisition and his future riches. After the banquet, he led his guests out to see the sheep, and it was only then that he realized he had killed and eaten the *pièce de résistance.*"[21] A somewhat surprising fact about the tribesmen of the Jibala, Gomara, and Senhadja was the high incidence of homosexuality among them. In fact, there were boy markets in Chaouen and at other places in the northwest as late as 1937, when the Spanish Protectorate officially proscribed them. The Rifians were generally of a very different sort, and Abd el Krim made sodomy punishable by death. On the occasion when two Jiblis were caught in flagrante delicto, the Rifians soaked them in gasoline and burned them alive.[22]

 Though outnumbered or beaten temporarily, the Berbers of the Rif had never been subjugated before the time of the Spanish Protectorate. Proud, brave, hardy, calling themselves *imazighen*— "the people"—they preferred death to alien domination. Sir John Drummond-Hay, British Minister at Tangier during the last half of the nineteenth century, said of these tribesmen, "[They] are wild and lawless, but most thorough sportsmen, and capable of great attachment and devotion."[23] And an anonymous Englishman, writing in the Tangier *Gazette* in 1905, said: "Pathetic as it may seem, there is not a man from the Rif to the Atlas but believes that he and his brethren, armed with rusty Remingtons and a hundred rounds of cartridges apiece, are more than a match for any force in the world that could be sent against them. These half million of hardy plainsmen and mountaineers believe, too, in a God . . . as earnestly as we believe in money, our Navy, and other tangible things . . . a God who fights for Islam. And they actually deem it better to earn paradise by falling in a holy war than to submit to any kind of interference in the affairs of Islam." A North African proverb has it that "the Tunisian is a woman, the Algerian is a man, and the Moroccan is a lion."[24] One might add that, once aroused, the Moroccan Berber is a particularly ferocious lion. These were the people with whom Spain and eventually France had to deal. Surely no imperialistic or colonial power anywhere in the world has ever encountered more formidable opponents than the Berbers of Spanish Morocco.

3. SPANISH RELATIONS WITH MOROCCO BEFORE 1912

A LTHOUGH Spain had held the northern Moroccan ports of Ceuta and Melilla for over 300 years, the Moroccans offered no concerted resistance to her presence there until the latter half of the nineteenth century, at which time the Spaniards suffered so many annoyances along the Moroccan coast and on the Mediterranean that harried officials, mostly aggressive militarists, decided to punish the Moroccans drastically and thus put an end to their depredations. There were other reasons, too, for beginning a military action in Morocco. The Spanish Government found itself so enmeshed in domestic difficulties at this time—issues of regional rights, political representation, constitutional procedures, and ownership of Church lands—that it needed a war on foreign soil to divert the people's attention.* As always when necessity demands it, a cause for war was readily found.[1] Spanish troops at Ceuta had constructed a redoubt on the outskirts of the city— much to the irritation of the Anjera tribesmen in the vicinity, who showed their disapproval by attacking the unfinished works in August 1859. They pulled down much of the construction, killed several Spaniards, and disfigured the coat-of-arms of Spain. The Governor of Ceuta immediately demanded that the Caid of the Anjera pay damages and punish the attackers. In addition, he ordered the Spanish Consul at Tangier to demand further reimbursement from the Sultan at Fez. The Sultan's court appeared willing to discuss the matter, but they allowed the proceedings to

---

* During the years 1858 to 1868, Spain had tried to win support and prestige abroad by means of an aggressive foreign policy. She became engaged militarily with France in Cochin China in 1859–63, with France and Britain in Mexico in 1861–62, in the reannexation of Santo Domingo in 1861–65, and with Peru in 1866.

drag along in the usual dilatory Moroccan fashion, which incensed the Spanish still more. Finally, Sultan Abderrahman died, which brought the court proceedings to a complete standstill. The Spanish, having received no compensation, took action, and in October 1859 declared war on Morocco.

The new Sultan, Mulay Mohamed, replied by proclaiming a *jihad*, or holy war, and sent an army under his brother to repel the Europeans at Ceuta. Meanwhile, since the war promised to be an expensive one, the Spanish government needed to sell its Moroccan venture to the Spanish taxpayer. The government hit upon the expedient of invoking Queen Isabel I's "last testament" of 1504, in which the Queen had advised her successors to persevere in their efforts to conquer Africa and to bring the Christian faith to the infidels there. Queen Isabel II was easily persuaded that it was her duty to carry out her predecessor's will. With the enthusiastic assistance of the press, the Moroccan campaign was presented to the public—a generally apathetic public, let it be said—as a religious crusade. Spain was inundated with chauvinistic propaganda, as journalists exhorted the public and the Army to make Ceuta and Melilla the stepping-stones to a new Spanish Empire.

The Spanish general Leopoldo O'Donnell gathered an army at Ceuta, then marched south toward Tetuan on New Year's Day, 1860. The advance guard under General Juan Prim was at once engaged by the Anjera. Although the Spaniards won this affair as well as all the subsequent battles in this little war, their losses were considerable, and it took the army more than a month to struggle the twenty-three miles from Ceuta to Tetuan. After securing Tetuan during the first week of February, the Spanish moved westward toward Tangier. In the meantime, a Spanish fleet had bombarded Tangier, Asilah, and Larache. Pressing their advantage, Prim's forces pushed through the hills around Fondak Ain Jedida, between Tetuan and Tangier. Finally, at the end of March, the Moroccans sued for peace. Both sides had taken a terrific beating. Moroccan losses are not known, but the Spanish counted more than 1,000 men killed and 3,000 wounded during this brief campaign.[2]

Spain gained little by this bloody venture. True, the Army earned a measure of prestige, but the indemnity of twenty million pesetas extracted from the Sultan failed to cover Spain's war expenses, and the political results were disappointing.[3] Ever mindful that Gibraltar was directly across the Straits from Ceuta, the British had limited Spanish action in the direction of Tangier. They had also quietly loaned the Sultan the money to pay the war indemnity.[4] The Spanish Army remained in Tetuan until it received this sum; then it promptly returned to Spain. With no colonial policy, no project for Morocco's future, not even an organized plan of occupation, there was little else they could do. The hard-won territory reverted to the tribesmen, who now had even better reason to fear and hate European invaders. Such acts as that of General O'Donnell, who had transformed the principal Moorish mosque at Tetuan into a Catholic church, particularly horrified and infuriated the Muslim Moroccans. The terms of peace extended the limits of both Ceuta and Melilla slightly inland, and by a treaty of commerce signed with the Sultan in 1861, Spain was given the right to begin economic development in northern Morocco. However, because the Spanish Government had no definite program for utilizing Moroccan resources, Spain failed to take advantage of this opportunity.

In 1893, fighting again broke out in Morocco—a repetition of the pointless hostilities of 1860. Whereas the first Moroccan war had been fought in the west at Ceuta and Tetuan, this new war was staged around Melilla in the east. The incident that set off the new action was similar to that which had been used as an excuse for the fighting in 1860. Spanish troops extending fortifications south of Melilla in September 1893 unwittingly desecrated the tomb of Sidi Aguariach (Auriach), a Rifian saint. When outraged tribesmen appealed to the Spaniards to stop the work, General Margallo, the commanding officer, referred the matter to the Spanish Government. The tribesmen did not wait for a reply, but tore down the Spanish works and attacked the workmen. Most of the soldiers were able to retreat into the defenses of Melilla itself, but General Margallo was cut off and surrounded at the small Spanish post of Cabrerizas Altas, just north of Melilla. In the ensuing attack, the leadership of Lieutenant Miguel Primo de Rivera, the young officer who would one day become the leader of Spain itself, saved the day. The only officer casualty in the whole encounter was General Margallo, who was shot in the head by a tribesman while engaged in reconnaissance outside the post.*

The skirmish at Cabrerizas Altas was over quickly enough, but because of it, Spain had put more than 25,000 troops in the field in Morocco; and just as in 1859, the cost of the brief show of force proved to be much greater than the benefits obtained by it. General Martínez Campos, who had replaced Margallo as commander in chief of the Spanish forces in Morocco, acted as Ambassador Extraordinary for Spain, and went to the Sultan's court at Marrakech to arrange a peace treaty. Because of his reputation for fair dealing and respect for the rights of Moroccans, Martínez Campos was well received. In the spring of 1894, he succeeded in concluding a treaty satisfactory to both Morocco and Spain; but he might have emerged with an even better agreement and heavier reparations had it not been for an unfortunate incident that took place in Madrid about the same time. The Moroccan Ambassador, Abd el Krim Bricha, was assaulted in a Madrid hotel by General Fuentes, a deranged officer of the Reserve. To Moroccans, Fuentes' act was unforgivable—a typical example of Spanish military arrogance— in spite of the fact that the Spanish press expressed great shame over the occurrence. In an effort to counteract the effect of the Fuentes incident, Spain gave Morocco somewhat more generous treaty terms than were at first contemplated. Even so, Morocco was forced to pay Spain an enormous indemnity, to accept an enlargement of the Melilla presidio, and to allow Spain to appoint consuls at Fez and Marrakech. Moreover, the appointments of Caids in the Rif were thereafter to be subject to Spanish approval.

* This version of Margallo's death is the one official records and all serious historians report; but Brenan, p. 61, quotes a story related by Manuel Ciges Aparicio, in which Ciges says that in a rage, Lieutenant Primo de Rivera shot Margallo because the general had secretly sold to the Moroccans the very guns they were using against the Spanish soldiers. Ciges was the Mayor of Avila, northeast of Madrid; as a Republican official, he was shot by the Franco rebels during the Civil War in 1936. Whether his execution had anything to do with the Primo de Rivera story is a moot question. Corruption in the Spanish Army was rife, and gross insubordination was no rarity; rifles certainly were sold by the Spanish to tribesmen; and in the past officers now and then had been attacked, and sometimes killed, by the men they commanded (see Payne, pp. 29, 51). However, there is no strong evidence to support Ciges Aparicio's claim, and all other works I have read assert that General Margallo was killed by enemy fire. See, for example, Herrera and García Figueras, p. 36; García Figueras, *Marruecos*, p. 94; Ballesteros, p. 383; Payne, p. 63; Mulhacén, p. 127.

In terms of political control, however, this right of approval meant very little, for the Sultan's jurisdiction in northern Morocco was nominal rather than real; both the Jibala and the Rif were overwhelmingly of the Blad s-Siba, and concessions from the throne were almost meaningless there. All things considered, the Spanish had gained even less from their second Moroccan campaign than from the first; and they had yet to produce a positive colonial policy.

In 1898, with the inglorious conclusion of the Spanish-American War, Spain lost whatever standing she might have had as a world power. National pride demanded that something be done to regain a certain measure of prestige. Where were there greater possibilities of glory than in Morocco? One had merely to look across the Straits of Gibraltar to see plainly the peaks of this unexploited land. The two presidios planted on its shores had been Spanish for over three hundred years; and moreover, the Spanish Army had easily won the recent brief military excursions. Now was surely the moment, when the other great nations of Europe were scrambling for choice pieces of the African continent, to rebuild the glory of Spain.

Alfonso XIII, whose antecedents included Bourbons and Hapsburgs, had ascended the throne of Spain at sixteen in 1902.[5] A slender, intelligent youth, Alfonso had hoped to re-create a prosperous and progressive Spain—but he was never a deep thinker, and he preferred balls, banquets, sporting events, and parades to council meetings.[6] He took a childish pleasure in uniforms and pageantry. His first tutors were Army officers, and military life greatly appealed to him: the young monarch once remarked that if he had not been King, he would have chosen to be a major in the Infantry. Possessed of an innate dislike of politicians, the King turned for comradeship and support to his military advisers.[7] He was genuinely interested in the welfare of his people; one of his first acts as King was to tour most of the large cities of Spain and the Balearic Islands and to speak personally to people of all social levels—industrialists, savants, labor leaders, peasants. Although he was generally popular, nine attempts were made on his life during his reign. On one occasion, a lunatic fired at him and his mother as they left a church in Madrid; and on another, an unknown assailant threw a bomb at his carriage as he rode through

Paris with the President of the French Republic, Émile Loubet.*
Alfonso's marriage in 1906 to Victoria Eugenia Battenberg, a
granddaughter of Queen Victoria, precipitated another attempt
on his life. The young couple had just left the Cathedral of Madrid
and were riding in their carriage through cheering throngs down
the Calle Mayor when a Catalan anarchist named Matteo Morral
stepped out on a balcony and threw a bomb at them.[8] It hit one of
the horses, bounced into the street, and then exploded, leaving the
King and his bride unharmed, but killing more than twenty people and wounding a hundred more. Undaunted, the King coolly
repeated his ride through the streets late that evening. Courage
and a desire to know the needs of his people were qualities that
helped offset Alfonso's less admirable characteristics and helped
make him, if not a great monarch, at least a sympathetic figure on
the stage of history. Sir Charles Petrie, an English historian of the
period, went so far as to claim that Alfonso was the greatest Spaniard of the twentieth century.[9]

In 1902, Spain remained divided over the question of future action in Morocco. Though many of the country's leaders were re-
luctant to become involved in further bloodshed, the nation, and
the Army in particular, had been humiliated by the overwhelming
triumph of American arms in the 1898 fighting in the Philippines
and the West Indies, and badly needed to rebuild international
prestige. The Army viewed Morocco as one of the few areas—perhaps the only area—available to Spain for conquest. It was important, too, that Morocco, a threat in the hands of any other
major power, be secured to protect the Spanish mainland from
attack, whether by England, France, or Germany. Finally, Spanish business interests were anxious to gain a better foothold in
Morocco's northern mountains, which were reputed to be rich in
mineral deposits and whose population constituted a ready market
for Spanish exports.

By and large, the Spanish masses were either apathetic or appre-
hensive about engaging in further military action. The long history of Spanish colonial adventures was a chronicle of bungling
and wastefulness, taxation and bloodshed. The burden of war al-

---

* A 1905 newspaper cartoon by Pasquino of Turin shows Alfonso and Presi-
dent Loubet riding in their carriage. A bomb goes off nearby, and the King asks:
"Is it for me or for you?" The President replies: "For both of us, Your Majesty.
Aren't we in the country of equality?" See Fernández Almagro, p. 65.

ways falls heaviest on the common man, and the common man of Spain at this time was weary of misadventures abroad. Each time a new outbreak occurred among the northern Moroccan tribes, the Spanish people felt the pressure of greater taxes and the threat of military conscription, and yet could look forward to none of the "glory" or profits to which a capable Army and a competent national administration might have led them. As a matter of fact, many men of foresight suspected that Morocco was not the answer to Spain's problems at all.[10] To split up the Army and the fleet, both dependent logistically upon the mother country, would be to repeat the errors of the past. Moreover, the Ceuta and Melilla presidios were far apart, accessible only by sea, and therefore difficult to maintain. A conquest on the grand scale in that mountainous terrain could only be achieved at great cost of life and matériel; and it was far from certain that the returns from such an undertaking would be worth the effort. Nevertheless, in the long run the imperialists—the "africanistas"—had their way. The secret treaty concluded by Spain with France in 1904 clearly demonstrated the Spanish Government's intention of establishing a colonial empire in northern Morocco.

As these decisions were being reached in Madrid, there was a serious uprising against the Sultan in the Taza district of Morocco between Fez and the Algerian frontier. The leader of this revolt was an Arab tribesman—a former clerk from Taza named Jilali ben Dris.[11] Jilali had been convicted of forging important signatures while employed as a scribe at the Moroccan court. Upon being released from jail, he had moved to Algeria, where he lived with the Darkawa sect and immersed himself in the study of religion. Eventually he decided to return to Morocco. A convincing speaker, he became a widely known religious leader, and was reputed to be able to work miracles. He set himself up as Rogui—pretender to the throne of Morocco—by spreading the rumor that he was the lost son of former Sultan Mulay Hassan I. (The Sultan's son was, in fact, neither lost nor dead, but simply living in quiet retirement.) In any case, the Rogui's claim was easily foisted upon the unsophisticated tribesmen; it was well known that Mulay Hassan's son was blind in the left eye, and though Jilali was not blind, a drooping left eyelid made him seem so. At all events, the Rogui rallied most of the Giata, Tsoul, Branes, Meknasa, and Howara tribes of the northeast to his banner, and attacked and defeated the Sultan's forces at Ain Mediouna, in the hills north of Fez, in December 1902. As a result, Jilali, or "Bu Humara,"* as he was known, held sway over northeastern Morocco, from Fez to Melilla. With French connivance and support, he proclaimed himself Sultan at Taza.[12] For more than six years, he fended off the Sultan's forces, but maintained a wary friendship with the Spanish Army at Melilla. The Spanish Government, of course, could not openly recognize him, since they were bound to support the Sultan. The Rogui's organization was loose and undependable, and the homage rendered to him by the various tribes in his territory was never more than the absolute minimum necessary to stave off wholesale massacre. But when the Rogui awarded a French company a 99-year lease on a factory site in the Restinga, a long peninsular strip just south of Melilla, both military and business interests in Spain were alarmed, for the factory, though ostensibly a commercial enterprise, was actually turned over to the manufacture of munitions for the Rogui's forces.[13] When Sultan Abdul Aziz landed a *harka* in the Restinga in the summer of 1907 to put down Bu Hamara, he requested supplies and assistance from the Melilla garrison, and received them. Nevertheless, the Rogui's irregulars all but destroyed the Sultan's troops, and it was only because the Spanish allowed the refugees to enter the safety of Melilla's walls that they escaped at all.

A short time later, in July 1907, the Rogui gave the Spanish Compañía Española de Minas del Rif a 99-year lease on the iron mines at Monte Uixan, as well as the right to build a railroad connecting the mines to the port of Melilla. The very next month, the Rogui sold a similar lease to the lead mines at Monte Afra to the Franco-Spanish Compañía del Norte de Africa.† These mines,

---

* Literally, "the man who rides on a female donkey." Gavin Maxwell reports that in Moroccan mythology *bu hamara* meant a *jinn* who fools the people with money and presents, and leads them to disaster. See Maxwell, p. 84.

† The sale of mining concessions to Europeans was nothing new in the Rif, according to Auguste Muliéras, pp. 96–99. During the 1880's, a Beni Urriaguel *amghar*, or tribal councillor, and a *cadi* from Targuist had sold the rights to an alleged gold mine in Jebel Hamam, the lofty mountain in the heart of the Beni Urriaguel, to a French concern. After making a down payment, the Frenchmen landed at Alhucemas Bay intending to travel inland and take possession of their new mine; but the Rifian tribesmen did not intend to allow foreigners, especially Christians, to enter their tribal area, and a large force chased the French-

which were exceedingly rich, were located about twelve miles southwest of Melilla among the hills of Beni Bu Ifrur. According to Ruiz Albéniz, there was also a remarkable group of hills at Monte Uixan, said to be composed of almost solid hematite ore assaying 72 per cent pure iron.[14]

Much of the early prospecting in northern Morocco, and most of the engineering and mining development, were the work of Belgians, Dutchmen, and the enterprising agents of the German Mannesmann brothers. The Mannesmanns at one time suggested that they operate the whole of northern Morocco on a 100-year concession basis, but Madrid demurred; why, after all, give Germany, or anybody else, the benefit of anything worthwhile in a Spanish Protectorate?[15] While the Spanish seem never to have lost their admiration and high regard for the Germans, both France and England rightly regarded Germany as a competitor in the economic field, and Anglo-French diplomacy was constantly directed toward restraining German activity in Morocco.[16] This proved a difficult task in the northern part of the country, which as far back as 1902 had been tacitly considered an exclusively Spanish sphere of influence. Over the years, the Germans there had won the respect of both the Spanish administration and the Berber tribesmen for their honesty and efficiency. Because they maintained good relations with tribal leaders, they were able to entrench themselves firmly in the Moroccan economy. This posed a considerable threat to further French control of Morocco—a threat that persisted until the end of the First World War. After Spain had declared herself a neutral in that conflict, Germany

---

men away. A French complaint to the Sultan produced the answer that Morocco's natural resources belonged to the Sultan; that only the Moroccan Government had the right to dispose of these resources; and that therefore the mine had never belonged to the French at all. The Sultan promised to deal sternly with the *amghar* and the *cadi*, and to reimburse the French; if he kept this promise, it has not been recorded. But the Beni Urriaguel, having heard the story, burned down the *amghar*'s house and chased him into neighboring Beni Tuzin. When the Tuzinis refused to turn him over to the Urriaglis, a fight ensued. The *cadi*, on the other hand, fled back to his own tribe, and lived well on his portion of the French money. Muliéras says that the Sultan sent troops into Beni Urriaguel to investigate the gold mine, but this is almost surely apocryphal, since the Urriaglis, always part of the Blad s-Siba, would never have let the troops in. In any case, though the mountains of Beni Urriaguel may glitter, and though even Abd el Krim believed that Jebel Hamam contained precious metals, geologists have long since proved there is no gold there after all.

used Spanish Morocco as a base from which to distribute anti-French propaganda, deliver arms to the Rif and the Jibala, and in general threaten the security of the French Zone and build ill will against France. Men like Raisuli, Abd el Malek, and Abd el Krim the Elder were all apparently won over to an anti-French bias as a result of German machinations. France accused Spain of helping Germany during the war, but Spain countered later by claiming that half her troubles in the Rif stemmed from the French having run guns and bullets to the Rifians in an effort to win the tribesmen over to their side.[17] Walter Harris stated that most of the capital for the Colonizadora was supplied by German financiers.* The Colonizadora was one step behind the Spanish Army, and as the troops advanced, first south from Melilla, then slowly westward from 1909 to 1921, this organization bought land: near Melilla, then in the desert around Monte Arruit, then at several places along the Muluya River, and then even further west, around Tistutin.[18] It was the Colonizadora, too, that by 1918 had constructed the Ceuta–Tetuan railroad in the western part of the Protectorate.

Although the Rogui had acquired a degree of prestige in the north, his sales of mining rights to foreigners had helped to denigrate it, especially in the Rif. Foreign experts were welcome only so long as the tribes on whose lands the mines were discovered held control; otherwise, tribal resentment skyrocketed. But no one paid much attention to Abd el Aziz's protestations that Bu Hamara was usurping his authority—least of all the French, who secretly welcomed anything that weakened the Sultanate and thus brought their own début on the Moroccan scene that much closer. But the Rifian tribesmen interpreted the sale of mining concessions to Christians as treachery, and it was this that finally wrecked the Rogui's soaring ambitions. Bu Hamara had launched an invasion of the Rif from Zeluan in June 1908, and his *harka* had actually been able to penetrate into the mountains of Temsaman, where the tribes were badly split by *liff* factions.[19] At this point, the Beni Urriaguel united as a tribe for the first time in their history, called on their Beni Amart neighbors to help them,

* "Colonizadora" was the popular name for the Spanish Colonization Company, which set out to develop the new Spanish settlements in Morocco.

and met the Rogui's forces at the Nekor River in the autumn of
1908. Bu Hamara's commander was a Negro named Jilali Mul-
l'Udhu, and the Rifians were especially outraged at the thought of
being opposed by a man of color.[20] They trapped Mul-l'Udhu's
plains cavalry in the mud of flooded gardens and cut them down.
Inspired by the Beni Urriaguel victory, other tribes rose against
the Rogui. By summer of 1909, his forces had all been either
routed or destroyed, and he himself had become a fugitive. He
was ultimately captured by the Beni Mestara far over in the Wazzan region, and handed over to the new Sultan, Mulay Hafid, at
Fez in August 1909. At first the Rogui and his adopted son, who
had been captured with him, were treated well, for Mulay Hafid
intended to appropriate the fortune he presumed the Rogui had
salted away, and he knew he would need the Rogui's signature
in order to get hold of it. (The adopted son had been treated to
a sexual debauch, during which he had boasted that the Rogui
had more than a million dollars in Spanish banks.) Apparently
the signature was not forthcoming, for the Rogui's fate was a hideous one.* He was confined in a cramped wooden cage and paraded through the labyrinthine streets of Fez as though he were
a wild animal. Then he was fiendishly tortured, in hopes that he
might reveal where he had put his supposed booty. According to
Maldonado, he was then thrown into a pit with a lion, which
mauled him but did not kill him; and finally he was stabbed by
a slave, then burned to death.[21]

The Rogui's defeat proved that Rifian tribesmen, although they
were prone to squabble among themselves, were nevertheless capable of closing ranks and presenting a solid front to invaders.
One result of the defeat was the rise to power of some of the *imgharen,* who became little dictators in their own backyards; Hadj

---

* Horrible tortures were the usual fate of criminals or enemies of the Sultan
in Morocco in those days. Pierre van Paassen relates some of the ways in which
El Mansour, a terrifying dwarf who became Sultan around 1590, killed his
enemies. He once put a rival in a glass cage and had him smeared with honey;
then he and the victim's wives laughed and applauded while the man was eaten
alive by ants. On another occasion El Mansour had a rival cut to pieces so slowly
that it took the man a week to die. (Van Paassen, p. 251.) Patrick Turnbull is
one of many travelers who report that well into the twentieth century, the main
gates of the larger Moroccan cities were often decorated with the decomposing
heads of those who had challenged the governmental power (Turnbull, p. 31).

Mohand Biqqish of Geznaya was among the outstanding new leaders of this type. Having driven out the Rogui, the Rifians saw no reason to stop fighting. Why not drive all the foreigners out of the country? In July 1909, they attacked the Spanish workmen who were building a bridge for the Compañía Española de Minas near Monte Uixan, killing seven of them and forcing the others to flee for their lives.[22] General Marina, the commander at Melilla, decided to retaliate, and asked for reinforcements from Spain. This request provoked a violent reaction from the Spanish people, who still mourned the sacrifice of so many lives in the Philippines and Cuba. While the politicians bickered, the press screamed that the youth of Spain was being sacrificed for the sake of the mining interests and the military. To make matters worse, the government was so badly advised as to call up 850 reservists, the majority of whom were from Catalonia, where anti-government feeling ran highest. Most of these men had believed they were exempt from further military service; none had had any training for a number of years, and many had married, set up households, and entered civilian occupations.[23] As the reservists marched to board ship at Barcelona, a mob of wailing women and children tried to oppose their departure, pleading with the soldiers to lay down their arms and refuse to fight. The event precipitated a general strike, which was followed by some furious rioting, much of it directed against the Church. Dozens of convents and monasteries were burned, and it was only after a week of fighting between the Army and the crowds—a week that came to be known as "Tragic Week" in Spanish history—that order was restored. According to Joan Connelly, 136 civilians, policemen, and soldiers were killed, and many more than that were arrested.[24] Francisco Ferrer, intellectual anarchist and friend of the would-be regicide Matteo Morral, was accused of leading this insurrection.[25] Guilty or innocent, Ferrer was shot; and the government was once more in control.

Meanwhile, just outside Melilla the Spanish Army ran into stubborn opposition. In bloody skirmishes from July 23 to July 27, it lost ninety officers, including a general and two colonels, and over a thousand men. According to Ruiz Albéniz, the majority of these casualties were directly attributable to the lack of foresight shown by General Pintos. When the general's troops arrived in Morocco, still slightly groggy from a rough sea passage, they were taken directly to the front in a swaying train. Toiling up the slopes of Monte Gurugú wore them to the point of exhaustion, and when they pleaded for a rest and a chance to eat, the general gave them permission. The tribesmen immediately struck from ambush at a ravine called Barranco del Lobo. General Pintos himself was among the first to be killed.[26] It took the Army the rest of the year to gain control of Monte Gurugú and to occupy the villages of Nador and Zeluan, a short distance south of Melilla. The hero of the 1909 campaign was Corporal Luis Noval, who, as a captive of the Rifians, was forced to lead a contingent of them to an important post in the Spanish line. When Noval and his captors had stolen to the very edge of the position, the corporal suddenly stood up and shouted: "We are Moors! Fire on us!" The resultant volley killed Noval, but it also broke up the attack and helped save the situation for the Spanish.[27]

It had long been obvious to the military authorities that control of Melilla lay with whoever held the heights of Monte Gurugú, largest of the series of peaks and bluffs that stretch south and southwest of the city. The Army, 40,000 strong by September, surrounded Monte Gurugú, and in the last ten days of the month pushed the tribesmen out of these high salients. A few weeks before this, Colonel Larrea and a Spanish force had invaded the Quebdana tribal area south and southeast of Melilla—an area almost unknown to Europeans—and in a savage six-day campaign of killing and crop-destroying, had completely subdued the tribe. Throughout most of October and November, the Spanish tried to negotiate with the tribal leaders, but it was not until after another brief offensive during the last few days of November that the tribes agreed to negotiate. Since much of their land was occupied by the Spanish, and since they had no strong allies or further resources for fighting on, peace was the only alternative. The war had cost Spain more than 4,000 casualties, yet her hold on northern Morocco was as tenuous as ever. The heights of Gurugú were fortified in a number of places, but the posts were small, badly placed, and poorly manned. General Pintos' downfall had demonstrated how inept Army field leadership had become, and yet nothing was done to remedy the situation, or to provide a better system of fortifications.

Although King Alfonso visited the Melilla area just after the cessation of hostilities in order to familiarize himself with the problems faced by his commanders, it did little to improve his popularity, which seems to have declined steadily from 1909 onward. The Army accused him of giving the majority of promotions to desk soldiers instead of to the fighters in the front lines; and the Spanish people bitterly resented the personal and financial sacrifices that had been demanded of them in consequence of his latest Moroccan campaign.

As a result of the Act of Algeciras, the Spanish had signed an accord in 1910 with the Sultan by which he promised to establish a native police force to reduce banditry and to prevent any major rupture of the uneasy peace. But the Sultan had been unable to create such a body, and so the Spanish Army did it for him. In June 1911, the Regulares, a force composed of native tribesmen loyal to Spain, was founded at Melilla.[28] This command was destined to be the training ground of some of Spain's finest military leaders, among them José Sanjurjo, Manuel Gonzáles Tablas, and Francisco Franco. Also in 1911, the Spaniards quietly extended their lines westward from Melilla. This slight advance was enough to touch off another uprising among the tribes, led by a chief called El Mizzian.[29] He proclaimed a *jihad* against the Christians, and began hostilities by attacking a Spanish topographical party at the Kert River in August 1911. A Spanish offensive had carried across the Plain of Garet all the way to the Kert by winter, but the combination of bad weather and enemy pressure finally forced the Spanish all the way back to the Zeluan-Melilla area. The struggle dragged on until the spring of 1912, when El Mizzian's death in a minor skirmish deprived his men of a leader. They dispersed, and the fighting came to a gradual close. It was during this campaign that the Spanish General Staff first seriously discussed the feasibility of landing troops at Alhucemas Bay—the only area on the whole Mediterranean coast where large numbers of troops could be disembarked, and thus the obvious key to control of the Rif. But the details of the carelessly guarded plan had leaked out, and the Bucoya and Beni Urriaguel tribesmen who lived there had hastily fortified the lowlands around the Bay. The Spanish did succeed in raiding these shores, and in the process they burned down the house of an Urriagli notable named Abd el Krim, father of the future Rifian leader; but the Kert campaign terminated inconclusively. At its end, the Spanish Army held a line a bit farther to the west than before, but the rebel tribes were unsubdued, and the Rif remained inviolate.

At this juncture the Spanish chose to move into the western sector of Morocco. Two dynamic figures were to hold the center of the stage—Lt. Col. Manuel Fernández Silvestre, and Mulay Ahmed er Raisuli. Silvestre entered the western Moroccan scene in 1908 as the chief Spanish instructor of the indigenous police force newly organized at Casablanca, in the French Zone, under the provisions of the Act of Algeciras.[30] The colonel was a handsome, powerful man with a bushy black moustache—an impetuous soldier with a preference for cavalry charges and man-to-man encounters. He had served in Cuba when he was only nineteen, and had been so badly wounded in his first battle that he had barely survived. Silvestre had originally been assigned to Morocco in 1904, at Melilla; now he was thirty-seven years old, battle-scarred, and very ambitious. Before his assignment in Morocco, he had been an aide and a personal favorite of King Alfonso. Tremendously popular, both with his troops and with the ladies, Silvestre was a real-life character as flamboyant as any to be found in the pages of a romantic novel.

Raisuli was equally extraordinary.[31] He was called "The Eagle of Zinat," after the hill village of the Fahs tribe east of Tangier where he was born about 1871. He was descended from Mulay Abdeslam ben Mshish, the revered saint of Jebel Alam, a holy mountain in the central Jibala, in the tribal lands of Beni Aros.* Raisuli's father was a prominent Sherif known throughout the northwest as a man so powerful that he would lend his allegiance to the Blad l-Makhzen only when it suited him to do so. That any Sherif could maintain this extreme independence is understandable if one remembers that Morocco had always been a country

---

* Mulay Abdeslam ben Mshish is the Jibala's greatest saint. It is said that seven annual visits to his tomb in consecutive years are as meritorious as a pilgrimage to Mecca.

where the strong did as they pleased, and the weak prayed that Allah would reward them in Paradise for the miseries they had to endure on earth.

As a youth, Raisuli studied religion and Koranic law, displaying unusual perception and definite qualities of leadership. But religion was far too tame for him. He became a combination Robin Hood, feudal baron, and tyrannical bandit. On occasion, Raisuli would deliberately ride through and destroy growing crops just to prove he was somebody to be reckoned with. People said, but not very loudly, that his entire education had consisted of the Koran, horses, and women, and he was notorious for his carousing at Tetuan. While Raisuli was still in his twenties, Ba Ahmed ordered the Pasha of Tangier to arrest him for his acts of brigandage. To accomplish this, the Pasha, who was Raisuli's foster brother, paid a visit to Raisuli's little palace at Zinat, about twelve miles east of Tangier. There he was hospitably received, in accordance with Islamic custom. When Raisuli repaid the call by visiting the Pasha at Tangier, he was seized, beaten insensible, and thrown into prison. His own men thought Raisuli had been killed, but in fact the Pasha had sent Raisuli far down the Atlantic coast to Mogador, where he kept him imprisoned for four appalling years.[32] At Mogador, Raisuli was fastened to a stone bench, and heavy chains were fixed around his neck, feet, and hands in such a way that in all those years he was never able to bring his hands together. His feet festered, and were often black with flies and lice, and rats ate the feet and legs of a dead man chained beside him. Luckily, Raisuli was saved from insanity or a miserable death by the ministrations of relatives and faithful friends, who were allowed to bring him food and news of the outside world. When Abd el Aziz came to the throne at the turn of the century, he granted amnesty to numerous prisoners all over the country, and Raisuli was one of them. His release was brought about mainly through the efforts of Leo Gentile, an Italian diplomat at Tangier who had known and entertained Raisuli in former days, and who was a friend of the new Sultan as well.

Raisuli was free again, but he bore the marks of those chains upon his soul as well as his body. Rosita Forbes thought that "lust of war and lust of gold" were the two strongest passions in Raisuli's heart after his imprisonment. He had become appreciably more cruel and relentless. The Jibala had never forgotten him, and even though all his property had been confiscated, he had no trouble in rounding up a new band of freebooters. For the next quarter of a century, until his capture by Abd el Krim and his subsequent death in 1925, Raisuli was the scourge of the northwest. He kidnapped whom he would, pillaged his own tribesmen, and shrewdly fought off the Spanish forces who sought to move into the Jibala or, when it seemed expedient, fought alongside them. Like his father before him, he ignored or used the Sultanate as the mood or the need occurred; for Raisuli, like many Moroccans before him and since, had learned to hedge his bets. His relatively long career was proof of his acumen and agility.

Raisuli's exploits were legendary. He kept a fleet of small ships on the Atlantic and the Mediterranean for preying on coastal traffic. He once chopped the ears off a messenger merely because the unfortunate man had brought him bad news. He shaved the beard of another man who displeased him—a humiliating thing to do to a Muslim even today, because it signifies negation of the man's virility. He is supposed to have bought a man against whom he had a grudge from a rival chieftain for the equivalent of $1,500, for the sole purpose of having the pleasure of cutting the man's head off at the door of his own house. He murdered his brother-in-law, who had taken a second wife, to spare his sister the humiliation of being supplanted by a rival.[33] He levied an annual tax of $15, a huge sum then as now in Morocco, on every peasant household; and what is more, he collected most of it. Many tribesmen believed that nothing less than "a gold pistol ball made in Mecca" could kill him.[34]

If on some raid Raisuli and his henchmen took prisoners who were poor and worth nothing, they usually butchered the captives or made them slaves. Valuable captives were held for fantastic ransoms. Three of Raisuli's kidnappings brought him not only small fortunes but worldwide notoriety and, eventually and paradoxically, an appointment as Governor of the Atlantic Zone of Morocco. In 1903, Raisuli's raiders ran off with Walter Harris; but since Harris and the bandit chief were old acquaintances, and since the prisoner had always been generous and hospitable to the neighboring tribesman, Raisuli held him in the hills for a mere three weeks. Harris was finally exchanged, not for money, but for several

of Raisuli's own men who had been imprisoned by the Pasha of
Tangier.[35]

The most sensational kidnapping of the brigand's long career
was that of Ion Perdicaris, a wealthy Greek-American citizen of
Tangier, and Perdicaris's stepson, Cromwell Varley.[36] On the night
of May 18, 1904, Raisuli's band swooped down on the Perdicaris
estate near Tangier, seized Perdicaris and Varley, and carried the
two men off into the hills. The older man was allowed to write to
the American Consul at Tangier and explain his predicament. At
the same time, Raisuli sent a letter to the Sultan demanding
$70,000 ransom for the release of the prisoners. In addition, he in-
sisted that those of his own men who were held in Tangier prisons
be immediately freed; that the Imperial Army units in the north of
Morocco be withdrawn; and that he himself be installed as Pasha
of Tangier.*

Word of Raisuli's impudence was flashed to the United States,
where President Theodore Roosevelt was attending the Republican National Convention at Chicago. The convention promised
to be a dull affair, since it was a foregone conclusion that Roosevelt
would be renominated, and the President was desperately pondering what he could do to arouse public interest in the proceedings.
The Perdicaris kidnapping was a godsend, for it provided exactly
the kind of spectacular situation that T.R. knew how to exploit.
After all, Perdicaris was supposed to be an American citizen, and
nobody was going to push Americans around any place in the
world if T.R. could do anything about it. The President ordered
his Secretary of State, John Hay, to draft a cable to R. S. Gummeré,
the American Consul at Tangier. That famous message, "I want
Perdicaris alive or Raisuli dead," made history. T.R. read the
cable to the convention with his typical dash and ardor, and the
delegates thunderously acclaimed him. To prove that he meant
what he said, Roosevelt dispatched seven warships of the South
Atlantic Fleet to Tangier Bay. He let it be known that he might

* G. H. Selous, the British Consul at Fez, who was well acquainted with the
Sultan's court and army, tells us that "Imperial Army" was an unduly imposing
title, for the Sultan's forces were rabble dressed in vivid coats, baggy trousers,
and red fezzes. Their weapons were antiquated, and their ideas of drill and formation were laughable. Selous admits, however, that two squadrons of the
Sultan's horse guards were relatively efficient. (Selous, pp. 125–27.)

land U.S. Marines and unleash them on Raisuli, and made it sound as though he meant to declare war on Morocco if Sultan Abd el Aziz did not act quickly to free Perdicaris and Varley. Abd el Aziz's plight was a frustrating one, caught as he was between the clever Eagle of Zinat on the one hand and the might of the United States on the other. It took almost two months for the harried Sultan to arrange it, but Perdicaris and Varley were eventually returned alive and well to their home in Tangier. Perdicaris, who was over seventy, seems to have enjoyed himself thoroughly. He and Raisuli knew each other well, and Leo Gentile, the Italian diplomat who had helped free Raisuli from the Mogador dungeon, was Perdicaris's son-in-law. Perdicaris had talked a good deal with his captor, and considered Raisuli neither a bandit nor a murderer, but a patriot forced into brigandage to save his native soil and his people from the yoke of tyranny.[37] Meanwhile the frantic Abd el Aziz, whose *mehalla* was ineffective against Raisuli's forces, had acceded to every one of the bandit's demands, and had actually appointed him Pasha of Tangier and Governor of the whole Jibala. Raisuli was delighted with the international furor he had created. He emerged from the affair $70,000 richer, and glowing with new prestige. He was now legally, as well as actually, the most important man in northern Morocco. The irony of the Perdicaris kidnapping, which was not revealed until some time later, lay in the fact that two weeks before T.R. sent his famous cable, the State Department had discovered that Perdicaris was a Civil War draft dodger, and furthermore, that he was not even a citizen of the United States. At the beginning of the American Civil War, Perdicaris had registered in Athens as a Greek citizen in order to avoid military service. Roosevelt was well briefed on the facts, but he sent the cable anyway—perhaps because the dramatic possibilities of the affair were just too great for him to resist.

Raisuli lasted only a short while as Pasha of Tangier. His administration was one of deliberate terrorism and corruption. He cut off the city's electrical power whenever it suited him, and tried to blackmail the more prominent Europeans in the community. He killed much too readily, and his choice of tortures aroused horror among the foreign diplomats stationed there. Abd el Aziz had the courage to relieve Raisuli of his office in 1906, but the

vengeful bandit further embarrassed him the next year by kidnapping the Caid Maclean, who had been sent to Raisuli's camp
as liaison officer by the Sultan.[38]

Donald McKenzie agrees with Selous on the state of the "Imperial Army" and its efficiency, and he reports that despite all the
efforts of Maclean and a few other European instructors, the Sultan's forces—which were, after all, the main instrument of order
in the Blad l-Makhzen—were badly equipped and poorly disciplined. Each man received a penny a day, and had to furnish his
own food.[39] Thus, through necessity, the "army" became a veri-
table band of robbers, who were incidentally employed to collect
taxes forcibly when and if they could. It was seven months before
the Sultan succeeded in obtaining the release of his Scots adviser,
and even then it cost him $100,000 in ransom.[40]

When Mulay Hafid rose against Abd el Aziz in 1908, Raisuli,
sagely bet-hedging, chose the former; and when Hafid attained
the throne, Raisuli was astute enough to hand over to the new,
tougher Sultan the ransom he had received for Maclean.[41] Raisuli
then made a personal visit to the new Sultan at Fez in 1908, swear-
ing a secret oath with him that he would "never cease from protecting the Moslem land and the Moslem people against the Christian."[42] Hafid rewarded Raisuli by reinstating him as Governor of
the Jibala and part of the Lukus, and making him Pasha of Asilah
as well. Neither Raisuli nor anybody else had ever before held
complete control over the unruly tribesmen of this region, but
Raisuli was feared and respected wherever he went. No other man
could have contained the constant ferment in the Jibala.

After receiving his new titles and new responsibilities, Raisuli
settled down to a pseudo-respectable routine. He had palaces large
and small at Tangier, Tetuan, and Chaouen, at the small Atlantic
ports of Asilah and Larache, and in the hills at Zinat and Tazrut;
and his harems of beautiful wives and concubines were the peers
of the Sultan's own. For all his high-handedness and cruelty, Ahmed er Raisuli appears to have been a man of vision, with a shrewd
understanding of the political situation in which Morocco found
itself.[43] More than anything else—after his own personal advance-
ment, of course—Raisuli wanted an independent Muslim Morocco. But in view of the debility of the Sultanate and the widespread anarchy (to which he himself had contributed), it seemed

to him inevitable that Europe would interfere further in Morocco; and he preferred what he hoped would be temporary domination by the comparatively inefficient Spaniards to the better organized and more strongly enforced control of the French.

While some Moroccans may have supported Raisuli's political views, few of them were pleased by his methods of enforcing them. The Spanish at Ceuta received a constant stream of complaints from the people of the Tetuan area imploring the Army to protect them from Raisuli as well as from lesser but equally ruthless adventurers like Ash-shaja'i, "the Brave One," in the Anjera. Further south, the town of Alcazarquivir was a target for pillage by the nearby Sumata tribe; and these townsmen, too, asked for Spanish protection. In 1911 a French detachment arrived at Alcazarquivir, claiming that they had come to recruit soldiers for the Sultan's Army at Fez.[44] This interference by the French in a territory that was clearly about to become a Spanish sphere of influence had to be stopped. Spanish marines under a Lieutenant Colonel Dueñas made a difficult landing at Larache on June 8, 1911, and continued inland and south to Alcazarquivir several days later.[45] Spain at once notified all powers signatory to the Act of Algeciras that she had disembarked troops on Morocco's Atlantic coast. This announcement unleashed a stormy reaction throughout Europe, particularly in Spain itself. The Spanish people had not forgotten the fiasco at Melilla in 1909, and they greatly resented being hustled into yet another military venture for which they were ill-prepared, and which would bring little glory and much suffering to an already burdened nation. Few understood why Spain was in Morocco, and almost no one had any hope that the Spanish government, indecisive and disorganized as always, could plan and execute a successful campaign of occupation. The French, for their part, accused Spain of violating the Franco-Spanish Accord of 1904, in which Spain had agreed not to move into any part of her future protectorate without first consulting France. Spain replied simply that growing anarchy in the area had forced her to act too rapidly for prior discussion.[46]

It was obvious that a man of strength and experience in Moroccan affairs was needed to direct the Spanish effort at Larache. The choice fell on Lieutenant Colonel Silvestre, who arrived at Alcazar in June 1911. The situation was touchy there, for several minor

incidents had occurred, including the arrest by Spanish troops of
the French Consul at Alcazar on charges of carrying a pistol. But
since the Spanish were now on the scene in force in what was pri-
vately acknowledged to be their own province, the French detachment had no choice but to retire to Fez. Silvestre was left with a
fait accompli, and the problem of cooperating with Raisuli in
maintaining order.

Silvestre and his staff made their initial visit to Raisuli at his
Asilah palace in August. The Spanish were deferentially received,
and smooth relations between the two leaders seemed assured. But
by the time of Silvestre's second visit in October, Raisuli's characteristic despotism and misuse of power were beginning to revolt
the colonel. Silvestre had a somewhat naïve eagerness to make good
in his new post, and he proposed to correct some of the wrongs he
thought he saw on all sides. Once when Silvestre paid a surprise
call at Asilah to investigate stories of Raisuli's extortion and to see
for himself what prison conditions were like, he was shown a cell
containing nearly a hundred men, all chained together, some of
them dead or dying. The whole place reeked of decay and excre-
ment. "God!" exclaimed Silvestre. "Are all the men in the country
criminals? This is horrible, inhuman. I will not stand it in a country which is under our protection!"[47] The glaring abuse of authority that Silvestre thought he saw was interpreted by him simply in
terms of good and evil, and not in terms of the background against
which it was being perpetrated. Raisuli, after all, was the Sultan's
legally appointed deputy in the Jibala and Lukus, and his methods,
no matter how cruel, were better understood and accepted by his
countrymen than any infidel invader's acts could ever be. In Morocco, the law of the strongest had always held sway, and harshness
and brutality were the normal conditions of everyday life. Most
of the tribesmen who attempted to conciliate Silvestre were doing
so in hopes of settling old scores with Raisuli: far from allying
themselves with the Spanish in order to enforce a greater degree
of justice, these men were cannily counting upon Silvestre to free
them from an authority that they found inconvenient. Silvestre
did not understand that the more the Spanish tried to foist European standards upon the comparatively primitive Moroccans, the
more they weakened Raisuli's prestige and power, and that if Raisuli's hold on the people weakened, Spain would be forced to keep

order in his place. Moreover, Silvestre seemed to forget that he had been sent to northwestern Morocco, not to oppose or to interfere with Raisuli, but rather to support him in his position as a regional chief of the Sherifian Empire.

At the beginning of 1912, Silvestre was appointed a full colonel for "exceptional and meritorious service"—a promotion that seemed to vindicate his aggressive conduct of affairs around Larache. Nevertheless, the colonel had begun to realize that Raisuli was the real power in the Jibala; and after the setting up of the French Protectorate in March 1912, when it was clear that the establishment of a similar Spanish Protectorate was only a question of time, Silvestre recommended to higher authority that Raisuli be chosen as the first Khalifa of the Spanish Zone. In spite of this recommendation, which he repeated in August, Silvestre's private feelings about Raisuli were still ambivalent, and he soon plunged himself and Spain into an awkward situation. Exasperated by Raisuli's continued attempts to exact money and goods from various communities, Silvestre with a detachment of his troops actually fired on some of Raisuli's tax collectors. To make matters worse, the Spanish commander then removed Raisuli as Pasha of Asilah, and gave the post to one of Raisuli's traditional enemies, a man named Ermiki. Raisuli sped to Tangier in a fury to protest to his old friend the Spanish Minister, Zugasti. How, asked Raisuli, was it possible that the "protected" people of a Protectorate could be attacked by the very "protectors" themselves? Zugasti persuaded Raisuli that Silvestre was wrong in this instance, and that Spain's intentions were friendly; but Raisuli returned to Asilah in a resentful and suspicious frame of mind.

Thus the new Spanish Protectorate began to take form at the end of 1912 in an atmosphere of uneasy accord. In reality, the Protectorate existed only on paper. Spain held a few miles of territory around Melilla in the east, a similar area around Ceuta in the north, and the small Asilah-Larache-Alcazarquivir triangle in the southwest. Spain's various clashes with the Rifians had demonstrated how difficult it was going to be to occupy the new zone. Candido Lobera, editor of *El Telegrama del Rif*, the newspaper at Melilla, wrote: "If Beni Wariyagel [Beni Urriaguel] is reduced to submission, peace will reign in the Rif. We can never penetrate the heart of the Rif without previous disembarkations at the coast of Alhucemas."[48] Lobera, some of the military chiefs, and a few others knew that this was the only possible solution to the occupation problem, but no one in authority was prepared to take so drastic a step. Meanwhile, far from "protecting" the inhabitants from various chimerical dangers, the Spanish Army in Morocco had its hands full protecting itself from the Rifians in the east, and from the opposition gradually developing behind Raisuli in the west.

4. THE SPANISH PROTECTORATE
1912–1921

Now that Spain had legal right to her protectorate in Morocco, she was faced with the problem of occupying it and governing it effectively. As Stanley Payne points out, Spain was poorly prepared to do either. "Had it not been for the vigor of French imperialism, Spain would probably never have become deeply involved in Morocco. It cannot be said that creation of the Spanish Protectorate was produced by a groundswell of expansionist sentiment in Spain. Rather, this decision was an act of the minority ministry then in power, and was encouraged, it would seem, by the King."[1] In fact, there was widespread disillusionment with the Protectorate treaty in Spain; despite offers of higher pay and the chance for promotion, few Army officers volunteered for service in Morocco.[2]

The first High Commissioner of Spanish Morocco was the former commander of the Ceuta garrison, General Felipe Alfau, a soldier of sound judgment and experience, who had served in Morocco for many years.[3] In response to the pleas of the inhabitants of Tetuan, who were constantly being harried by Raisuli, Alfau had marched south early in 1913.* The general's strategy of a gradual and well-prepared advance met with hardly any opposition, and the Spanish Army entered Tetuan on February 19. There was little fighting, and losses were negligible; and as they moved down the peninsula, the Spanish had time to build a road and to

---

* Tetuan, which had been chosen as the capital city of the new Protectorate, lies against sloping hills on the north side of the Martín River, only a few miles west of the Mediterranean. The city commands a superb view of the mountains to the south. On the south side of the Martín, the land slants steeply upward to a formidable wall of rock that terminates in high mesas and a series of sharp peaks and crags. These stone bastions are called the Gorgues, and they fall within the tribal boundaries of Beni Hozmar.

install telephone and telegraph lines connecting Tetuan with Ceuta.

The Spanish troops who occupied Tetuan behaved themselves badly there, looting, raping, and generally terrorizing the native inhabitants. The officers, some of whom comported themselves little better than their men, did nothing to control the situation, and to make matters worse, allowed Spanish prostitutes and other riffraff to pour into the city in the wake of the military forces.[4] It is no wonder that many Moroccan families fled from Tetuan and took refuge in the nearby mountains, joining forces with the rebels there, and that others sought asylum within the neutral precincts of Tangier. This was an inauspicious beginning for the Spanish program of "peaceful" colonization.

Most Spanish writers of the day had little to say for their countrymen as colonizers. Major Augusto Vivero, one of the new band of *africanistas*—those Spaniards, mostly Army officers and politicians, who favored Spanish expansion in Morocco—felt that the results of the Colonizadora (the colonial venture) were important. He praised the Spanish for constructing water and market facilities, and insisted that Moroccan land values shot up wherever the Spanish settled.[5] Louis Bertrand noted that Spain had built three hundred miles of roads behind the Kert River before 1921.[6] But better-qualified observers, including the few Spanish who lived and worked in Morocco and who realized how little was known about the tribesmen and the hinterland, tended to be skeptical about Spain's position in the Protectorate. Victor Ruiz Albéniz, for example, who worked for eight years as a doctor at the Monte Uixan mines, wrote that the Spanish had no understanding at all of the Protectorate or its needs. How, he asked, could the Spanish build a successful protectorate in Morocco when none of them had the least notion of the country's geography, its resources, or the condition of its people?[7]

Antonio Azpeitua, a Basque intellectual, agreed with Ruiz Albéniz. The State, wrote Azpeitua, should properly serve as the instrument of society, but in Spain it served only the particular ends of individuals.[8] In his opinion, the Spanish could not possibly succeed in improving the lot of the Moroccans, since their own educational and economic standards were so low, and their concept of the Moors so distorted. Moreover, the Spanish people were used to thinking of themselves as conquerors, not colonizers. Most of them viewed the Moroccans with implacable hostility, and the administrators themselves showed little enthusiasm for their task. According to Francisco Bastos Ansart, a major of the Engineers, the Spanish lacked the energy to govern well, and were almost totally uninterested in learning either the history or the needs of their new charges. There was a general belief among the Spanish occupation forces that the Moors were sworn enemies of all Christians, and therefore could not be trusted.[9] Prince Aage of Denmark, who fought as a captain in the French Foreign Legion in Morocco from 1923 to 1925, claimed that the Spanish were looked down upon by the French as poor colonizers.[10] Arturo Barea, a middle-class Spanish intellectual who served as a sergeant with the Spanish Army in Morocco for the better part of four years, tells us that through incompetence or through lack of enthusiasm, the Spanish administrators failed to bring any sort of order to Morocco during the first twenty-five years of the Protectorate's existence. He characterizes the Protectorate of that period as a combination of battlefield, tavern, and brothel. No provisions were made, says Barea, for supporting the native economy. His commentary on Spain's fitness to be a colonial power was bitter: "Civilize the Moroccans ... we? We from Castile, Andalusia, Gerona, who cannot read or write? Nonsense! Who is going to civilize us? Our village has no school; its houses [are] clay; we sleep in our clothes ... in the stable ... to keep warm. We eat an onion and a chunk of bread in the morning and go to work on the fields from sunrise to sunset ... we crack up with hunger and misery. The boss robs us, and if we complain, we are beaten by the Civil Guards."[11]

For administrative purposes, the Protectorate was divided into three *comandancias,* Larache, Ceuta, and Melilla; and because communications among them were difficult, the commanding officer of each *comandancia* was given local autonomy except over matters of general policy.[12] But who knew what "general policy" was? Although the heads of the *comandancias* were technically under the authority of the High Commissioner at Tetuan, they received orders directly from the Ministries of War and State in Madrid as well. In the Larache *comandancia,* the Spanish legation at Tangier added its voice to the general confusion. Civilian administration in Spanish Morocco was supposed to function through three special departments—those for Native Affairs, Economic Development, and Financial Affairs—but since few Spanish colonists lived in the Protectorate, and few native tribesmen were actually under the control of Spanish authority, the civilian administration was virtually powerless to effect changes or to enforce order on a significant scale.*

There were at least three opinions about the best way to solve the problem of occupying the Jibala. (The Melilla sector was expected to present a more formidable problem, and consequently the Army had decided to defer operations there.) High Commissioner Alfau wished to proceed as cautiously and as peacefully as possible in winning over the Jibli tribesmen and in adding their tribal areas to the territory controlled by Spain. Colonel Silvestre, on the other hand, advocated nothing less than an all-out war, for he hoped to crush Raisuli permanently and thus put a speedy end to opposition in the Jibala. The Spanish Minister at Tangier, Juan Zugasti, was of the opinion that the whole matter could be settled by flattering Raisuli and persuading him to be received with honors by King Alfonso at Madrid. Raisuli knew of the controversy between the Spanish commanders; he knew, too, that he had little chance of being named Khalifa of Spanish Morocco, though he was convinced that his qualifications were the best. He was a Sherif; he had been Pasha, Caid, and Governor; there was no more influential or knowledgeable person anywhere in northwestern Morocco. He would never be satisfied with empty honors bestowed by a Christian king.

At this juncture, it was Silvestre's impetuosity that further complicated the Spanish position in the Jibala.[13] In March 1913, Rai-

* Many Moroccans lived and died without even knowing who the reigning Sultan was. According to Coon, the Ait Atta of the Jebel Sarro, in the High Atlas Mountains of southeastern French Morocco, the last tribe to submit to the French (in 1933), revered a local holy family, because they believed that by their intercession these people kept them free of the Blad l-Makhzen. Most Moroccans had never seen a Western foreigner, much less a foreign soldier, nor had they any knowledge of international treaties affecting their country. Their first knowledge of the Spanish Protectorate would have been the excited tale brought home by some itinerant merchant, or the sudden sight of a file of alien soldiers. In view of this, it was easy for the various tribes to believe that Spain was coming to Morocco to conquer the country, to abrogate all Islamic institutions, and to destroy the traditional tribal way of life.

suli had charged the village of Jaldien, in Beni Aros, the sum of
25,000 pesetas in ransom for the release of some villagers whom he
had confined at Asilah. Silvestre was angered by what he felt was a
perfect example of Raisuli's corruption. He marched to Asilah,
where he not only prevented payment of the ransom, but forced
Raisuli to free the prisoners. Then, after Raisuli had ridden off
to protest to Zugasti at Tangier, Silvestre put the chieftain's family
under guard at Asilah. These high-handed tactics were too much
for Madrid, and the Minister of War sent a telegram relieving Silvestre of authority.[14] Meanwhile, the Spanish minister at Tangier
tried to mollify Raisuli by arranging for the release of his family,
but to no avail. Incensed over the Jaldien incident, resentful at
being rejected for the office of Khalifa, alarmed over the misbehavior of Spanish troops at Tetuan, and perhaps hopeful that by
playing hard to get he could still find some personal gain, Raisuli
slipped away to Tazrut, deep in the Beni Aros mountains. In an
interview with Silvestre just before his flight, Raisuli had made his
position plain: "You and I," he said to the impatient colonel,
"form the tempest. You are the furious wind; I am the calm sea.
You arrive and you blow irritatingly. I am disturbed, and I burst
into a fury of foam. Now we have a great storm. But between you
and me there is a difference. I, like the sea, never leave my place,
while you, like the wind, are never in yours."[15]

The new Khalifa, selected by the Spanish and duly appointed by
the Sultan, was an unremarkable man by the name of Mulay el
Mehdi, whose grandfather had been Sultan during Morocco's
struggle with Spain in 1860, and whose father was a Caid of the
northern provinces.[16] The Spanish breathed a sigh of relief when
El Mehdi was installed at Tetuan in April 1913, for they felt that
in him they had found a Khalifa who would neither oppress and
alienate the natives through corrupt practices nor rock the Moroccan boat by opposing Spanish colonial policy. But Silvestre's
treatment of Raisuli and his family and the misbehavior of the
Spanish troops at Tetuan had not been forgotten, and in spite of
El Mehdi's appointment, opposition to Spanish occupation grew
on all sides. In the neighborhood of Ben Karrich, only a few miles
south of Tetuan on the slopes of the Gorgues, a group of rebel
tribesmen menaced the local Spanish outpost; and in the hills half-

way between Tetuan and Tangier, a Spanish detachment from
Fondak Ain Jedida was forced to retire to the capital city because
of harassment by guerrillas.

Through the summer of 1913 there were attacks on both Asilah
and Alcazar, all along the Ceuta–Tetuan road, and upon small encampments wherever Spanish troops happened to be. The Spanish
public blamed General Alfau, since his unopposed occupation of
Tetuan had led them to believe that here, at last, was a general
who combined the qualities of tact with those of military finesse
in such a way that Spain would soon occupy the whole Protectorate
without paying the familiar heavy price in casualties and taxes.
The disillusionment was great. General Alfau, a good soldier
nevertheless, was recalled in August, and General José Marina y
Vega, the commander at Melilla, was substituted for him.[17] Silvestre, in spite of his capacity for embarrassing the high command,
not only was retained in Morocco but was promoted to the rank
of brigadier general. His troops occupied a line of small posts in
the west, extending from the edge of the Tangier Zone south to a
village called Tenin de Sidi Yamani. Meanwhile, in the Melilla
comandancia, General Gómez Jordana had advanced gradually
into the country of the Beni Sidel and the Beni Bu Yahi, encoun-
tering little resistance along the way. Jordana, one of the few able
and enlightened generals in the Spanish Army, had a real interest
in bettering the lot of the Moroccans. He set up native schools
and granaries, and built roadways throughout the territory under
his command.

Unlike his hotheaded subordinate General Silvestre, Marina
believed that an understanding with Raisuli was a basic condition
for any sort of lasting peace in the Jibala. To this end, he sent mes-
sages to Raisuli at Tazrut in May 1915 by the hand of Ali Akalay,
an intimate friend of the Caid.[18] But en route to Tazrut, Ali
Akalay and the servant who had accompanied him mysteriously
vanished. Some days later, their bodies were found floating in a
small stream near the southern borders of the Tangier Zone, in the
Larache *comandancia.* They had been robbed, strangled, disfigured, then thrown into the water. Enraged, the High Commissioner appointed an investigating committee, which soon traced
the murders to Ermiki, the newly appointed Pasha of Asilah.

Ermiki assumed guilt for the murders, saying that the idea had
been his alone, and was summarily executed. However, it soon
came out that he had acted at the prompting of certain Spanish
officers who had no desire for a peaceful settlement with Raisuli.[19]
In the face of this revelation, General Marina had no choice but
to resign his post. Silvestre, in whose *comandancia* the murders had
occurred, and who could hardly have been entirely ignorant of a
plot so closely linked to the political action he advocated, was recalled to Spain. Apparently, Alfonso approved his favorite's aggressive qualities while overlooking his impulsive behavior, and
expected substantial accomplishments from him in the future.[20]

In July 1915, Francisco Gómez Jordana, the capable commander
who had slowly and skillfully consolidated Spanish gains in the
Melilla *comandancia,* replaced the hapless Marina as High Commissioner. It was at this point that Spanish neutrality in the European conflict came into question. These were particularly perilous
years for Spain, underscored by the titanic struggle of World War I
in Europe and by the irritating involvement in Spanish Morocco,
where Spain wished to preserve an uneasy peace. Not only were
the problems of Raisuli and the Occupation unsolved, but there
was now added the further complication of German agents operating against France from the relative protection of the Spanish
Zone. It will be recalled that while Spain held nominal control
of the population, the Khalifa, as the Sultan's representative, was
not only the spiritual leader of the tribesmen, but also the agent of
French policy in Morocco. Furthermore, the Treaty of Fez stipu-
lated that the French Resident-General should serve as Minister of
Foreign Affairs for *all* Morocco. Morocco as a whole, then, was
under the authority of the French-controlled Sultan. But Spain,
while harboring Germans in its Protectorate, was not at war with
Germany. France was; therefore the Sultan, along with all his subjects, including those living in the Spanish Protectorate, was technically at war with Germany. There was but one way out of the
dilemma for Spain, and she took it in January 1916, sending diplomatic notes to each of the foreign chancelleries in the Protectorate
announcing the autonomy of Spanish Morocco in determining its
own foreign policy.[21] Although this act was in direct violation of
the Treaty of Fez, there was little the French could do about it

without attacking Spain directly. Caught up in the European struggle, France could not challenge Spain at this time, and so Spain was left with a *fait accompli*.

Although the Spanish nation continued to maintain its neutrality conscientiously enough, it is undeniable that many of its most prominent citizens, including some in the Protectorate, had pro-German sentiments. For this reason the Kaiser's agents in Spanish Morocco were able to pursue a definite program aimed at inciting certain tribes to harry the French. The Mannesmanns, for example, were friendly with many Moroccan leaders, including Raisuli and the elder Abd el Krim. While the government and the Protectorate looked the other way, the Germans brought guns, ammunition, and propaganda into the Rif and the Jibala by means of submarines at Tangier, Ceuta, and Melilla.[22] The Spanish seem not to have sensed the possibility that these materials might one day be turned against them by resentful tribesmen. German gold kept Raisuli temporarily quiet, though he was canny enough not to become a mere pawn of the Germans. Rather, he used them—as he used almost everyone with whom he came in contact—for his own benefit. An incidental result of the anti-French campaign was that it distracted hostile tribesmen from incursions against the Spanish.

At the end of September 1915, Raisuli and Gómez Jordana reached a secret agreement. Raisuli, in the name of the Sultan, was to be given authority over whatever tribes would submit to him. He thus became unofficial but actual co-equal with the Khalifa at Tetuan.[23] This expedient satisfied both Raisuli and the Spanish; what the Khalifa thought of it is not recorded, and would have made no difference anyway. But if the Spanish had hoped that Raisuli would now become docile, they were mistaken. True, his forces fought by the side of Spanish troops against the Beni Hozmar and the Beni Musuar, and they helped take Fondak Ain Jedida, thus securing the military trails between Tangier and Tetuan and isolating the dissidents of Wad Ras and the Anjera; but Raisuli could never be relied upon for long, and since he was always more interested in personal power and aggrandizement than he was in abiding by agreements, he was soon brewing new schemes. Having been given authority over those tribes that would submit to him, he systematically began to win

over by force those that were disposed to acknowledge the Khalifa. And he continued to harass the Spanish whenever possible.
A glaring instance of his treachery and his disdain for agreements
was the ambush and annihilation of a Spanish column in the
Wad Ras country not far from Tangier.[24] While advancing along
a small valley, a column of Spanish soldiers observed what they
took to be a Spanish officer and several troopers on a nearby
hill. The "officer"—actually a shaikh of the Wad Ras harka—
directed the column up the bed of a nearby stream and into an
exceptionally narrow ravine. As soon as the Spanish soldiers had
obediently entered this natural trap, they were assaulted on all
sides by tribesmen, and the whole column was massacred.

Madrid viewed General Jordana's constant complaints about
Raisuli's treachery as signs of his inability to cope with the demands of his new office, and the Spanish press joined in by accusing
Jordana of spending too much of the Army's budget.[25] Although
he was bitterly resentful of the injustices he was forced to endure
as the result of Madrid's refusal to let him act against Raisuli,
Jordana was powerless to do anything but renew his explanations
and pleas. Frustrated at every turn, he became ill, and died suddenly one day at his desk in the very act of writing still another
report to his superiors in Spain.[26]

To the difficult post made vacant by Gómez Jordana's death
came General Dámaso Berenguer, in August 1919. An outstanding
officer, Dámaso Berenguer was cultured, deliberate, reserved, and
technically able. He was born in Remedios, Cuba, in 1873, while
his officer father was serving there, and was graduated as a cavalry
officer from the General Military Academy in Spain. Although he
was only forty-six at the time of his Moroccan appointment, he had
already enjoyed a long and distinguished military career. Berenguer had fought on the Melilla front through the campaigns of
1909 and 1911, and it was his personal command that had defeated
El Mizzian in 1912 in Beni Sidel.* Berenguer served as colonel on
the staff of the first High Commissioner, General Alfau, in 1913,

* It was Berenguer who created the Regulares of Melilla in 1911 out of elements of the indigenous Moroccan police. The Regulares were usually used as
guards in areas newly occupied by the Spanish Army in Morocco. (According to
Antonio Azpeitua, a severe critic of Spain's Moroccan venture, the men who volunteered for the Regulares were likely to be outcasts from their own tribes, and
were therefore of questionable dependability. Azpeitua, p. 60.)

and had written a treatise on Spain's military problems in Morocco. In 1916 he was promoted to the rank of brigadier general and appointed Military Governor of Málaga. One of King Alfonso's favorites, Berenguer was made a major general in 1918 and appointed to the post of Minister of War.[27] His administrative experience and interest in the Moroccans made him an excellent choice for the job of High Commissioner, and his appointment seemed to mark a turn for the better in Spanish fortunes in the Protectorate.

At the end of December 1918, the three *comandancias* in Morocco were reapportioned under two commands, Ceuta and Melilla. To the Ceuta post, the Army sent the veteran general Manuel Fernández Silvestre, who took command just a few weeks before Berenguer became High Commissioner.[28] The relationship between Dámaso Berenguer and Manuel Silvestre, companions at arms for many years and both royal favorites, was a complex one. Silvestre was two years older than Berenguer, and he had been in Morocco even longer than the new High Commissioner. He had once been Berenguer's commanding officer, and actually outranked him (though by a single number) on the Spanish Army's seniority list. It was rumored that Berenguer's appointment as Minister of War was partly attributable to Silvestre's special influence with the King. Although Silvestre had risen from the ranks, he had been a royal aide and a personal friend of King Alfonso, who would have liked all his generals to be as forthright and as uncomplicated as Manuel Silvestre.

There had long been rumors of keen rivalry between the two generals, though Ruiz Albéniz claims that Berenguer appreciated Silvestre's good qualities, and was neither afraid nor jealous of Silvestre's royal support.[29] Silvestre appears to have liked Berenguer, but not enough to curb his own tendency to insubordination in the field. The two generals held widely different opinions as to how Spanish Morocco could best be pacified. A superior administrator, Berenguer, who had served under Alfau, believed in a cautious, well-prepared advance. He had visited the brilliant French Resident-General Marshal Hubert Lyautey at Rabat, and had studied the Marshal's peaceful methods with approval. Berenguer was particularly aware of the price in lives and goods that war exacts, and aware too of Spain's past mistakes in military strategy.

He was convinced that the most prudent course lay in presenting a peaceful show of force. He neither expected nor wished to use this power against the Moroccans in the fashion of a conqueror.[30] He did expect to establish an indigenous administration in Spanish Morocco and to achieve Spain's ends through it. Berenguer viewed the pacific occupation of the Spanish Protectorate as a political rather than a military problem. Especially after the taking of Chaouen, he was convinced that he need not ask for one more Spanish soldier, because he could reach his objectives in the easiest way with the least sacrifice by using only troops already at hand.

Silvestre—who, it is said, had expected to be appointed High Commissioner and was keenly disappointed when Berenguer got the job—was a fighter all the way. Never patient or subtle, he wanted a showdown with the Rifians in order to get the matter over in the shortest possible time. What is more, he wanted all the glory for himself.[31] Flamboyant and egotistical, Silvestre was undeniably popular. He was overly familiar with his staff, allowing them to address him as "tu," and even to call him by his nickname, "Manolo."[32] He was not a strict disciplinarian, and as command-ing general at Ceuta, he allowed his troops considerable leeway. Berenguer was appalled by their loose conduct; he ordered the Ceuta casino closed, and he tried in other ways to impose a greater degree of military decorum. When Berenguer recommended Sil-vestre for command of the Melilla *comandancia* after a mere six months at Ceuta, it was popularly believed that the High Commis-sioner was purposely sending him as far away as possible. Almost surely, however, the transfer occurred because Berenguer genu-inely felt that Silvestre was an outstanding leader, and that it would be in Spain's best interests to give the aggressive general more autonomy.[33]

With the conclusion of the First World War, Spain found herself entangled in new difficulties with France. France had re-sented Spain's complaisant "neutrality" during the war, and she now demanded that Spain give her "complete freedom of action in Morocco"—by which France meant that she should be allowed full sway over the entire country. And in Spain itself the leftist Catalan extremists, who were dominated by the separatist intellectuals of Barcelona, clamored for Catalan independence—the "self-determi-nation for ethnic groups" called for in President Wilson's famous

Fourteen Points.[34] Catalans were traditionally separatists, and their desire for autonomy gave them a certain sympathy for the Moroccans as well as a corresponding antipathy for any military project the Madrid government might have in mind for North Africa.

Madrid might have been accused of error on several counts in assigning General Silvestre to the Melilla *comandancia*. For one thing, his conduct of affairs in the old Larache *comandancia* had been consistently embarrassing. Then, too, with more time and experience in Morocco than the distinguished new High Commissioner under whom he was serving, Silvestre might well have been expected to resent being placed in a subordinate post. Finally, the dashing general enjoyed a popular reputation that the more staid Berenguer could never hope to equal. It was debatable whether men of such disparate character could be expected to work harmoniously together.

As might have been predicted, now that his harkas dominated more of the Jibala than those of the Khalifa, Raisuli refused to come to any new terms. Indeed, the Spanish area of control in the Ceuta *comandancia* was so restricted that no Spaniard dared to venture outside the walls of Tetuan for fear of snipers. Communications between Ceuta and Tetuan were cut so frequently that Tetuan townsmen often made wagers, not as to whether the evening express train from Ceuta would arrive on time, but as to whether it would arrive at all.* Still, the year 1919 ended successfully for Spain, with Spanish forces reestablishing peace in the Anjera, Wad Ras, and Hauz districts to the north, and cutting Raisuli's line of supply from Tangier to Harrub, between the Jebel Habib and Beni Aros tribal areas. At the beginning of 1920, Berenguer's troops occupied the heights of the Gorgues, just across the Martín River south of Tetuan. Fortunately for the Spaniards, these heights were not defended; it is highly doubtful that the majestic and steep escarpment could have been taken by frontal assault. The occupation of Ben Karrich, low on the slopes at the

---

* The Ceuta–Tetuan railroad, a single, one-meter-gauge track, was completed in the spring of 1918. The only train that was never interfered with was the early morning "fish express" from Rio Martín, a village on the Mediterranean near Tetuan; the Moroccans in Tetuan were so used to eating fish that their rebellious co-religionists acceded to custom and allowed the daily supply to reach the city markets. (Pryne, p. 79.)

entrance to the valley of the Beni Hassan, where there was some opposition, was not accomplished until June.

Early in 1920 the Spanish General Staff decided to create a unit of shock troops for duty in Africa. This was the Spanish Foreign Legion, better known as the Tercio, named after a Spanish military organization of the sixteenth and seventeenth centuries. The idea seems to have originated with Major José Millán Astray y Terreros, a forty-year-old veteran of the Philippine campaign. The Tercio was to be a special corps of seasoned shock troops, trained and organized in the tradition of the French Foreign Legion, upon which, in fact, it was patterned. In proposing this elite unit, Millán Astray said that Spain would gain doubly from its establishment, for anybody joining the Tercio would be likely to be a hard character, and for every foreigner who joined, a Spaniard would be spared. Millán Astray had spent some time in Sidi bel Abbes, the French Foreign Legion's headquarters in Algeria, and in Tlemcen, studying the organization of France's famed corps, and his reports were impressive. The Spanish Legion was created late in January 1920, and Millán Astray, promoted to the rank of lieutenant colonel, was named its first commander.

The Legion's leader was a handsome fellow and a strange one. He was born of middle-class parents in 1879 at Coruña, and graduated from Spain's Infantry Academy when he was only sixteen. His father had held some fairly important positions, including those of chief of police in Barcelona and director of the Model Prison at Madrid. His career at the prison came to an end when an inmate whom he had temporarily allowed outside committed a murder, and he himself was jailed as punishment. This incident apparently affected Millán Astray's whole life, for it seems that he never gave up trying to restore the family honor.[35] He made a fighting reputation for himself in the Philippines. According to Arturo Barea, his devotion to duty verged on the fanatical. Brave to the point of recklessness, Millán Astray was high-strung and puritanical.[36] He wrote "The Legionary's Creed," an ethical code for the Tercio, which stated that the best soldier is the one who dies for his country. "Death in combat is the greatest honor. One dies only once. Death arrives without pain, and is not so terrible as it seems. The most horrible thing is to live as a coward." Millán Astray's personal record in Morocco perfectly exemplified this belief, for before he left the Rif, he had lost an eye, an arm, and a leg, and most of the fingers on his remaining hand. He is remembered today in Spanish history books as "the glorious mutilated one."[37]

By April 1920, the Tercio was ready for action. Recruits, who were chosen from volunteers between the ages of eighteen and forty, were promised the equivalent of sixty cents a day (far better pay than ordinary Spanish soldiers) plus an enlistment bonus of $70 to $100. The Tercio was composed of men from many nations, including Spanish soldiers, riffraff, and criminals, an American Negro, and a Russian prince. As might be expected, Antonio Azpeitua had nothing good to say about it, claiming that the Foreign Legion attracted the very worst types,[38] and Arturo Barea called it "a cancer in the Army." Nevertheless, the black and yellow flag of the Tercio was to be prominent in all the ensuing campaigns in Morocco. Life in the Spanish Foreign Legion was brutal, and some inkling of the mentality of Millán Astray's men is revealed by the fact that they used to run into battle shouting, "¡Viva la Muerte!"—"Long Live Death!" Their favorite song was called "El Novio de la Muerte"—"The Sweetheart of Death."[39] When Patrick Turnbull visited Tetuan many years after the Abd el Krim Rebellion, Captain Hernández, an ex-Legionario, told him, "You don't join the Tercio to live—you join it to die."[40] Over the years, the Tercio's losses were higher than those of any other unit in the whole Army, which must have made Millán Astray smile with sanguinary satisfaction.

Among the Spanish Foreign Legion's most distinguished officers was a young major destined for glory named Francisco Franco Bahamonde.[41] Born in 1892 at El Ferrol, a small port in the northwest corner of Spain, he was the second son of a Navy paymaster. Franco's boyhood ambition was to attend the Spanish Naval Academy in his native city, but by sheer chance there were no vacancies at the time he applied for entrance, and he was sent instead to the Infantry Academy at Toledo's famous Alcazar. Franco was commissioned a second lieutenant at seventeen, and was sent to Morocco in 1912 when he was nineteen. Fighting in the battles against El Mizzian, he early established his reputation as a valiant leader. But even as a youth, Franco was a realist all the way, and he once declared forcefully, "I don't want medals. I want promotion!" He won both in profusion, and became one of the foremost *africa-nistas*. He was nearly killed in 1916 when he sustained severe wounds during a skirmish near the village of Biut, in the Anjera Hills west of Ceuta. Shot several times in the abdomen while leading a charge against a machine-gun emplacement, he was not expected to live, and only his youth and determination saved him.[42] He was invalided back to Spain and assigned to garrison duty at Oviedo, where he remained for four years. When he had recovered, he returned to Morocco. With his splendid fighting record, he was a natural choice for the new Tercio, and it was within the Tercio's ranks that he built the military career that eventually led him to the supreme command of the Spanish nation. Photographs of Franco taken in his youth reveal him as a notably handsome man. The little major was only 5′ 3″ tall, and had a high-pitched voice. He did not drink, and he was not a womanizer. He was a first-class organizer, a harsh disciplinarian, and a fearless fighter. In the opinion of Sergeant Barea and his companions, Franco was not quite human: "he had no nerves," and he was not friendly, not even to other officers.[43]

High Commissioner Berenguer's plans for 1920 called for the occupation of Chaouen—a major undertaking whose successful conclusion would not only mark the deepest Spanish penetration of the Moroccan hinterland but also sever communications between Raisuli in the Jibala and whatever allies he had in the Gomara. Chaouen is a picturesque little village hidden in the mountains about forty miles south of Tetuan. As one of the first Englishmen to visit it soon after the Spanish occupation wrote: "An unforgettable [experience] is rounding the corner of a rock and suddenly coming upon the holy city of Xauen, built by Moorish exiles from Spain in the year 1300. Tucked away in a crevice between two towering slabs of rock, its roofs covered with a golden moss, circled by red machiolated walls, and framed by a leaping cataract of water, Xauen [is] ... a sight to take the breath away."[44] The approach to this little town lies in the valley of the Beni Hassan. The valley itself is hemmed in, especially on the east, by vast buttresses whose stony crenellations form a superb natural fortress. Chaouen is an Arab "holy city," which supposedly had been visited by only three Europeans before the arrival of the

Spanish troops. The French explorer De Foucauld spent a desperate hour there disguised as a Jewish rabbi in 1883; Walter Harris, in the guise of a tribesman, visited the city in 1889; and William Summers, an American missionary, was poisoned there in 1892 and died of the effects some time later.[45] The Ahmas tribe, within whose territory Chaouen lies, has a cruel reputation; and there exists to this day a street in Chaouen called the Way of the Burned, in commemoration of some Christian prisoners who are said to have been burned alive in the main plaza.

With Chaouen as his target, Berenguer left Tetuan on September 19, 1920.[46] His main force marched straight up the valley, while other troops offered flanking support from the heights on both sides. The major effort went smoothly, and there was no real opposition. Berenguer entered Zoco el Arba, a marketplace about halfway to Chaouen, at the end of September, and reached Dar Koba during the first week of October. By October 14, the main force of 15,000 men had clambered up to the niche that holds the holy city. The Beni Hassan had given way even before the Army reached Zoco el Arba, but they had merely yielded the valley floor and were waiting behind the ridges in wary indecision. The Spanish flanking details found the going much too rough among the heights, and they soon climbed down and joined the main force. Another Spanish column from Larache was assigned the task of marching over the mountains from the west and cutting through Beni Aros to rendezvous with the Tetuan troops at the target city. This force advanced past Teffer, in the far southwestern corner of the Protectorate, but when the violent rainstorms of late autumn set in, the Spanish could not push past the barrier of stubbornly resistant tribesmen to their front. Having subdued the dissidents of Beni Sakkar and Beni Isef, the Larache column decided to retire to the coast instead of linking up with the High Commissioner's command at Chaouen.

Meanwhile the able General Castro Girona, one of the few Spanish officers who were genuinely interested in the welfare of the Moroccans, had effected an almost bloodless occupation of Chaouen.[47] Disguised as an Ahmas charcoal burner, the General stole into the city, made his way to the chiefs in charge, and by alternately threatening bombardment and offering remuneration, was able to negotiate a peaceful surrender.* On October 15, 1920, Berenguer's soldiers ran up the Spanish flag over Chaouen's alcazar, while the trumpets played the Spanish Royal March and cannon boomed a twenty-one-gun salute.† A surprise Ahmas counterattack on October 21 ended in death for eleven officers and one hundred twenty men of the new Spanish garrison. However, there was no question but that the Spanish were in control; and no further large-scale attacks upon the city by the mountaineers developed. Meanwhile the Spanish set about constructing small blockhouses (*blocaos*) at strategic points in the area. It seemed that at last the Spanish Army was moving ahead in a manner designed to gain the respect of the tribesmen. But Antonio Azpeitua says that the effect was soon ruined, for Spanish whores were installed at Chaouen only three days after the Army got there, a souvenir-hunting officer removed a lamp from the local mosque, and Spanish soldiers shouted insults at Moroccans on their way to pray.[48] The Army did allow one of its doctors to operate on twenty tribes-

* In his book *The Track,* an account of his years in the Spanish Moroccan Army, Arturo Barea presents a soldier's-eye view of the Spanish officers prominent in the Chaouen campaign. In view of subsequent events, one may assume that these men were typical of their kind elsewhere in the Spanish military hierarchy. General Berenguer is described as being fat, remote from his men, and possessed of an unctuous voice. General Marzo was even more obese, and had to wear a corset. Easily angered, he was frequently brutal to his troops. General Serrano was "a stout fatherly man adored by his troops for his ... humor ... and his fearlessness." Lieutenant Colonel González Tablas was tall, energetic, and aristocratic, in contrast to the other commanders of the Regulares, who in the main were lethargic and middle-class. General Castro Girona was deservedly popular with the rank and file, since his exploit at Chaouen had saved untold numbers of lives; but many of his brother officers were jealous of him, for he spoke several Moroccan dialects and had immense prestige among the Moors. Such was the caliber of some of these Spanish generals that they could not even read military maps—when maps indeed existed. Barea, who worked in the maps section, says that even after seven years of Spanish occupation, no map existed of the city of Tetuan. (See Berea, p. 284.)

† García Figueras, *Marruecos,* p. 283. Strangely enough, Raisuli had made no attempt to resist the march on Chaouen. Some observers felt that this could be attributed less to the threat of Spanish arms than to the consideration of nearly $300,000 given to the chief by the Spanish Government to ensure his neutrality. Since the Beni Aros, staunch followers of Raisuli, were hostile religious rivals of the more numerous Ahmas with regard to ceremonies and pilgrimages to the tomb of Abdeslam Ben Mahish, Raisuli may have been glad to see the Spanish overcome them. See Barea, p. 426; Sheean, *An American Among the Riffi,* p. 287.

men afflicted with cataracts, but in general the military behaved as unwisely as ever.

Over in the Melilla *comandancia,* General Silvestre had taken up his new command early in 1920. The Berenguer plan here called for the same sort of careful advance that had culminated in the taking of Chaouen. This time the military objective was Alhucemas Bay in Beni Urriaguel. Since Alhucemas lay at the very center of the Rifian rebel movement, it was considered to be the most important objective in Spanish Morocco. With characteristic aggressiveness, Silvestre had pushed westward, and by the summer of 1921 he had almost doubled the area that Spain had occupied since 1909. Between May and September 1920, Silvestre's men took Dar Drius, Tafersit, Azru, Azib de Midar, Isen Lassen, and Buhafora; and in November they added Ben Tieb and several smaller places in Beni Said to their score. In January 1921, Silvestre occupied what was to be his main forward base—Anual, a hamlet in a small valley of Beni Ulichek.[49] According to Ruiz Albéniz, Silvestre had gone to the Melilla *comandancia* with one end in view —the rapid conquest of Alhucemas and the eastern zone of Spanish Morocco.[50] Berenguer constantly urged caution upon his colleague, but caution had never suited the headstrong Silvestre, who proceeded as though there were nothing to fear.[51] Silvestre considered the Rifians a rabble: a kick in the pants would get rid of them; they were not serious enemies. Reflecting the opinion of his chief, Silvestre's adjutant had declared publicly, "The only way to succeed in Morocco is to cut off the heads of all the Moors." It was known, too, that King Alfonso shared his favorite's impatience with the idea of a slow, peaceful occupation of the central Rif. In any case, by the late spring of 1921 it seemed that Spain was finally well on the way to solving her Moroccan problem. Silvestre had pushed forward rapidly through Beni Said and Beni Ulichek in the north, and into Metalsa and Tafersit farther south. By May 1921, he was poised to invade the territory of the powerful tribes of Temsaman, Beni Tuzin, and Beni Urriaguel. Behind the lines, Silvestre depended upon a string of blockhouses and small posts to secure the country he had overrun. True, most of these outposts had been hastily set up without much regard for lines of supply— but the important consideration seemed to be that Spanish troops now stood where none had ever been before.

In the west, Berenguer had split the Gomara off from the Jibala by the investment of Chaouen, and had divided the Anjera from the rest of the Jibala by the action at Fondak Ain Jedida. Although he had not engaged Raisuli in an open fight, the General had effectively bottled him up in his own Beni Aros hills. Of course, the Chaouen garrison could never be considered invulnerable—it was forty hilly miles out in the wilds from Tetuan, connected to the capital by only the most elemental of roads—and Berenguer had not succeeded in subduing the surrounding tribes.[52] But these matters were considered secondary to the fact that Spain was definitely on the move in the Protectorate.

From the inception of Spain's active interest in Morocco, government policy had been lacking in cohesion. Madrid often took a conciliatory point of view, but ambitious officers in the field, of whom Silvestre was the prototype, frequently ignored or interfered with government directives. That important commanders could get away with such effrontery was an indication of a serious weakness in Spain's conduct of Moroccan affairs. The tribes were alternately cajoled and harassed, and therefore regarded Spain with suspicion and distrust. From Melilla to Larache, the Caids and their warriors watched the enemy and bided their time. Powerful forces led by unusual leaders were building up in the Rif. Unfortunately for Spain, few of her military authorities understood what this portended.

5. ABD EL KRIM

THE only sustained, disciplined, and centrally organized rebellion in the history of the Rif was the revolt led by the extraordinary brothers Mohamed and Mhamed ben Abd el Krim.[1] Historians and biographers usually assert that the father of these two men was either a *caid* or a *cadi* (a Muslim judge);* but David Hart and Andrés Sánchez Pérez, whose more intimate knowledge of the Rifians is based upon several years' study of the tribes and residence among them, claim that the elder Abd el Krim was a *fqih,* or schoolteacher, at a mosque in the village community of Ajdir, near Alhucemas Bay.[2]

The Abd el Krim who became known to history as the leader of the Rifian Rebellion was the elder of the two brothers—Mohamed ben Abd el Krim el Khattabi.† This was the Abd el Krim of the newspaper headlines—the Abd el Krim of Moroccan myth and legend. Mhamed, his younger brother by about ten years, was at least as remarkable and intelligent as he, and as much responsible for the successes of the Rifian tribesmen, but he was more retiring, and hence less well known. The similarity between the names of the two brothers stems from the fact that Rifian sons are customarily named for their paternal grandfather—Mohamed and Mhamed are simply different modes of the same name. In this work, the name "Abd el Krim" will refer specifically to the older

---

* The confusion may stem from the fact that the Arabic words *fqih* and *cadi* are variants of the same term; a *fqih* specializes in religion and a *cadi* in law, although religion and law are inseparable in Islam. According to David Hart, a *cadi* is something like a *fqih* with a Ph.D., for a *cadi* must have a degree from a Muslim university. Although his father had no degree, Abd el Krim graduated from one of the biggest and certainly one of the best universities in all Africa—the Qarawiyin at Fez.

† His name meant "Mohamed, son of Abd el Krim [the generous one] of the Khattabi double-clan [in Beni Urriaguel]."

brother, the internationally famous Rifian leader. The few facts that are known about the Abd el Krims' earlier years are elusive and conflicting.

Abd el Krim was born about 1882 at Ajdir, in the Beni Urriaguel clan of Aith Yusuf u Ali. In later years, after he had left the Rif, Abd el Krim told Roger-Matthieu that his family had been established in Beni Urriaguel since the year 900;[3] and David Hart asserts that Abd el Krim claimed to be of Arabian ancestry, from Yenbo in the Hejaz, and a descendant of Omar Ibn Khattab, the seventh-century Caliph of Islam.* However, Pessah Shinar, an Israeli scholar, says that Abd el Krim was neither Arab nor Sherif, but pure Berber;[4] and Andrés Sánchez Pérez believes that Abd el Krim's father originally came from the Geznaya tribe south of Beni Urriaguel. Since in the Rif the purchase of tribal land by strangers automatically makes them bona fide tribal members, it may be that the Abd el Krims bought their way into Beni Urriaguel.[5] In any case, the elder Abd el Krim was an influential man, and his wife was the daughter of a *cadi* from a clan having a *liff* alliance with her husband's clan.

Abd el Krim's early schooling was that of any Berber boy—simply studying the Koran, and thoroughly memorizing its 114 Suras. According to Rupert Furneaux, the elder Abd el Krim became involved in a blood feud which he did not, for moral reasons, wish to pursue, and he therefore moved his family to Tetuan in 1892.[6] The ambitious father had great plans for his sons, and he sent them both to Melilla to attend Spanish schools. The curriculum they studied there—history, geography, simple mathematics, some literature, and the Catholic catechism—provided them with an education immeasurably superior to that of their Rifian contemporaries. Unlike the vast majority of his comrades at Melilla, Mohamed Abd el Krim was sent upon graduation to study in Fez, at the Qarawiyin *medersa,* where, in his own words, he was further educated "in the Koran, in musketry, and in horsemanship."† Even as an adolescent he was considered well enough educated to begin to qualify as a judge. The younger son, Mhamed,

---

* Hart explains, in a letter dated June 12, 1967, that altering one's genealogy to prove illustrious Arab ancestors is a common practice among Berbers. According to neighbors, the family were Sherifs from Geznaya.

† A *medersa* is a Muslim university.

was a brilliant scholar, and at the expense of the Spanish Government he was sent to Madrid in 1917 to prepare for a career as a mining engineer.[7] For almost three years, Mhamed lived in a European environment, studying mineralogy and military engineering.

In 1906, when he was twenty-four, Abd el Krim took his first job, that of editor of the Arabic supplement of *El Telegrama del Rif,* the Spanish newspaper in Melilla. In the following year, he became a secretary in the Bureau of Native Affairs, under Gabriel Morales, the Spanish officer in charge. By 1912, he had become an assessor in the same office, where most of his work concerned the legal aspects of rights and title deeds to the iron deposits in Beni Tuzin territory, which bordered his own Beni Urriaguel tribal area. By 1914, Abd el Krim had been appointed *"qadi l qudat"*— chief *cadi*—for the entire Melilla area, and by 1915 he was acting as an editor for *El Telegrama del Rif.*[8] As the son of a Beni Urriaguel notable, as a highly educated Rifian who stood well with the Spanish, and as a *cadi* and an editor, Abd el Krim was an important young man. It was he who was responsible for inciting the Beni Urriaguel against the Rogui.[9] While he was teaching Arabic at the Hispano-Arabic school in Melilla, one of his Spanish students revealed to him the Rogui's plans for the Urriaglis. Abd el Krim took leave as soon as he could and went home to his native village, where together with his father he urged the Beni Urriaguel to unite against the Pretender, charging that the Rogui intended to conquer the tribe so that he could sell their mining rights to Europeans for his own benefit. The subsequent uniting of the Urriaglis, the tribe's defeat of the Rogui, and the continued belief that Beni Urriaguel possessed mines of great value that must be defended against foreign exploitation combined to help build the idea of Rifian nationalism in the minds of the tribesmen.

Despite his having been born near a region partially overrun by the Spaniards—Alhucemas Island, on the doorstep of Beni Urriaguel, not far from Ajdir, less than a mile from the mainland, had been occupied by the Spaniards since 1668*—where outrages and

---

* Approximately eight hundred feet high, this small rock was completely covered with installations, although the garrison never numbered more than five hundred persons, women and nonmilitary included. From the day the Spanish took Alhucemas Island until 1926, the Beni Urriaguel kept a constant watch on it.

punitive attacks against tribesmen were not uncommon and where hatred of the Spanish was a natural inheritance, Abd el Krim appears not to have been hostile to them as a young man. It was his work at Melilla that revealed to him not only the mineral potential of the Rif but also the shockingly corrupt and exploitative manner in which the Spanish conducted affairs in the Protectorate. He developed an increasingly unfavorable view of his employers. He became convinced that the Spanish intended to exploit the Rif and its mines for their own profit entirely. His cynicism was fed by the statements of certain high Spanish officials, one of whom said, "We're content to let murder go unpunished as long as it is just a matter of Rifs killing other Rifs." One of Abd el Krim's former classmates, Dris Said, a man with strong nationalist feelings, seems to have had a decisive influence upon him during this period. At all events, the future leader decided that it was hopeless to expect fair play from Europeans. "They will never consider us as equals; they will always treat us like dogs,"[10] he said.

Abd el Krim's father had long been aware of the commercial possibilities of the Rif. Surveys had been made showing that the mineral deposits of the Rif included copper, antimony, and silver, in addition to iron and lead lodes even more valuable than those being worked in the Beni Bu Ifrur country near Melilla.[11] The *fqih* had long been suspected by the Spanish of gunrunning and contraband trading, and they thought it more than probable that in these escapades he had acted upon information supplied by his well-placed sons. In fact, he had been trading with the Mannesmann Brothers. Finally realizing that the Germans might have been responsible for some of the trouble they were having with the Rifian tribesmen, and yielding to French pressure in the matter of punishing German-oriented tribesmen, the Spanish instituted a policy of retribution against Rifians who had collaborated with Germany.[12] This sudden change of policy—or rather the establishment of a policy where none had been before—struck the Rifians as a further example of Spanish hypocrisy. When a Spanish raiding party burned the *fqih*'s house, he rallied a band of followers around him and retreated into the Beni Urriaguel mountains in a vindictive mood. In the meantime, the younger Abd el Krim was indiscreetly voicing his opinions about France and Spain. He said openly that he could not view with calm a Sultan

who reigned under French domination; that he would prefer German rule to French. He also said that Spain should not extend her
sovereignty past her presidios, and that she should enter some sort
of treaty arrangement with a new Rifian State.[13] This was going
too far, and the Spaniards tried Abd el Krim, sentenced him,
and imprisoned him at Rostrogordo, north of Melilla, in August
1917.[14] Here the story grows complicated. Abd el Krim himself
told Roger-Matthieu many years later that General Aizpuru had
had him sentenced because he refused to fight with the turn-
coat Abd el Malek against the French.[15] Another explanation for
Abd el Krim's detention was that he had quarreled with General
Silvestre. (This story is entirely apocryphal, for Silvestre did not
take command at Melilla until January 1920, by which time Abd
el Krim had left the city.)[16] At any rate, Abd el Krim's brother-in-
law was able to smuggle a rope to him, and with it he attempted
to escape from Rostrogordo. But as he was descending from the
prison wall, the rope became tangled, and he was left dangling
ninety feet from the ground. He was able to hold on for almost
an hour, but then he dropped, breaking his left leg (he walked
with a limp for the rest of his life).[17] He was, of course, easily recaptured, and was forced to serve eleven more months before he was
finally released. Toward the end of 1918, after he went back to work
in Melilla for *El Telegrama del Rif*, he became alarmed over the
fact that members of the Beni Snassen, who had fought against the
French under Abd el Malek and had been living in Melilla to
escape French persecution, had been handed over by the Spanish
to the French authorities. This convinced Abd el Krim that, in
view of his outspoken criticism of France during the war, he too
might be extradited. No proof exists that the Spanish would have
turned the prominent Rifian over to France, but Abd el Krim did
not intend to take the chance. He applied for a twenty-day leave
in January 1919, and simply never came back.[18]

Before his flight, Abd el Krim had written to his brother ex-
plaining the situation and urging him to return home. Mhamed's
career in Madrid was going very well, but nevertheless he responded at once, and by the spring of 1919, the brothers had joined their
father in his mountain exile. There, these three exceptional men
took stock of the Spanish position in Morocco, and began recruit-
ing tribal support for the rebellion that was to make the name of

Abd el Krim known throughout the world. In September 1920, in the midst of these preparations, the father died from eating poisoned eggs served him in an ostensibly friendly Rifian household. The host, a young man of Tafersit, was said to have been bribed by the Spanish with a promise of a new rifle to eliminate the *fqih*, whom the Spanish had suspected of plotting to stir up the tribes of the Rif against them.* Surprisingly, no revenge seems to have been sought or taken against the alleged Tafersiti poisoner by Abd el Krim's sons.

The brothers Abd el Krim held no official political power in Beni Urriaguel; they were neither *caids* nor *imgharen*. Their background, experience, and skill at organization gave them an effective superiority, and they attained leadership through sheer force of personality and intellect. Abd el Krim was not just another *marabout* conducting a *jihad* and promising paradise—he was a local leader who had enlarged his ambitions to include the idea of a national state. The Rifians listened to him because they thought he had the three qualities necessary in a true war leader—audacity, courage, and the ability to size matters up quickly.[19] The brothers intended to do much more than merely resist the encroaching Spanish troops. They had a vision of an aggressive war—a carefully planned and coordinated effort far greater than anything either the Rif or Spain had ever seen before. They would use their natural advantages to the full, and Abd el Krim would exploit the propensity of his Rifians to rise against outside domination. The brothers had carefully observed Spanish military organization and method at first hand. They had lived through the troubled days of the Rogui's adventures, the piecemeal Spanish campaign of 1909, and the later battles against El Mizzian. They knew the Spanish thoroughly. Right now they were following Silvestre's dash westward with intense interest, for they noted that the general was spreading the same number of troops over a larger and larger area, extending his lines of supply ever thinner. If the general could be lured still further west, away from the Melilla entrepôt, a Rifian attack might have a good chance of success.[20]

The brothers knew their own limitations, too. They had spent so much time in the employ of Spain that many tribesmen sus-

---

* According to David Hart, the Spanish seem to have thought that opposition to them in the Rif would end with the death of the elder Abd el Krim.

pected they might have sold out to the Spanish (or that they had
made a deal with France to let Spain come into the Rif). The Abd
el Krims went to a good deal of trouble to reassure their followers.[21] Though it was no problem in the Rif to enlist a harka that
would fight the Spanish any day of the week, such a group might
disperse suddenly for any of a number of reasons. The tribes of the
Rif had never before fought together as a unit against outside invaders, or submitted to central control; indeed, hardly any of them
had done more than feud internally. But to defeat Spain, central-
ized control would be needed. Moreover, after a military merger
of the tribes, the Rifians would need to accumulate stores of food,
ammunition, and medicine, and they would have to ration these
supplies against the number of years it would take to win political
recognition. They would have to create a diplomatic corps to explain their cause, win friends and money abroad, and represent
them when they dealt with foreign powers. All this would have to
be accomplished with a minimum of trained personnel, experience,
equipment, and funds, and with inferior numbers. On the other
hand, the Rifians would be fighting on entirely familiar terrain.
Their native mountains presented vast difficulties for a European
army dependent partially on mechanized transport and artillery
support. The Rifian warrior needed little more equipment than
a rifle, a bandolier of bullets, a few dried figs, and a loaf of bread.

Apologists for Abd el Krim feel that he was entirely justified in
his rebellion. Powell, for example, believes that Abd el Krim and
his people, incensed by the cruelty, corruption, injustice, and exploitation meted out to them by their Spanish "protectors," were
right to rebel.[22]

Even nature seemed to favor the Rifian cause. The winter of
of 1920–21 had been even colder than usual, and it followed the
fourth consecutive autumn of poor harvests. In Beni Urriaguel, the
most infertile part of the Rif and yet the most densely populated,
the people were particularly restless.[23] By the spring of 1921, Abd
el Krim had succeeded in establishing the nucleus of a potent fighting machine. Most of these men came from Beni Urriaguel, and
the remainder were from Bucoya, Temsaman, Beni Tuzin, and
Beni Amart. This force suited the purpose of the moment, but the
Abd el Krims were not satisfied, and continued to try to enlist
support for their intertribal confederation.

Because of the particular military problems involved in their projected campaign, the Abd el Krims opted for an overall strategy based on guerrilla warfare. They would fight the way they fought their feuds—the way they always had fought. Stress would be placed on surprise, ambush, and mobility—on arriving at the military objective more rapidly and in stronger force than the enemy. The invaders would be allowed to overextend themselves, exactly as Silvestre was now in the process of doing, so that not only their troops and outposts were vulnerable, but also their lines of supply. Pitched battles in the open would be avoided whenever possible. The Rifians were to be elusive and lethal—striking, then vanishing into the mountains before pursuit could be organized. Considering the rough terrain, these were tactics of the most practical kind —tactics ideally suited to the experience and temperament of the tribesmen in the Spanish Protectorate.

The Abd el Krims were much too intelligent not to realize that some strong, permanent political organization was absolutely necessary if they and the Rif were to survive. To this end, they cleverly manipulated the *liff* system of alliances when it was to their advantage to do so, and crushed it when it proved troublesome. They dealt almost solely with *liffs* on the local level, appointing *caids* of equal standing to head each *liff*, and thus ensuring harmony and winning support.[24]

About Abd el Krim's personal life, few facts are known. He was of medium height, undistinguished in appearance and inclined to obesity, with brown eyes, brown hair, and a dark complexion. His face was round and sleek, and he habitually wore a mild expression, though he could be direct and forthright or crafty and evasive, as occasion demanded. He customarily wore the simple clothing of the people—a dark brown *jellaba* and a white wool turban. He resembled a comfortably established merchant, and, like Raisuli, he looked anything but the incisive leader he was. Abd el Krim seems to have been friendly and fair-minded until the latter years of the Rifian war, when he had to contend with the growing pressures of European armies in the field as well as with mutiny and treachery among the allied tribes. Although he ruled a land where extravagance, intemperance, and licentiousness were common among the powerful, he took only the four wives allowed him by the Koran, and had no vicious habits. At the time of the rebellion, he had three children, all boys. Both his mother and his sister were dear to him. Only a few Rifians and a handful of other tribesmen knew their famous leader, even by sight. The Abd el Krim who inspired his people was, for most of them, a glamorous legend—an omnipotent chieftain leading his people to unheard-of accomplishments.

Mhamed, the younger brother, had the same heavy physique and wore the same ordinary garments as Mohamed. But Mhamed was more ascetic, possessed greater dignity, and apparently made a stronger impression on observers. By European standards, Mhamed was the most civilized Berber in the Rif. It was rumored that once the Rif had obtained its independence, Abd el Krim meant to turn over the leadership of the government to him. Together the brothers shared the responsibility for the Rifian state they were creating. Abd el Krim was the central figure, the legend; while Mhamed, who acted as both his brother's adviser and commander in chief of the Rifian Army, was the shrewd power behind the throne.

By the summer of 1921, the Rifians could count on approximately 3,000 to 6,000 fighting men—the pick of the Rif. The Spanish had more than four times that many soldiers in the Melilla *comandancia* alone, and another 45,000 men in the Jibala. Moreover, they could count on certain reserves of manpower and matériel from nearby Spain. The tribesmen had a small quantity of smuggled French rifles, as well as Spanish Mausers that they had pilfered or bought outright from the Moroccan troops fighting for Spain.[25] But though they were vastly outnumbered, utterly lacking in technological assets, and poorly supplied, the Rifians were eager to fight—to challenge and defeat the might of Spain and drive the Europeans forever from their shores.

6. ANUAL

A CASUAL glance at the map of eastern Spanish Morocco in May 1921 might have beguiled the observer into believing that Spain was well on her way to total occupation of her Protectorate. Even though less than a third of the territory was actually under the control of the Spanish Army, General Silvestre's advance westward from Melilla toward the central Rif had brought as much new territory under Spanish dominion in less than a year and a half as had been gained in the twelve preceding years. His forward line of posts stretched in a line roughly north to south from Sidi Dris on the Mediterranean, over the mountains, through Anual, and south to Zoco el Telata de Metalsa—about thirty-five land miles. From Melilla, the point of furthest Spanish military penetration was about eighty miles west to the forward posts of Buy Meyan and Anual in Beni Ulichek. Silvestre had 25,700 men—20,600 Spaniards and 5,100 Moroccan Regulares—strung out in this area, garrisoning approximately 144 outposts, blockhouses, and small forts.[1] The usual garrison for a Spanish blockhouse was made up of twelve to twenty men, but centers like Batel, Dar Drius, Buy Meyan, and Anual each had a garrison of eight hundred men or more.

On the map, the Spanish position looked good. In the Melilla newspaper reports and in the Spanish press, it sounded good. On April 7, 1921, *El Telegrama del Rif* predicted that the Army would soon be at Alhucemas Bay,[2] for the tribes in that region were now disposed to be friendly to Spain. This optimism was probably the result of statements given out by High Commissioner Berenguer, who had personally inspected the Melilla front in March.[3] Berenguer had been well received by the tribesmen in Beni Said, at Ben Tieb, and at Buy Meyan, and had also met with a group of Urria-

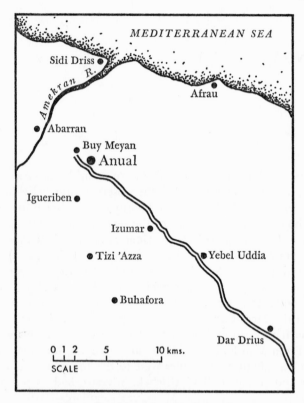

Map 2. Road from Anual to the southeast

guel chiefs on the beach at Alhucemas. After discussing the situation with General Silvestre, he had returned to his headquarters at
Tetuan under the impression that, for all his impulsiveness, the
commanding officer of the Melilla *comandancia* was doing a mas-
terful job with a minimum of losses. In fact, Berenguer had told
Vizconde Eza, the Minister of War, that the occupation of Alhucemas—and, by inference, the subduing of the powerful Beni
Urriaguel—would now be an easy task.[4] Eza was so delighted with
Berenguer's report of Silvestre's progress that he chuckled, "We
must reward Silvestre's discipline. He has been able to contain his
desire to advance [recklessly]."[5] A new empire seemed to be in the
making on Spain's very doorstep.
   Although the High Commissioner was primarily concerned with

his personal efforts to subdue the Jibala, he was characteristically cautious in his discussions with the impetuous Silvestre concerning the Army's penetration of the Rif. It would seem that Berenguer's recent trip to Alhucemas Bay and his cordial reception there by the Rifians had so impressed him that he did not see the true state of affairs. The truth was that by far the greater portion of the area held by the Spanish was rugged, arid, and mountainous—accessible only by rude trails, and poorly supplied with water. Moreover, the tribes among whom the Spanish posts were scattered had never been decisively beaten in battle, nor had Silvestre bothered to disarm them. The apparent submission of these tribes was the result not of military defeat, but rather of a vagary of nature. Harvests had been so poor for several years that a great many of the tribesmen, particularly in Beni Said and Beni Ulichek, had migrated temporarily to Algeria in search of work.[6] Thus weakened by the loss of many of their fighting men, these tribes were in no condition to resist. Silvestre had made many enemies by burning crops and even a few houses in the Kert in order to compel submission; moreover, he had confiscated cattle freely, without paying compensation to the tribesmen. Many tribesmen were in danger of starving, and some had no other dwellings than caves in the hills. Silvestre eventually distributed a small amount of food in Beni Said, Beni Ulichek, and Beni Tuzin, but the tribesmen remained wary and unfriendly, ready to fight at the smallest excuse.[7]

The poor condition and morale of the Spanish Army in Morocco were common knowledge, at least in Melilla and Ceuta. While there had been a substantial pay raise in June 1918, and another small one, which mainly affected lieutenants, in the spring of 1920, the ordinary soldiers remained underpaid, underfed, and poorly equipped.[8] High Commissioner Berenguer had written a long report to the Minister of War in February 1921 discussing the deficiencies in supply and matériel, and sanitary services, as well as the misuse of credit.[9] War Minister Eza, in turn, had reported these facts to the Cortes, adding that the martial spirit of the troops in Morocco was good, but that conditions there were very bad. He stated that in the Teffer sector, inland from Alcazarquivir in the west, soldiers were sometimes kept on duty in blockhouses without relief for months at a time. The Larache and Melilla barracks, he said, were filthy, and so were the hospitals everywhere in the Protectorate. Losses to malaria were excessive, and medical services in general needed a drastic overhaul. Eza suggested that, since both the native Moroccan police and the Regulares were permanent troops, they should be given better pay and better living conditions than conscripts were.[10]

The men who governed Spain must have known that there was a shocking lack of discipline and efficiency among the military in Morocco, yet they did practically nothing to remedy the situation. Not all Spanish officers were inefficient or undisciplined, but so many of them were that the general level of leadership was low. Many officers were aristocrats or scions of wealthy families who owed their rank to family influence rather than to their fitness for military responsibilities. Army pay was so pitifully low, even after the raises of 1918 and 1920, that many officers took second jobs to make ends meet. Spanish officers in Morocco frequently spent more time away from their garrisons than in them, had little or no contact with their military inferiors, and cared nothing about their needs. The situation of the common soldiers was abysmal. The scanty equipment they were issued was often faulty, and they were poorly trained in its use. Army food was almost inedible, and field hospitals and medical supplies hardly existed. Yet in spite of all this, the average Spanish soldier endured his lot with fortitude, and fought bravely.

If the military picture in Morocco showed serious flaws, the Spanish civil administration there presented nothing better. Civilian officials had failed to produce any dams, public works, or schools to speak of. There were few good roads anywhere in the Protectorate, and the narrow-gauge railroad from Melilla had been extended across the Plain of Garet only as far as Tistutin.[11] It was clear that the civil administration was in no hurry to make improvements or to bring the so-called blessings of European civilization to the people whose land they had preempted.

In spite of all this, Berenguer optimistically watched while Silvestre drove deeper into the Rif. One of Silvestre's intimate friends, Gómez Hidalgo, quotes him as saying at this time, "We need a victory so overwhelming that it will convince the Moors that they cannot afford the price of resistance to Spanish domination." Gómez Hidalgo questioned the wisdom of sending Silvestre, who lived only for war, to Morocco to impose peace.[12] With so much at stake, however, Silvestre was forced to proceed peacefully, whether he liked it or not. To this end, he sent Colonel Gabriel Morales,

chief of the native police and one of his staff officers, to Alhucemas
Bay to treat with the Beni Urriaguel. Morales, who had been Abd
el Krim's superior at the Native Affairs Bureau in Melilla, spoke
thamazighth and was respected by the Rifians. He favored High
Commissioner Berenguer's strategy of cautious advance in the Rif,
believing that the present posts of Anual and Izumar represented
the westernmost points that the Army was capable of holding at
the moment, and that the pacification of Temsaman and Beni
Tuzin, alone, would take all summer. Still, if the Beni Urriaguel
could be persuaded to remain peaceful, the Spanish position would
be infinitely more secure. Morales went to Alhucemas Bay in April
with Professor Antonio Got of Tetuan (by water, for the Rifians
would not let them approach by land) to discuss future arrange-
ments for mining concessions with the Beni Urriaguel. The Spanish emissaries were so cordially treated that they returned several
times, hoping to effect a firm agreement. On one occasion, Don
Horacio Echevarrieta, the Basque millionaire and Mannesmann
associate, went with Got. His mission was the rather delicate one of
selling Abd el Krim a deal by which Spain would give the Rifian
leader $7 million, in addition to modern arms and munitions with
which to resist the French, in return for his allowing Spain to
occupy the Alhucemas Bay area.[13] Abd el Krim was not interested,
and Morales and Got were unable to conclude any kind of arrangement with him.

   Abd el Krim had long ago decided that he did not want Spanish
hegemony in the Rif. He meant to keep the Spanish out and at the
same time secure for himself the best possible arrangement with
regard to mining rights for foreigners in the central Rif.[14] But
when reports of Berenguer's statements that the Beni Urriaguel
were now disposed to treat peacefully with the Spanish reached
him, and when he learned that Silvestre had told the Rifian
notables at Alhucemas Bay in March that Berenguer would eventually arrive by land, Abd el Krim was alarmed, for it looked as if
Temsaman and Beni Urriaguel would be neutralized by the Spanish in the meantime. Thus it seemed to Abd el Krim that now the
only possible way to keep Spain out of the Rif was to fight. To raise
war funds, Abd el Krim demanded—and received—a fine from
every Rifian chief who had met with Berenguer in March. The fact
that Abd el Krim could assess fines and then collect the money
proved the degree of prestige he now held. Although Silvestre was

enraged when he heard of these fines and wanted to move against Abd el Krim at once, Berenguer had forbidden him to do so. Abd el Krim had warned him through Antonio Got that if the Spanish crossed the Amekran River, both the Temsamanis and Tuzinis would resist in full strength. To this Silvestre remarked, "This man Abd el Krim is crazy. I'm not going to take seriously the threats of a little Berber Caid whom I had at my mercy a short while ago. His insolence merits a new punishment."[15]

1921 —— This was the state of things in the Rif in late May 1921, when a delegation of Temsamanis unexpectedly presented themselves at Silvestre's headquarters and asked that the Spanish cross over the Amekran River and establish a post on the hill of Abarran in Temsamani tribal territory. Though he was warned by certain other tribesmen to refuse the invitation, Silvestre accepted immediately.[16] A Spanish detachment invested Abarran on June 1, but that very afternoon, the native police among them mutinied and, together with the tribesmen, attacked the rest of the detachment. Of the 250-man Spanish force, 179 were killed, including the commander, Captain Salafranca. The survivors struggled back across the river to Buy Meyan.[17] On the same day, the Rifians assaulted Sidi Dris, a small coastal base that had been occupied by the Spanish only two weeks before. After a day and a night of fighting, in which 100 Spanish were killed or wounded, the Rifians abruptly withdrew.

As soon as Berenguer got word of these attacks, he sailed from Ceuta to confer with Silvestre. The generals met on board ship off Sidi Dris on June 5. Silvestre convinced the High Commissioner that the Abarran mutiny and the attack at Sidi Dris were isolated episodes of the sort that all invaders had to contend with. According to Robert Sencourt, the interview was anything but pleasant.[18] Silvestre's volatile temper got the better of him, and he became so angry at one point because Berenguer refused to permit him to push forward with his troops that he actually tried to throttle the High Commissioner, and had to be forcibly restrained by staff officers. Berenguer gave firm orders that the forward movement of the Spanish Army in the Rif was to cease altogether until the Jibala could be conquered. Although he now felt that Beni Urriaguel, Temsaman, and Bucoya would have to be handled with special care, Berenguer agreed with Silvestre that the situation was not serious. Silvestre for his part, apparently thinking that just one more step forward would not be a violation of his specific orders, began the construction of a support base in the hills at Igueriben, about three miles south of Anual, the very day after the interview.[19]

Silvestre's appearance at Igueriben convinced the Abd el Krims that the Spanish meant to advance, whatever the risk. The Spanish were now in a position to launch an attack from Anual in conjunction with a seaborne invasion of Alhucemas Bay. It therefore seemed to the Abd el Krims that a preemptive strike offered the best chance of stopping the Spanish. For months, Abd el Krim's agents had been lauding his abilities and whipping up the already great resentment against the invaders. The tribes listened. The Rifians found in Abd el Krim the qualities they sought in a war leader. He had said, after Abarran, "Oh Muslims, we have wanted to make peace with Spain, but Spain does not want it. She only wants to occupy our lands in order to take our property and our women, and to make us abandon our religion. Do not expect anything good of Spain. . . . The Koran says, 'Who dies in holy war goes to glory.' "[20] The tribesmen had responded, "You have taken Abarran by surprise. Now we are ready. If you can take another position, we will follow you as chief."[21] According to C. V. Usborne, Abd el Krim had circulated the following proclamation among the tribes on June 21 (Silvestre knew of it, but for his own reasons had not reported it to Berenguer): "The Spanish have already lost the game. Look at Abarran. There they have left their own dead mutilated and unburied, the souls vaguely wandering, tragically denied the delights of paradise."[22] The feeling against Spain had never been stronger among the tribesmen. The memories of eight hundred years of resistance to foreign intrusion were evoked and made the basis of Abd el Krim's propaganda.[23] The Rifians had an unusually able leader. Now was the time to strike Spain.

The strength of the Rifian buildup was imperceptible to the Spanish. There was a small skirmish at Anual in mid-June, some intermittent sniping at Igueriben, then nothing. Satisfied finally that the Spanish could be beaten in detail, Abd el Krim, whose harka was made up of his own Beni Urriaglis and groups from Temsaman, Amart, Beni Tuzin, Geznaya, Targuist, and Ketama, suddenly struck all along the Spanish line on July 17, 1921. Berenguer had only just been quoted in the Madrid daily *El Sol* as saying that the Spanish people could be sure that the work of pacification in Morocco was proceeding successfully, with only isolated losses, and that therefore no new troops would be needed.[24]

The initial Rifian assault was so unexpected that Silvestre's monthly report to the High Commissioner, sent on the very day of the uprising, carried only routine information.[25] Immersed in his daily paper work at Tetuan, Berenguer did not know that anything had gone wrong until he received the first of a battery of anguished telegrams from Silvestre on July 19, pleading for reinforcements, a diversionary attack by units of the Spanish Navy in the neighborhood of Sidi Dris, and air support.[26] Meanwhile, Igueriben had been besieged, and although it was clear from the outset that the uncompleted defenses would never hold back the Rifians, Major Julio Benitez, the commander there, refused to surrender. In answer to a message flashed over the hills by heliographs from General Navarro, second in command to Silvestre in the Melilla *comandancia,* who was down at Dar Drius— "Heroes of Igueriben, who honor the name of Spain, resist"— Benitez replied, "Your heliographs have been received with *vivas* for Spain. This garrison swears to its general that it will surrender only to death."[27] The major's response was valiant and prophetic. His men fought a good fight, but they were three miles away from the nearest water supply, which was at Anual. As the fight raged on and they were assailed by the heat and the stench of the unburied, they drank the juice from used pimiento and tomato tins, then vinegar, cologne, and ink, and finally even urine with sugar in it.[28] Anual sent down a relief column, which got close enough to Igueriben to be seen by the defenders; but the only access to the post was through a deep gorge heavily defended by the tribesmen, and the relief column was forced to retire after losing 152 men in two hours. Igueriben was overwhelmed, and Benitez was hacked to death along with most of his men. Of the twenty-five soldiers who made it back to Anual, sixteen later died of exhaustion and other causes, including the sudden shock of drinking too much water.

Anual, a camp ranging over three small slopes in an enclosed valley, had been under steady fire since the 21st, when an alarmed Silvestre and his staff arrived from Melilla. Artillerist Bernabé

Nieto, who was in the Anual garrison, records that when Silvestre got news of the last heliograph from Igueriben he gnawed his mustache and swore mightily.[29] As the attack on Anual increased in ferocity, Silvestre called a council of war with his officers. Ammunition was critically short, and almost all the officers considered the local position hopeless. Silvestre sent a final telegram at 4:55 A.M. on the 22d, announcing his intention of withdrawing to Ben Tieb if possible, after which he ordered a full-scale retreat.

For twelve long years the Spaniards had been slowly advancing ever deeper into the Moroccan hinterland, always victorious. To receive an order to retreat from the commanding officer himself, and from such an aggressive general as Silvestre, while under attack, was unprecedented, and the shock seems to have broken the already badly strained morale of the Spanish troops. They panicked. What might under other circumstances have been an orderly withdrawal became a rout.[30] Soldiers threw away their rifles and ran off in all directions through the terrible heat and dust of the Moroccan summer. Scores of them ran into the knives of Rifians waiting in ambush. Hundreds were shot down like rabbits by marksmen hidden among the rocks. Silvestre, who at the last minute refused to abandon Anual—although his son, a lieutenant, had done so at his father's order—is said to have screamed over the parapets of the fort to his stampeding troops, "Run, run, the bogeyman is coming!" The general, the well-liked Colonel Morales, and the rest of Silvestre's staff disappeared in the maelstrom of the battle, almost certainly massacred and not, as some prefer to believe, dead by suicide.

Silvestre's body was never found. According to Rifian myth, it was chopped into pieces, which were then scattered to the wind. Another story has it that the general donned his chauffeur's uniform, shaved his mustache, and tried to escape from Anual in this disguise.[31] According to Captain Fortea, one of the few Spaniards captured at Anual, Abd el Krim wore Silvestre's brilliantly colored sash throughout the later stages of the Anual debacle, and also cut off the general's head and had it carried through the mountains all the way to the walls of Tetuan as proof of the great Rifian victory. Abd el Krim himself told Roger-Matthieu that a tribesman brought him Silvestre's belt and insignia, but there is no more evidence for this story than for the others. The body of Colonel

Morales was found after the battle, and Abd el Krim had the remains delivered to the Spanish at Melilla, out of respect for his former friend.

Lieutenant Colonel Pérez Ortiz, a survivor of the rout, described it as a "human avalanche." As the few survivors found their way into posts farther to the rear, they only increased the panic by their own demoralized conduct and the horrors they described. News of the Spanish annihilation at Anual and Igueriben spread like a prairie fire among the tribal communities, and from all sides the Rifians and many others, aflame with thoughts of revenge and wild with the successes of the *mujahidin,* joined the rebels. Everywhere the Spanish soldiers fell before their onslaught. Everybody who could—soldiers, the few colonists, the merchants living at the Spanish posts—fled in the direction of Melilla, leaving the sick, wounded, and exhausted behind to be stabbed, beaten, or choked to death by the tribesmen, who preferred to save their bullets for more elusive targets.

The tidal wave of panic rolled on for days. In the mountains around Anual the posts of Buy Meyan, Izumar, and Yebel Uddia were overrun, and at Ulad Aisa, Dar Hach Buzian, and Terbibin the garrisons were slaughtered almost to a man. At Dar Quebdana, where the troops were wholly out of touch with events, the commander parleyed with the attackers and agreed to hand over his men as prisoners, whereupon he and the whole of his small force were slashed to pieces in cold blood. The Spaniards at Timayast and Sidi Abdallah escaped to Tizi Johoren, but were shot down there almost to a man. From Ras Tikerman, Tisingar, and Ain Mesaouda survivors escaped to Sbuch Sbach, where only a handful lived through the subsequent Rifian attack and escaped to safety. No one survived the hail of fire at Kandusi, Buhafora, Azru, and Ishafen. At Yart el Bax the native troops deserted to the Rifians after cutting the throats of their officers. At Ben Tieb, the Spanish burned their stores of munitions and fled toward Dar Drius.

General Navarro, Silvestre's second in command, who had been in Spain until July 17 and had gone forward to Dar Drius on Silvestre's orders, tried to exert some control over the remains of the Spanish forces. For a few hours he thought of holding on at Dar Drius with the two or three thousand survivors who had arrived there from all sides. But such was their physical and mental condi-

tion that Navarro thought he would be better off retiring as close
as possible to Melilla and to the relief he was sure would come
from that city. Consequently on the 23d he crossed the Plain of
Garet as far as Batel; then pressed on to Tistutin on the 27th. He
literally drove the worn remnants of his faltering command into
the safety of the walls of Monte Arruit on July 29. Meanwhile, at
Dar Drius an engine pulling several cars filled with refugees toward
Melilla was derailed, and those who escaped the crash alive were
spitted by the Rifians in a matter of minutes. The post at Tafersit
was swept away on July 23. Up at Sidi Dris, the garrison of 500 men
made a break for the ships that had sailed to their rescue, but only
five succeeded in getting aboard, while the rest were cut down or
captured. At Afrau, on the coast, the Spanish were lucky; most of
the people there were rescued by naval units on July 26. But far
down in the south, the large complement at Zoco el Telata de
Metalsa, afraid to dare the rough road to Batel, simply abandoned
the base at the first frightening news from the north, and fled five
miles south across the zonal border to safety under French Army
guns at Hassi Ouenzga. Only about a third of the 1,200 people who
left the Zoco arrived at Hassi Ouenzga unharmed.

On August 2 the stockade at Nador, just a few miles south of
Melilla, fell, and only a few soldiers escaped. The fall of Nador
practically doomed the garrisons at Zeluan and at Monte Arruit,
further south, where frantic concentrations of troops and refugees
still managed to hold out. Zeluan was rushed the next day, and
over five hundred desperate people were barbarously cut down.
Captain Corrasco and a Lieutenant Fernandez suffered typically
ghastly fates: they were gagged, tied together, shot several times,
and then burned alive before their companions.

General Navarro at the garrison of Monte Arruit might have
brought his command through to Melilla if he had been willing to
abandon the wounded. His refusal to do so sealed their fate. Monte
Arruit, a slight eminence on an almost treeless plain, where the
Spanish had built one of their typically rambling adobe forts,
was their last stand. The nearest water supply was almost two-
thirds of a mile away; one can only conjecture why the Spanish
military repeatedly made such incredible miscalculations. Navarro's command was so worn that it could hardly defend itself, and
many deaths were due to heat prostration, sunstroke, and asphyx-

iation in the dust. There were no medical supplies of any kind at Monte Arruit—another incredible fact—and up to the time that the base was overrun, 167 people had died of gangrene alone.

The sole military unit to stand and fight during the entire disaster was Lieutenant Colonel Fernando Primo de Rivera's Cazadores de Alcántara.* These courageous troops had saved Navarro near Batel by repulsing the Metalsa cavalry, the only horsemen the Rifians had; and they carried on now as the heart of the defense.† Planes from Melilla tried to drop food to the besieged garrison, but they could neither drop enough nor drop it accurately, and the defenders had to stand by and watch the exultant Rifians pick up supplies meant for them. On August 9 Monte Arruit, the last fort outside Melilla, fell to the tribesmen. Navarro had agreed to a formal surrender, but as soon as the miserable defenders had stopped resisting, the Rifians swarmed into Monte Arruit and massacred most of them. General Navarro and about six hundred of the command were taken prisoner. Every other living thing was killed, and all the installations, including some airplanes and hangars, were set afire.

Although Zeluan and Monte Arruit were both less than twenty miles south of Melilla, no attempt had been made to send troops to their relief. For one thing, the heights of Gurugú, which dominated Melilla, were infested with rebels; for another, the 1,800 Spanish troops left inside the city were recruits so poorly trained and so inexcusably undernourished that they were incapable of serious fighting. Melilla was swarming with terrified survivors of the rout, some of whom had lost their minds as a result of the atrocities they had seen and experienced. Fortunately for the citizens of Melilla, the Beni Sicar, north of the city, were being held back by their pro-Spanish *caid,* but he had warned the presidio that if the Rifians broke into Melilla, he would not be able to restrain the Beni Sicar from joining in the slaughter.

By the second week of August, the Rifians had actually pene-

---

* Fernando was a cousin of the future dictator Miguel Primo de Rivera.

† On July 30, a Rifian grenade severely lacerated Fernando Primo de Rivera's left arm, but the gallant colonel continued fighting as long as possible. Finally, in order to prevent gangrene, and although there were no anesthetics anywhere to be found, he stuffed a handkerchief in his mouth to muffle his agony and allowed his comrades to amputate his already torn arm with a razor. (He developed gangrene anyway, and died a few days later.)

trated the outlying streets of the city, which, if they had only known it, was altogether at their mercy. Melilla consisted of two sections—the old fortified town, built high on a huge rock bastion jutting out into the sea, and the modern city, which was connected to the older one by a narrow isthmus. The lower city was almost empty at this time, for most of the city's 40,000 inhabitants had fled in terror to the higher, fortified area or onto small boats in the harbor at the approach of the Rifians.

But the tribesmen did not sack Melilla.[32] There were various reasons for their abrupt halt. For one thing, the Spanish were so well defended by the thick walls of the old fortress that an assault upon them would have been costly. For another, the Rifians had no mobile cannon. Furthermore, by this time the tribesmen were tired of fighting: the Moroccan's volatile character is not one that lends itself to siege tactics, and the several tribes involved in the rout of the Spanish were simply not used to cooperating with one another. Now that the pursuit had ended, and ended in such un-dreamed-of success, the tribesmen wanted to go home with their plunder. There was a harvest coming up, and reaping the harvest was far more important at the moment than knifing more Spaniards. As more than one grizzled Rifian was reported to have said later, the mountain warriors were simply bored with cutting throats. At all events, instead of attacking Melilla, Abd el Krim's army melted away into the interior, and by the middle of August 1921, the Rifian forces had left the outskirts of Melilla entirely.

Abd el Krim later told Roger-Matthieu that he had decided not to take Melilla because he was afraid its seizure might have international repercussions.[33] But in view of what the Rifians had already accomplished, it is hard to see how their taking Melilla and completely eradicating Spanish influence in eastern Morocco would have made any appreciable difference internationally. The loss of Melilla would have denied Spain its only base in the northeast and set the seal on Abd el Krim's success; and it would probably have been impossible for the Spanish to have recaptured it by military action at that time. His failure to take Melilla was one of Abd el Krim's very few major errors, for with its possession or destruction he might have gained the time to create a Rifian State strong enough to defy Spain—and if he had, the course of history in Morocco would have been very different.

The reaction to Anual—the name by which this unprecedented military rout has been known to the West ever since—was intense both in Spain and in Morocco.[34] The High Commissioner suspended operations against Raisuli, sent what troops he could by sea to Melilla, and called for reinforcements and supplies to be rushed down from Málaga. Berenguer himself had arrived at Melilla on July 23, but the situation was so confused and so fluid that there was little he could do until help arrived from Spain. "All is lost, including honor," he grimly told a group of journalists.[35]

As soon as reinforcements arrived at Melilla, General Berenguer appointed General José Sanjurjo to succeed the unfortunate Silvestre, and placed tough and experienced officers like Millán Astray, Franco of the Tercio, and Lieutenant Colonel González Tablas of the Regulares in support positions. When Millán Astray landed at Melilla, he attempted to reassure the terrified citizens by shouting dramatically, "People of Melilla, the Legion is ready to die for you! There is no danger now. Long live Spain! Long live the King! Long live Melilla!"[36]

The catastrophe at Anual represented an immense loss for Spain, not only in lives, matériel, and territory, but in national morale and prestige as well. Although the news was withheld from the Spanish public as long as possible, and the final report to the Cortes listed 13,192 killed,[37] other sources have placed the losses as high as 19,000. There is some evidence to show that the real loss was closer to the higher figure, but when one considers that the Spanish Army did not even know exactly how many posts it had strung out in the Melilla *comandancia,* one can see the hopelessness of trying to establish accurate casualty statistics. Matériel lost by the Spanish included more than 20,000 rifles, 400 machine guns, and 129 cannon, plus substantial stores of ammunition and canned food—enough supplies to keep the Rifians fighting for at least a year. With the sole exception of the presidio at Melilla, the whole of the Spanish gamble in eastern Morocco—the railroad, the mines, the agricultural scheme, the few schools and dispensaries, all the military positions, the hard work of twelve years, everything—had been engulfed and destroyed by a band of primitives in a matter of twenty days. The Rifian triumph was even more astonishing in that the original Rifian attack force at Anual numbered no more than 3,000 men.[38] Spanish airmen who flew over the wide area of the rout a few days after the fall of Monte Arruit reported Spanish corpses everywhere, lying butchered along the trails, festering in heaps on the slopes, and scattered among the still-smoking ruins of burned-out *blocaos*.

Spain's humiliation was great. Her leaders had boasted for years to her international rivals about how well the occupation was progressing and how prosperous Spain's portion of the Protectorate had become. Her military were enraged, because they felt that the politicians had denied them the material basis for prosecuting war, and were now trying to blame them for the defeat. As soon as the dismal facts of the debacle were known in Spain, there arose a nationwide cry for revenge, followed by the demand for a full investigation into the causes that had led to such an unparalleled disgrace. But the government did not officially admit the stunning setback until October, by which time the Army was already struggling on the long road back to reconquest. By October, it had reoccupied Zeluan and the Spanish line of 1909, thus giving the government some small gain to point to.

Meanwhile, on August 4, Vizconde Eza had established a commission under General Picasso to investigate the events leading up to the disaster at Anual and to single out those responsible, as well as to look into the conditions of military life in general. But long before the official report was released, enough facts had leaked out to alarm and dismay the Spanish people. Several thousand depositions were taken from survivors of the debacle, but the results were so confused and conflicting that no clear picture of what had happened could be formed. Although it must be emphasized that not all Spanish officers were inefficient or corrupt and not all Spanish soldiers were unskilled or ineffectual, what did emerge was a sorry picture. For example, it was found that soldiers and the wives of officers had long been openly bartering guns and ammunition with Moroccans in public marketplaces in return for fresh vegetables. While many officers in Morocco were becoming rich in mysterious ways, the men in the ranks were starving.[39] It was alleged that the money voted by the Cortes for roads and barracks had gone into the pockets of colonels and generals, and that junior offi-

cers had pilfered soap, building materials, and food from Army
stores and sold them for their own gain.[40] Officers had spent hardly
any time with their troops, but a good deal on leave in Spain, or
gambling and whoring in Melilla. Even the priests were corrupt:
they had spent as much time sitting around in the cafés drinking
wine as the officers had. In the main, the Spanish Army was a conscript army composed of privates who had been too poor to buy
substitutes for themselves, or who lacked the necessary education
or connections to escape military duty. Arturo Barea wrote that
about 80 per cent of the Army recruits as a whole were illiterate.
Barea also was impressed with how pitifully undernourished most
of the troops appeared to be.[41] Many recruits, untrained and poorly
clothed, were armed with the oldest rifles in the Spanish Army—
guns that had been used in the Cuban War of 1898.[42] Some of these
rifles had never been fired or cleaned since their issue. A Lieutenant Arango testified to the Picasso Commission that of the thirty
men under his command, nineteen had been issued rifles in such
bad condition that bullets fired from them would travel no more
than a hundred yards.[43] Some of the cannon used against the
Moroccans were so antique that they would have served better as
museum pieces. Sanitation facilities were primitive in the extreme,
and the louse was lord and master of the Spanish camp. Barea
relates that just after taking Chaouen, General Berenguer complained that there wasn't any meat for dinner, and General Castro
Girona replied by reaching under his armpit, producing a handful
of lice, and remarking that these were the only cattle in the
vicinity.[44]

The Spanish conscript was ridiculously underpaid. Privates were
given one and one-half pesetas a day (about twenty cents), and
another peseta per day (fourteen cents) was allegedly put into
their food fund. A captain, however, made twelve pesetas a day, or
about $1.70. This pay difference seems even more absurd when one
considers that even the Jibala tribesmen working as laborers on
the Tetuan–Chaouen road received five pesetas a day for their
work. (It is pertinent to note here that most of the tribesmen saved
this money to buy rifles from the Spanish.) The average Spanish
soldier subsisted on a meager fare that included coffee and bread
in the morning, and beans, rice, and coffee, with now and then a
bit of sausage, at other meals. There was an incredible amount of

graft in connection with food supplies, but the shrewdest men tried to be assigned to road-building companies, where the real money was to be made. Civilian contractors made a practice of splitting their fees three ways—a third each for the contractor, the officer in charge of the section, and the senior sergeant. The typical attitude here was that only the State's money was involved, and that therefore it was no great crime to accept a rake-off. Should some rare sergeant declare himself against this easy pilfering of public funds, he would almost surely find himself demoted, or sniped at, or sent off to a dangerous area.

Spanish soldiers in Morocco learned all sorts of ways to avoid front-line duty. There were practically no doctors at the front, and a bullet in the stomach meant agonizing death. Troops resorted to such stratagems as eating tobacco to produce the sickly yellow color of jaundice, and holding garlic cloves under their arms to produce fever. They deliberately contracted venereal disease in Tetuan brothels, or else inserted small mustard rolls into their urinary tracts to produce painful inflammations that looked like venereal disease symptoms. They put nettles in minor wounds to make them swell and fester. They held red-hot coins to their legs, thereby producing sores that resembled ulcers. Viewed in the context of the Moroccan situation, this catalog of malingering loses its quality of excess; indeed, given so demoralizing a situation, it is a wonder that so many fought so bravely. As the Picasso Commission continued its investigations, more and more shameful facts were revealed. It was proved that many officers had hidden in Melilla cellars during the battle of Anual, only to appear later and claim that they had been held prisoner by the Rifians. When the Rifians struck, some officers were in Melilla for the opening of the new *kursaal*. Others were on leave in Málaga, and did not bother to return to their commands. It was said of one officer stationed at Monte Arruit that as soon as the alarm was given, he ran for the first car he could find and fled back to Melilla.[45] Airmen on duty were allowed to sleep far away from their planes, and those stationed near Monte Arruit were not able to get back to the airfield there in time to save their planes from destruction or get into the air to aid the defenders. When warehouses and military stores at Melilla were opened for emergency issues during the height of the panic, many were found to be empty, their contents having long ago been secretly sold to smugglers. On and on went the catalog of betrayed responsibilities.

The Maura government, in office at the time of the defeat at Anual, claimed that it would have been impossible to have sent a relief force to Monte Arruit, since the 1,800 raw recruits in Melilla were the city's only defense. Critics pointed out that the 1921–22 military budget had provided for almost 900 generals and 21,000 other officers on active duty, and had contained additional funds amounting to more than a billion pesetas, or about $143,000,000;[46] yet all this had not prevented a complete fiasco in the final show-down at Anual.* Salvador de Madariaga spoke of "Praetorian-ism," which he described as the rule of a body of officers, by no means a caste, who controlled the political life of the nation, giving but little thought to foreign affairs, and focusing all their attention on the preservation of power and the enjoyment of a dispropor-tionate amount of the budget.[47] There had been somewhere be-tween 130 and 150 posts and blockhouses flung up haphazardly around the Melilla *comandancia*. Most of them were small, and lacking in storage facilities: food, water, and supplies were carried uphill from a distance on trails that led through gorges or ravines. These small *blocaos* were usually constructed by piling sandbags about chest-high, adding a wooden wall and a wooden or corru-gated iron roof, and stringing a few strands of barbed wire around the outside. Ordinarily such a blockhouse consisted of a single room about 12 by 18 feet in area, with loopholes left between the sandbags, or cut through the walls. Each blockhouse sheltered 12 to 20 men. Nobody had any privacy, and since there was little to do except to wait for infrequent sniping attacks, boredom was a major problem. Except for small bunks or pallets, the blockhouse was almost bare. One oil barrel held drinking water, and another was used as a toilet. Both had to be cleaned, filled, and emptied outside, where there was no protection from enemy bullets. Although men were often assigned to such a life for months at a time, Army law was so stringent and fear of the tribesmen so great that desertions

---

* At the fall of the monarchy in 1930, the Spanish Army, which numbered about 100,000 soldiers, had 195 generals on active duty and 437 on reserve, as well as 6,500 colonels and majors, over 5,000 captains, and more than 6,000 lieu-tenants—or an average of approximately one officer for every five men, a pro-portion twice that of most armies.

were very rare.[48] Only the larger positions had doctors, and even such simple items as laxatives, cotton, and quinine for malaria were seldom available. Supply procedures were so faulty that many of the men wore summer uniforms all through the terribly cold Moroccan winters, simply because nothing warmer was provided for them. Some fifty trucks had been dispatched to the Melilla *comandancia* for use in transporting supplies to outlying positions, but only five were ever seen in the Rif.[49]

At Igueriben and Anual, the garrisons had been comparatively large, but the troops there had been issued only 40 cartridges apiece —scarcely enough for a day's combat—and only 600 shells in all for their cannon. At Igueriben, the fort had been so poorly situated that the enemy had been able to penetrate as far as the barbed-wire entanglements without being seen. The unfinished post at Abarran was 70 yards long and 13 yards wide, and the parapets, made of damaged sandbags, were only three feet high. The large garrison that disgracefully abandoned Zoco el Teleta de Metalsa and fled toward the French lines to the south was under fire all the way. Nobody stopped to save the column's wounded, and stragglers were ignored. It was found that most of the wounds inflicted on these men were in the back or side, which implied that they were running away from the fight. After the survivors had reached the safety of the French lines, the Spanish officers refused to care for their troops, and instead spent most of their time drinking at the French canteen. When Marshal Lyautey heard about Anual, he said, "The Spanish soldier, who is as brave as he is long-suffering, can, under another command, know better days."[50]

The Committee of Inquiry was said to have discovered a letter from King Alfonso to his favorite, General Silvestre, in which the King urged the general onward in the Rif, saying, "Do as I tell you, and pay no attention to the Minister of War, who is an imbecile."[51] Among the papers supposed to have been found in Silvestre's Melilla headquarters were two telegrams allegedly sent by the King, reading "On the 15th [July 15, 1921] I expect good news," and "Ho, you fellows, I'm waiting!"[52] Opinion was divided as to whether these telegrams really existed, those friendly to the King claiming that Silvestre would never have left such papers lying around in any case. There was also a story current that at a banquet in Madrid in the spring of 1921, Silvestre had promised

Alfonso that he would be at Alhucemas Bay by the anniversary of Santiago de Matamoros, July 25.* When it was known that the King and his family had been vacationing at San Sebastián and Deauville while Spanish troops were being massacred in the Moroccan mountains and deserts, the King's popularity waned.[53] In spite of the news from Morocco, the King had stayed on at San Sebastián, discussing plans for refurbishing the beaches and building new hotels and a casino. Barea says that after Anual, a host of unsavory stories about the King were spread: for example, that a wealthy Spaniard named Marquet had paid the King millions for a license to build a casino; that the King had shares in a motor supply business and an importing firm that brought German and American machine tools to Spain; that the King was in on the Rif mining schemes with the Mannesmanns and Conde Romanones. More and more Alfonso was referred to by the unflattering nickname "Narizotas"—Long Nose—and he was alleged to have said, when told about Anual: "Chicken meat is cheap."

No matter how many of the allegations against King and Army were questionable, it is certain that Anual marked Spain's lowest ebb in modern times. A member of the Cortes who had just returned from active service in Morocco neatly summed up the Spanish position in 1921 when he said that Spain was open to attack from anybody. "If we continue like this, we shall soon have no more Morocco, no more Army, and no more Spain."[54]

Anual represented the greatest victory the Rifians, or any other tribally organized society, had won against Europeans in modern times. Probably no more than 4,000 tribesmen were under Abd el Krim's orders during those fateful July and August days, though it is true that an unknown number of other tribesmen throughout the Rif and the Kert quickly joined in the fight once the Spaniards were on the run. The Rifian losses during Anual were never reported, but it is probable that they amounted to less than a thousand. Abd el Krim became a world figure overnight—a hero without parallel among the tribes of northern Morocco—a new and mighty menace to both Spain and France.

* The name means, ironically, "St. James Kill-Moors."

7. THE SLOW ROAD BACK

WITHIN a few days of the fall of Monte Arruit, the Spanish Army, heavily reinforced with troops from the mainland, moved back into action. The forces at Melilla now numbered 36,000; led by Generals Sanjurjo and Cavalcanti, the Spanish slowly pushed their way to Nador, which they retook on August 13.[1] Under intermittent attack from snipers, the Spanish struggled slowly onward; it took them almost two months to advance the few miles between Nador and Zeluan. Arturo Barea tells how they came upon bodies burst by the sun; bodies mutilated, without eyes or tongues or genitals; bodies violated with the stakes from barbed wire, or with their hands tied up with their own bowels; others beheaded, armless, legless, sawed in two.[2] When the advance guard finally reached Monte Arruit at the end of November, it found 2,600 corpses in and around the vast wreckage of the fort.[3] The hills between Monte Arruit and Anual were strewn with the rotting remains of men and horses, and littered with twisted wheels, half-burned caissons, broken rifles, and bloodstained clothing. It is no wonder that Arrarás described the reconquest as "the dolorous road to Anual."[4]

General Berenguer had tendered his resignation as High Commissioner, but the government at Madrid refused to accept it, and kept him in the field. No one was better qualified than he to fill the post, for during his long tenure in Morocco he had proved himself an able and politically trustworthy administrator. But after Anual, public opinion had turned against him, and his confirmation in the office of High Commissioner was met with infuriated protests, both in the Spanish press and in the Cortes. In addition, the public was demanding that the Army somehow arrange for the return of the prisoners captured by Abd el Krim at Monte Arruit, and accusing Berenguer of doing nothing to obtain their release. It was in this atmosphere of recrimination and conflict that Spain embarked on what amounted to a full-scale war against the rebel tribesmen in the Protectorate.

Over in the Jibala, Raisuli had been saved from almost certain capture by the Spanish disaster at Anual. Spanish troops had closed in on his camp in the hills at Tazrut, but on the very day on which they were to have made their final assault on the village, they received word of the massacre in the Rif, and withdrew at once to Tetuan. Abd el Krim's great victory had a major effect in the Jibala. The Spanish immediately canceled their operations in the hinterland, and concentrated their forces in or very near the larger posts and towns. The success of the Rifians touched off an explosive reaction among the Sumata, Beni Isef, and Beni Sakkar tribesmen of the Lukus, who were eager to join in the killing begun at Anual. A surprise attack by Ahl Serif and Sumata rebels on August 27 and 28, 1921, overwhelmed the Spanish garrison at Akba el Kola in Beni Isef, and left 200 Spanish dead.[5] A relief column from Alcazarquivir managed to fight its way to Akba the next day, but all they found were the smoking ruins of the post and the butchered corpses of its defenders. Trouble for the Spanish in the west increased in October when Mhamed Abd el Krim and a picked harka of Rifians entered the Gomara, traveled as far north as Wad Lau, and exhorted various tribes to join the Rifians against the Spanish invaders. But General Berenguer acted everywhere with dispatch, and before the year was out, Spanish columns from Larache had again surrounded Raisuli in the midst of his own mountains.

In the east, the Rifians were busily consolidating their position astride the mountains, on a line that ran from the sea near Afrau south through Beni Said and Beni Ulichek, all the way down to Zoco el Telata de Metalsa. At first, no more than a dozen tribes actually admitted Abd el Krim's supremacy, and of these, only two or three aside from the Beni Urriaguel were represented in the assembly of notables who masterminded the Rif Rebellion. But after Anual, Abd el Krim's prestige was enormous, and many of the tribes that had been wavering began to consider throwing in with him. On the other hand, his victory had forced Spain to change her policy toward Spanish Morocco from one of outright conquest to the far less ambitious one of limited occupation and political control through bribery of certain caids and chiefs. Spain now had about 150,000 men under arms in Morocco, and yet the war was developing into a stalemate.

The Army had encountered little real trouble in plodding back toward Alhucemas Bay (they had retaken Tistutin, and Batel on the Plain of Garet, in December 1921, and they were as far as Dar Drius by the middle of January 1922), but stalled when they ran into the Rifian mountain positions.[6] As the High Commissioner knew only too well, Spanish troops of the line from the mainland were usually worthless as guerrilla fighters, and consequently as battalion after battalion of them poured into the Protectorate, he placed them on garrison duty along the coasts at Melilla, Ceuta, Tetuan, and Larache rather than committing them to the field. The shock troops who did most of the fighting and took the greatest losses were the men of the Tercio and the native Regulares. These forces struggled on against the Rifians in spite of tremendously high casualties. On more than one occasion, a battalion of the Tercio or the Regulares would lose in a single action as much as three-quarters of its effective strength.[7]

There was only sporadic fighting during the spring of 1922. On March 19, a Rifian harka, using captured cannon, sank the Spanish warship *Juan de Juanes* in Alhucemas Bay, thus proving that the rebels were not to be taken unaware in that highly strategic area, and that any Spanish attack from the sea would have to be a major and complex effort. Fernando de Valdesoto tells of an attack made by Rifians on several armored cars in the vicinity of Dar Drius at this time.[8] Armored cars were new to the mountaineers and, like airplanes, were at first regarded with terror; but the Rifians were nothing if not brave, and a band of specially selected tribesmen went into action against the cars. The Spanish opened fire as soon as the enemy appeared, but although the guns brought down some of the Rifian attackers, others dropped to the ground and waited until the cars lumbered closer. Jumping up, the Rifians surrounded each car, fired their rifles through the ports, and set fire to the gasoline tanks, thus completely destroying the armored cars. Thereafter the tribesmen felt confident that they could beat off any future Spanish mechanized attack.

In early May 1922, Raisuli's stronghold at Tazrut was finally taken by the Spanish, but Lieutenant Colonel González Tablas, one of Spain's most enlightened officers, died in the final attack.[9]

Raisuli himself fled farther up into the mountains to the village of Buhaxen and managed to escape capture. But now he was cut off on all sides except the east, toward the Gomara and the Rif, and he was forced to choose between surrender to the Spanish and flight into the arms of Abd el Krim. Raisuli hated Abd el Krim, both as a successful rival leader and as a Berber upstart whose claim of Sherifian ancestry Raisuli felt was dubious. To beg hospitality from such a man was unthinkable—better to die fighting the Spanish. It would be better yet to make a deal with the Spanish while still in hiding at Buhaxen. By August, Raisuli was still holding out, still pondering how he could deal with the Spanish, and the Spanish advance everywhere had ground to a halt. Berenguer now offered his resignation for the fourth time, and in this instance, since the High Commissioner was now under fire from General Picasso's Committee of Inquiry concerning the Anual fiasco, the government accepted it. To fill Berenguer's office, Madrid appointed General Ricardo Burguete, a greatly respected officer with a spotless record. Burguete at once tried to implement the government's current policy of settling with the various rebel leaders financially instead of militarily. No sooner had he assumed office at Tetuan than he reopened negotiations with Raisuli. That capricious rogue could not have been more surprised or more delighted. In September 1922, he welcomed the Spanish emissaries and accepted their terms. As usual, the Sherif left the conference richer than he came. In return for his own and the Jibala's submission to the Blad l-Makhzen, Raisuli was allowed to retain his power in the Jibala, his personal guard, and his residence at Tazrut (Spanish troops were immediately set to work rebuilding his small palace for him). In addition, Burguete gave Raisuli a large financial settlement. Although the fighting in the Jibala came to an abrupt halt as soon as this accord had been completed, it seems quite probable that the Spanish erred prodigiously by conciliating the wily Sherif. With only a little more effort, they could have captured or killed Raisuli and removed him forever from the Moroccan scene. By firmly occupying the Beni Aros tribal area, which lay in the very center of the Jibala, the Spanish could have disrupted Raisuli's loose organization and taken a positive step toward controlling the dissidents in the West. As it was, the Spanish actually removed many of their detachments from the Jibala and, with regrettable shortsightedness, failed to disarm the tribesmen and fortify the Beni Aros hills.

Evidently they failed to understand that their friendly agreement with Raisuli only served to increase his reputation with the admiring Jiblis, to whom it was plain that he had again outmaneuvered the Spanish invaders.

One of Burguete's first acts as High Commissioner was to visit ex-Sultan Mulay Hafid, now living at Málaga, and ask him to intercede with Abd el Krim for peace and for the return of the Spanish prisoners taken during the Anual fiasco. Burguete's efforts came to nothing. By the end of October, the Spanish Army's cautious advance in the east had brought them to the important position of Tizi Azza, in the mountains about halfway between Anual in the north and Dar Drius in the south, where the tribal territories of Temsaman and Beni Ulichek meet.[10] Tizi Azza, like so many of the Spanish posts, was situated on a wild and rocky summit. In spite of the recent brutal lesson of Anual, which should have taught the Spanish something about logistics, Tizi Azza was so placed that supplies could only be brought in by way of a deep, unprotected gorge. Burguete intended to use Tizi Azza as the springboard for a final invasion of the Rif. Instead, he sustained a severe setback there. Tizi Azza was situated roughly on the forward line Silvestre had occupied the year before, and, as we have seen, it was along this line that the Rifian strategists had decided to fight. After Anual, the Rifians had deliberately retired to the point where the Plain of Garet slopes abruptly upward to form a range of arid hills whose crests provide easily defended positions. The Rifian guerrillas fired from the boulder-strewn summits and higher slopes of the rocky passes around Tizi Azza down upon the Spanish, and the advance ground to a halt. The first battle of Tizi Azza, which took place on November 1 and 2, 1922, resulted in almost 2,000 Spanish casualties, and left Burguete no choice but to call off his forward movement for the remainder of the winter. The Rifians made a lesser attack on Tizi Azza in December, but by then the Spanish had dug in defensively, and the battle was bloody but not decisive. At about this time the Spanish troops made an odd discovery. Having overrun some Rifian trenches near Dar Drius, they were surprised to discover that the tribesmen, in their inexperience with this sort of defense, had dug their trenches by throwing the dirt backward, instead of forward where it would have made a protective barrier.[11]

Burguete had moved 30,000 men, 7,000 horses, and a number of

armored cars to the eastern front, for he had decided to blockade
and starve out the Rifians. He also intended to mount a heavy
bombardment from the sea all along the buttressed Mediterranean
coast from Wad Lau to Alhucemas. His plan was to bombard the
Rifian village communities along the coast until Abd el Krim
agreed to hand over the Anual prisoners. Units of the Tercio were
actually landed from the sea at Wad Lau, and eleven coast guard
vessels, several cruisers, a navy dirigible, and the small aircraft car-
rier *Dedala* were assigned to the Mediterranean coast to prevent
supplies and ammunition from being smuggled into the Rif. Abd
el Krim's answer to these punitive measures proved how little they
bothered him. He bombarded units of the Spanish Navy, whenever
they sailed within range, with cannon hidden in the caves and
rocks along the shore.

Other problems plagued the Spanish high command. One of the
main problems was that of Tangier. The Spanish had never been
able to entirely seal off this city, from which Abd el Krim's agents
could send a steady stream of supplies and money into the Rif
and a steady stream of propaganda out of it.[12] Then, in September
1922, there was the affair of the "Larache Millions," in which corrupt officers in the Larache sector were discovered to have em-
bezzled well over a million pesetas—more than $143,000—in funds
and supplies.[13] Finally, Colonel Millán Astray, founder of the
Spanish Foreign Legion and supposedly one of the darlings of the
military establishment, caused a sensation by resigning his commission in November. This entirely unexpected event focused public
attention, in turn, on the question of *juntas de defensa*, a development that had involved the whole Spanish Army if not the whole
of Spain.[14] The *juntas de defensa*, or military defense councils,
were born of the widespread discontent among Army officers during the winter of 1916–17. The first *junta* was formed by junior
officers of the Infantry garrison at Barcelona. By 1922, *juntas* had
been formed by officers of all the other major Infantry garrisons in
Spain, by the officers of other branches of the service, by noncommissioned officers, private soldiers, and even civilians. The *juntas*
represented an unofficial reaction, mainly among middle and junior grade officers, against low pay scales, desultory promotion,
and the favoritism shown to the Army's leading generals. In spite
of the inflation in Spain during World War I, there had been no

increase in Army pay. The situation worsened when industrial and government workers, as well as various other civilian employees, were able to force wage raises for themselves through strikes. Another thing that the *junteros* particularly resented was a system of promotion called *méritos de guerra,* or combat merits, based upon putative valor in action. This system had been reinstated in 1910 after being abandoned for more than a decade, and it had the personal endorsement of King Alfonso because it allowed him to reward his favorite generals and thus bind to him a small, powerful group that was completely loyal to the throne. To complicate matters, a significant segment of Army officers especially irked by the pay and promotion policies were those who had volunteered for active service in Morocco. Moroccan service was dangerous, after all, and officers who opted to fight there expected rewards above the ordinary, and certainly beyond those bestowed upon their brothers-in-arms stationed in Spain. Consequently, the officers serving in Morocco tended to favor promotion by *méritos de guerra;* they were loyal to the king, and opposed to the *junteros.* The *junteros* looked down on these *africanistas* as expedient and corrupt. Within the Army, the Artillery officers were foremost in insisting upon promotion by seniority, because they felt this system made for a more professional corps. In any case, the *junteros* demanded better salaries, a more equitable system of promotions, and the opportunity to air their grievances personally to King Alfonso. They were against their own generals and the palace clique in particular, against promotion by favoritism, and against the *africanistas.* The Infantry *juntas* had insisted that every Infantry officer must affiliate with them or suffer prosecution by a council of his brothers. It was in order to draw attention to the widespread insubordination and disorganization fostered by the arbitrary methods of the *juntas* that Millán Astray offered his resignation, saying that he could not serve the *juntas* and the legal government simultaneously.[15] Within a few days, Millán Astray had been removed as chief of the Spanish Foreign Legion, ostensibly because his numerous wounds incapacitated him for such an arduous command. The *junteros* were temporarily jubilant, but Millán Astray and the *africanistas* finally emerged the winners in their long duel. The King and the Cortes, their patience exhausted, passed a bill in November 1922 outlawing the *juntas.* Leading *junteros* suddenly found themselves without regular assignments, and all that the *juntas* salvaged from their long tilt with the government and the *africanistas* was the promise that, in the future, promotions by *méritos de guerra* would be carefully considered. Nevertheless, while their power and support were greatly diminished, the *junteros* were able to exercise a significant degree of pressure on the Spanish government for a number of years to come.

In Morocco, meanwhile, General Burguete was attempting to obtain the release of the prisoners taken at Anual. Popular demand for their release had become increasingly insistent as the months passed by, and in December 1921 a "rescue committee," whose purpose was to persuade the government to take immediate action, had been formed in Spain. The Cortes, eager to solve the problem, turned the matter over to the Red Cross. This organization sent Señor Fernández Almeyda into the Rif to discuss terms with Abd el Krim. The Rifian leader demanded the payment of three million pesetas, about $430,000, in ransom. Those to be repatriated were to include only those persons taken since July 1921. Furthermore, payment of an extra million pesetas in damages was to be made for losses suffered by the Rifians. Finally, all tribesmen held as prisoners and hostages by the Spanish were to be returned to the Rif immediately. The Spanish government found these terms completely unacceptable. To recover the prisoners by force was obviously out of the question for a long time to come, yet the Cortes reasoned correctly that it would be dangerous to give the rebels cash, and thus enable them to buy more war matériel. Worse, the weakness to which Spain would admit by handing over to the Rifians as much as a single *céntimo,* and the influence and prestige Abd el Krim would gain if his terms were met, were matters almost too shameful to contemplate. Madrid refused to pay. Abd el Krim, realizing that he held all the high cards, not to mention the prisoners, refused to change a word of his terms. Meanwhile, public pressure in Spain mounted. Late in 1922, the García Prieto government decided to humble itself and bring back the prisoners at whatever cost. Through the services of Horacio Echevarrieta, a Spanish millionaire banker who had bought up many of the Mannesmann mining claims in the Rif, the deed was done. The banker went to Alhucemas (he had been friendly with the Abd el Krims in the past) and became a voluntary prisoner for a few hours in order to guarantee the government's good faith. The four million pesetas was handed over to Abd el Krim, and the prisoners were brought to Melilla in January 1923.[16] Of the 570 Spaniards who had survived the Anual rout, only 326 walked out of the Rif. These numbered 44 officers, 239 soldiers, and 43 civilians, of whom 33 were women and children. The survivors arrived in a pitiable state, suffering from cold and undernourishment and bearing the marks of the chains they had been forced to wear during their captivity. Most of those who died appear to have been victims of a typhus epidemic that carried off some of their captors as well.[17] Several of the prisoners went so far as to praise the Rifians as fair-minded captors: if life had been hard for the prisoners, these people said, it had been equally hard for the tribesmen.*

At this point, Spanish public opinion was sharply divided on what course should be followed in Morocco. *Abandonistas,* those who wanted to get out of Morocco, including some prominent military leaders, insisted that the country be given back to the Moroccans; not another soldier or another cent should be committed there. A staggering amount had been spent, yet the Spanish were engaged in a major war and their attempt to pacify the country had failed. On the other hand, a large number of Spaniards, both in the military and in the government, wanted to revenge themselves on Abd el Krim at any price. These men believed that Spain could still win a decision in Morocco.

As the new year 1923 began, the Jibala remained quiet, and the dirt road from Tetuan to Chaouen had been completed. In the east, the Spanish had won back practically all the area formerly held by Silvestre. Nevertheless, the rebels were demonstrably stronger than they had been—strong enough to dictate terms to Spain, and strong enough to repel the best troops Spain could send against them. The central Rif remained inviolate, and the brothers Abd el Krim, far from considering themselves imperiled by the 150,000 Spanish troops massed against them, were more than ever convinced that they could succeed. They went ahead with their plans to form a new Rifian State—a state completely free of control by Spain, France, the Sultan, and every other outside influence. They intended to show the world that the Rifians were capable of governing and defending their homeland unaided.

---

* The number and condition of the Rifian prisoners held by the Spaniards seems not to have been formally recorded.

8. PRIMO DE RIVERA

During the last days of 1922, the García Prieto government, which was responsible for the return of the Anual prisoners, had come to the decision that the Moroccan Question could best be settled by a civilian High Commissioner. This was yet another blow at the Army and the *africanistas*.[1] Theoretically, at least, a civilian would have political talents that a general could not be expected to possess; since the Army chiefs had failed to settle the problems in Morocco, a civilian High Commissioner might better be able to handle the situation. Unfortunately for this line of reasoning, the government made two bad choices in a row. The first was Don Miguel Villanueva, who was so ill that he was never able to assume office. He was replaced in February 1923 by Don Luis Silvela, who knew almost nothing about Morocco or its problems. His appointment at a time when the fortunes of Spain were at such a low ebb was another in the long chain of blunders that successive Spanish governments made in the Protectorate.

Silvela faced the same two-front pattern that had defeated his predecessors. In the west, Raisuli was ostensibly in retirement as a condition of the pact signed with General Burguete a few months before, but in reality, he enjoyed as much influence throughout the Jibala as he ever had. While Spain's hands were officially tied by her accord with him, Raisuli exploited every situation to build his own prestige and fortune. Moreover, he let no opportunity go by to place difficulties in the Spanish path. In the east, the Army faced the rapidly growing and ever more cohesive federation of tribes led by the Abd el Krims. On February 1, 1923, Abd el Krim had had himself proclaimed Amir (prince) of the Rif in all the *zocos* and mosques of the territory he controlled, and his position appeared to be growing stronger every day.[2]

But the *africanistas* and the majority of the Spanish military were determined to avenge Anual. Having reoccupied most of the area taken by Abd el Krim in his 1921 onslaught, they felt that they were equal to the job of invading the Rif and permanently destroying the power of the Beni Urriaguel. The *africanistas* were enraged by the ransoming of the Anual prisoners, which they considered a direct reflection on their inability to beat Abd el Krim in the field and to force the release of the captives through the threat of military retribution. But they ran into resistance from Santiago Alba, the Spanish Secretary for Moroccan Affairs, a moderate who thought that friendly negotiation with Abd el Krim would produce far better results than continued warfare would.[3] To this end, Alba worked through a Rifian contact of some distinction, Dris ben Said, an old friend of Abd el Krim. In order to foil Alba's plans, the military brought the sinister General Martínez Añido out of retirement and made him chief of the Melilla *comandancia*.[*] It seems to have been more than a coincidence that shortly after Martínez Añido assumed command, Dris ben Said was mysteriously murdered.[4] Without his offices, Alba's plans for peaceful negotiation were all but doomed, and the generals could continue to accuse the government of inefficiency for not bringing the Moroccan situation to a swift conclusion.

Abd el Krim and his Rifians attacked the Spanish concentrations at Tizi Azza again in the first week of June 1923, but were beaten off after heavy losses. The Rifians continued to take the initiative, and the Spanish remained on the defensive. The June attack was delivered with such force that Spanish soldiers afterward described the battlefield as an inferno of fire and steel. Both sides knew that Tizi Azza was the key to the Spanish position in the Melilla *comandancia,* and that if the Rifians could break through and roll up the Spanish positions from this central point of vantage, another Anual could easily follow. The Army had no intention of letting this happen. Spanish planes were part of the defense at Tizi Azza, but the uneven terrain afforded excellent cover for the Rifians, and the bombing and strafing were generally ineffective. The rebels even bagged a low-flying plane piloted by Major Alfredo Kindelán, a Spanish Air Force ace, but Kindelán managed to escape alive.[†] The situation at Tizi Azza was saved

---

[*] According to Brenan, p. 73, Miguel Unamuno characterized Martínez Añido as "a brute."

[†] Kindelán later became chief of the Spanish Air Force.

largely through the bravery of Lieutenant Colonel Rafael Valenzuela, who had replaced Millán Astray as commander of the Tercio.
Valenzuela led his Legionarios in a stand-up charge, shouting commands and firing his revolver until he was struck down by a shot
in the head and another in the chest.[5] His gallantry inspired his
troops, and they charged up the most heavily invested slopes and
drove the Rifians back. Following the battle, Francisco Franco was
rewarded for his fearless leadership in it by being promoted to the
rank of Lieutenant Colonel and being given the command of the
Tercio in Valenzuela's stead.

One of Abd el Krim's most dangerous opponents within his own
mountains was Abd el Malek Meheddin.[6] This notable was the son
of an important Algerian family, and grandson of the famous Abd
el Kader, whose years of resistance to the French conquerors of
Algeria had established him as one of the great Islamic heroes of
modern times. Abd el Malek was born in Syria while his father was
in exile there, and was given a good education. He fought alongside
the Rogui in 1902, but deserted him when it became clear that the
Pretender was headed for disaster. After serving for a time with the
French Army in Algeria, Abd el Malek became an officer under
Sultan Abd el Aziz; but upon the Sultan's abdication, he was imprisoned by Mulay Hafid. It is hardly surprising, then, that Abd
el Malek trusted no one, and was not averse to accepting German
money to harass the French and, incidentally, the Spanish. For
some reason, Mulay Hafid, who had imprisoned Abd el Malek,
later made him chief of the Sherifian police at Tangier, but this
job seemed paltry to the ambitious Abd el Malek. In the opinion
of a German agent in northern Morocco, Albert Bartels, Abd el
Malek was aiming at nothing less than leadership of an independent Morocco.[7] Abd el Malek felt that he was far too important to
be wasted on a sinecure, and once again he deserted. After making
his way back to Taza, he led German-financed raids against French
troops throughout World War I. At one point, he tried to persuade
Abd el Krim to join him, but with no success. He did enlist the help
of Hadj Mohand Biqqish, the most powerful chief in the Geznaya.[8]
With the German defeat in Europe in 1918, Abd el Malek retired
to the Spanish Protectorate, where he was well received and soon
became the ranking native officer in the Regulares. Like Raisuli,
Abd el Malek was extremely envious of Abd el Krim. High Commissioner Burguete thought he saw an opportunity here, and he

attempted to use Abd el Malek's influence among the Marnisa and Branes tribes, southwest of the central Rif and just over the zonal borders in the French Zone east of Fez, to persuade them to strike at Abd el Krim from within his own mountains. But Abd el Malek's reputation for shifting allegiance was not conducive to trust, and he possessed nothing like Abd el Krim's prestige and consistently triumphant record against the Spanish. Burguete was unsuccessful; the struggle between tribes never developed, and Spain thus lost another trump.

Just after the June 1923 action at Tizi Azza, Abd el Krim dispatched delegates to Melilla to suggest a temporary cessation of hostilities. In doing this, Abd el Krim acted neither from fear nor from necessity, but from a hope that Spain, humbled and beaten as she had been at Anual, might be in a mood to accept this opportunity to get out of Morocco altogether, thus leaving him free to establish an independent Rifian nation. Primo de Rivera himself had often advocated getting out of Morocco, and it was well known to the Rifian leaders that many in Spain followed the *abandonista* line.[9]

In the middle of June, Rifian and Spanish delegates met briefly aboard a Spanish ship off the coast at Alhucemas, and for a month afterward a series of notes were exchanged and debated. The two positions were best illustrated by the letters exchanged between Diego Saavedra, Secretary General for Spanish Morocco, and Mohamed Azerkan,* Rifian Minister of Foreign Affairs.[10] On July 15, 1923, Saavedra wrote to Azerkan:

It is necessary to establish the points on which we shall negotiate. It must be as follows: There will be no negotiations nor discussion that takes into consideration the independence of the Rifian State, nor any mention of the Treaty of 1912. It is possible to grant a kind of independence—economic and administrative—to the Rifian tribes, and also to confirm the position and rank which Si Mohamed Abd el Krim enjoys at the present moment; also that of the governors of the tribes who rule under the provision of the Makhzen [Blad l-Makhzen] and under the protection of the Spanish Government.

The negotiations shall be confined especially to the means of

---

* The Spanish contemptuously called Azerkan "Punto" because as a boy he had cadged "puntos"—cigarette butts—from the Spanish officers.

developing commerce, industry and agriculture amongst the Rifian tribes, and to the granting to them of material and moral assistance by the Makhzen and the Protecting Power. If you agree to these conditions, I beg you to send me a document signed by your chief, and the final negotiations will begin.

Finally, I beg of you to consider me as being very desirous of bringing about a lasting peace, and of removing all your doubts that we are trying to deceive you. We desire to act with you in good faith and to prevent bloodshed. It is our hope and wish that the Rif should progress in wealth and enlightenment, not in the interests of Spain alone, but also in those of the Rifians themselves.

Above all I must inform you, by orders of the Spanish Government, that your reply to our terms must be in our hands forty-eight hours from the time that you receive this letter. I shall regret it if you turn a deaf ear to our propositions that are all to your benefit, and if you refuse what is to your advantage, taking instead a road which will bring calamity upon you. If you continue in error, Spain will adopt every means to put down this rebellion in a way that is less her choice than her duty to the civilized Powers that entrusted her with this mission. If you are sincere in your expressed desire of peace, choose without hesitation the road that leads to rectitude and progress.

When you have duly considered these words, and when all suspicion is removed from your minds, send your reply, and may peace be upon you all.

In spite of the 48-hour stipulation, no answer came from Abd el Krim in Ajdir until July 24, nine days after the dispatch of Saavedra's letter. At that time Mohamed Azerkan wrote:

Your letter resembles a final ultimatum, and as such its contents have caused us much surprise. As Minister of Foreign Affairs to the Rifian Government, I feel bound to inform you that our terms are as follows:

That the Rifian Government, established upon modern ideas and on the principles of civilization, considers itself independent politically and economically—privileged to enjoy our freedom as we have enjoyed it for centuries, and to live as other people live. We consider that we have the right to enjoy that possession of our territory in preference to any other nation, and we consider that the Spanish Colonial Party have transgressed and violated our rights, and that they have no justification for their pretense of a claim to make a protectorate of our Rifian State. We have never recognized this protectorate, and we shall never recognize it. We refuse it once and for all. We desire to be our own rulers and to maintain and preserve our legal and indisputable rights. We shall defend our independence by every means in our power, and we protest to the Spanish nation and its intelligent people who, we believe, do not dispute the legality of our demands.

We state—before the Spanish Colonial Party sheds the blood of more of the children of Spain in order to promote their private ambitions and their imaginary pretensions—that if only they will count with their consciences they will realize that they are greatly at fault, and that they have caused their country great losses through their colonial ambitions that are contrary to Spanish ambitions. Let them remedy their error before it becomes still more entangled. We protest against the wicked actions of the Colonial Party. We protest to the civilized world and to humanity. We are in no way responsible for the blood that has been shed nor for the money that has been wasted.

We are surprised that you ignore the interests of Spain herself in not making peace with the Rif by recognizing its independence, and thus keeping up neighborly relations and strengthening the bonds of union with our Rifian people, instead of infringing our rights, humiliating our people, and ignoring all the humane and legal doctrines of universal law such as are contained in the Treaty of Versailles, which was drawn up after the Great War.

This has taught mankind the penalty of ill-doing, of violation and of pride, and by it the world has learned also that no man is to be despised, and that it is a natural duty to leave every people to manage its own affairs. Power and force fail before right. The Treaty [Versailles] was drawn up by the chief men of great nations who had taken part in the war and experienced its terrible consequences. In the end they could not fail to recognize the truth, and they gave to all nations, even the smallest, the rights of self-government. Yet politicians have said that treaties are only ink upon paper, and that power rests with the sword. But truth is truth; otherwise the world would remain always in trouble and perplexity. Peace will not come until every nation is at liberty to defend its rights. It would be no disgrace to Spain if she were to live in peace with the Rifians after recognizing our Government and its independence, and thus increasing the common interests of the two countries. On the contrary it would be a noble action and an honor to her. It would form a magnificent record in her history, and we Rifian people are prepared to welcome a change in the Spanish Colonial Party, for their present attitude is unjust. We sincerely hope that the misunderstanding will be removed. The cause of it is due to the wrong methods that they adopt, to their violence and to their failure to look ahead or to appreciate the consequences that must ensue.

The Rifian Government will be truly sorry if the Colonial Party persists in its transgressions and in its tyranny. Imagine yourself to be the party that is being invaded, your homes in the hands of foreigners intent upon the possession of your property. Would you submit to the invaders because they claimed certain rights and asserted their pretensions? I think that you, and even your woman-kind, would defend yourselves and refuse to accept the humiliation of submission. Your history in this respect testifies for you that this is so. Know that the Rif and all its people are ready to die, and believe me we will die in the cause of truth. They will defend their honor to the last, and nothing will shake their determination unless the Spanish Colonial Party will abandon its wicked motives . . . otherwise the Rifians will die to a man.

I must declare once and for all that the Rif will not change its attitudes, nor give up the principles upon which we act, that is to say, we will not reopen negotiations for peace except upon the conditions of the recognition by Spain of the independence of the Rif.

With no moral basis for taking over the Rif, and with little to show for ten years of administrative efforts, Spain's position was a weak one. Many foreigners—and, indeed, many Spaniards—felt that Spain was irretrievably checkmated in Morocco and that she ought to get out. On the other hand, the gap between the Rifian government's ideals, as expressed in the foregoing letter, and the realities with which the Rifian people lived was as obvious as it was immense. It is not easy to imagine the humane sentiments and concepts of the Azerkan letter being applied in the wild and violent confines of the Rif. The concept of a Rifian state had little meaning for simple men of disparate tribes. Sincere as the expressions on both sides undoubtedly were, neither government would accede to the other's point of view, negotiations were broken off, and the war continued.

It was during this summer of 1923 that England, France, and Spain sent representatives to London to settle the status of Tangier and its international zone.[11] The conference opened on June 29, and it was apparent from the beginning that the three powers held divergent opinions. Gerald Villiers, chief of the African Section of the British Foreign Office and the leading British delegate, wanted a thoroughly internationalized Tangier; Pierre Beaumarchais, Sub-Director of the African Division of the French Ministry of Foreign Affairs, favored a zone protected by France alone; whereas Spain, represented by her Minister Plenipotentiary, the Marques de Torre Hermosa, wanted to incorporate Tangier into Spanish Morocco. After much wrangling, Spain finally adopted the broader English view. France was outvoted, and the Statute of Internationalization was signed in December 1923. (The Tangier International Zone went into actual operation on June 1, 1925.) The final draft of the Statute provided for an eight-nation government for the zone, which was only 147 square miles in area. England, France, Spain, Italy, Belgium, Holland, and Portugal took active parts in the Tangier Government. So did the United States, although she did not sign the Tangier Statute or surrender her extraterritoriality. Morocco was represented by a *mendoub,* or agent, appointed by the Sultan, but since the Sultan was completely dominated by France, France was assured of two votes instead of one.

This solution to the Tangier question was of no benefit whatsoever to Spain, since it failed to close the breach in the wall of the Rif. Abd el Krim's agents and well-wishers operated freely in Tangier, and much of the rebels' supplies seeped through that city. All that Spain gained in exchange for agreeing with Britain on the matter of Tangier was control of the mountains whose springs supplied Ceuta and Melilla with fresh water. These areas became legal parts of Spain, somewhat in the manner that Algeria later became a *département* of France, and ceased altogether to be a part of Morocco. The Spanish also won the right to expel from Tangier, at the whim of the Spanish Consul, any Moroccan born in Spanish Morocco.

On July 30, some of the leaders of the Bucoya tribe, whose territory extended to the western end of Alhucemas Bay, and who were neighbors of the Beni Urriaguel on the west, secretly approached the Spanish at Tangier and promised their assistance in any military disembarkation the Spanish might undertake at Alhucemas. The offer was turned down even though it came from the very

portals of the central Rif, partly because such a landing would involve complicated military and financial considerations that Spain
could not marshal at the time.

The Spanish government kept prodding the military clique to
draw up a blueprint for victory in the Rif, and to this end it authorized a special commission composed of members of the General
Staff to proceed to Morocco and bring back a workable formula.
This commission left for Melilla in August, and soon had drawn
up a project calculated to stabilize the Army's position while at the
same time providing it with a springboard for offensive operations.
The Army was to dig in along the currently held "Silvestre Line,"
the center of which was Tizi Azza, just a few miles south of Anual.
There were to be two lines instead of one, with mobile forces between them, so that the Army could either advance at any given
point with ready reinforcements or fall back upon a system of
defense in depth.[12] On August 22, 1923, as this plan was being
considered, Abd el Krim struck hard again, this time at a sizable
convoy en route to Tizi Azza. At Tifaruin, not far from the Anual
battlefield, an estimated 9,000 rebels threatened to annihilate the
supply column. But the Spanish drove off the enemy, and killed
600 Rifians. (Afterward, they claimed this purely defensive action
as a great victory.)

In Spain, on the same day, mutinies broke out at the ports of
Barcelona and Málaga among the troops being marched to boats
heading for Spanish Morocco. Public confidence in the Army was
so feeble that many refused to be called up for active duty in North
Africa. At Málaga, the troops refused to board their vessels, and,
led by a Corporal José Sánchez Barroso, they attacked several officers who ordered them forward, killing one and wounding three
others.[13] In Barcelona, mobs shouted *vivas* for Morocco and death
to Spain, and whistled down the Spanish flag. But the military
never entirely lost control, and both incidents were contained with
a show of force. The Army arrested Sánchez Barroso and sentenced
him to death, only to have the Madrid government annul the death
sentence. The Army looked upon this interference in a military
affair as a serious breach of conduct on the part of the government,
and one that could lead to an impossible situation by undermining
discipline and authority; but the government replied that it
wanted no martyrs. Meanwhile, the whole country was becoming

dangerously aroused. The Moroccan Question was uppermost in the minds of the people, who were clamoring for radical measures. The government, for its part, continually threw the blame for every problem, domestic and foreign, on the Army. The plight of the Spanish nation had never been more dismal.

It was at this moment of near-anarchy that Don Miguel Primo de Rivera, Captain General of Barcelona and a popular officer, brought off a successful, bloodless coup d'etat and took control of the government of Spain.[14] The new leader, born at Jerez de la Frontera in the southern province of Andalusia in 1870, the scion of an influential family, had known nothing but military life since the age of 14. He first arrived in Morocco as a lieutenant in 1893, and in the brief campaign of that year he personally captured a cannon that had been taken from the Spanish only a few moments before. For this and other deeds of exceptional bravery, Primo de Rivera was awarded the Cross of San Fernando, and was promoted to the rank of captain. Assigned to duty in Cuba in 1897, and then to the Philippines, he was back in Morocco by 1911, fighting in the campaign along the Kert River. Here Primo de Rivera was so badly wounded that he had to abandon active service for a time. Promoted to the rank of major general in 1913, and appointed to the post of observer with the French Army on the Western Front during the early part of World War I, he made a splendid record. But as Governor of Cádiz in 1917, the general brought down official censure upon himself by publicly condemning the government's conduct of Moroccan affairs and by suggesting that the presidio of Ceuta, or some other portion of Spain's Moroccan holdings, be exchanged for Gibraltar in a three-way deal with England.[15] This indiscretion cost him the governorship. But Primo was too talented to be permanently excluded from the public scene. In 1919, he was elevated to the rank of lieutenant general and made commander of the First Infantry Division at Madrid. Meanwhile, he ran for office in Cádiz, and was elected that city's senator to the Spanish Cortes in 1921. With typical candor, Primo de Rivera spoke out against the continued waste of manpower in Morocco, stating emphatically that Spain should be relieved of further responsibility there. The Cortes ousted the senator-general, but almost in the same breath urged him to accept the post of Captain General of Barcelona. Spanish nationalists, as well as his friends, hoped that such a resolute soldier could put a stop to the persistent separatist movements in Catalonia. His rivals hoped that he would lose a degree of popularity, because any successful policy of suppressing the Catalans would almost surely demand drastic methods. Primo de Rivera handled the insurgents with prompt severity, and the trouble ceased for the time being.

The Captain General's experiences in Barcelona convinced him more than ever that the incompetence of the politicians in Madrid was responsible for the nationwide unrest as well as for the impasse in Morocco. By the late summer of 1923, mass discontent in Spain was at its height, and the overall political situation was deteriorating. The Army, led largely by incompetents, was still poorly equipped; taxes were a constant burden, and the hue and cry for punishment of those responsible for Anual had not abated. The press called Morocco "the graveyard of the youth of Spain"—the "bottomless pit" down which the national wealth was being poured.

Behind the scenes, a radical change was being considered, with at least the tacit consent of King Alfonso. A group of royalist generals known popularly as "the Quadrilateral" had been formed under the leadership of José Cavalcanti, a highly respected Cavalry officer who was both an *africanista* and a favorite of the King.[16] Cavalcanti's associates in the Quadrilateral were General Antonio Dabán, General Leopoldo Saro, and General Federico Berenguer, the brother of the former High Commissioner. The group's goal was to establish a strong government capable of successfully prosecuting the war in Morocco, and they had come to the conclusion that such a government could only be established by means of a military coup. They therefore looked around for a popular leader. Primo de Rivera was interested in the role, despite his reputation as an *abandonista*. By assuring the Cavalcanti group that he intended above all to effect an "honorable"—that is, a face-saving— conclusion to the action in Morocco, he won their support. He convinced the Quadrilateral that it was necessary to promise many different things to many different groups in order to gain support. By promising autonomy to the Catalans, relief of responsibility to the royalists, and honor to the military, he was able to win support from many factions. The Quadrilateral accepted him as the logical man to lead Spain out of her difficulties. Social unrest and

General Manuel Fernández Silvestre
Fot. Kaůlak

General Dámaso Berenguer
UPI Photo

Spanish corpses at Monte Arruit after the Moroccan evacuation of the post, 1921
UPI Photo

Mohamed Abd el Krim (seated) and
his brother Mhamed, 1924
Mansell Collection

Major Francisco Franco and General
José Sanjurjo in the Melilla zone, 1921
Ministry of Information, Madrid

King Alfonso XIII making a radio address, 1925
UPI Photo

Spanish gunners at Tetuan firing on Moroccans on the heights of Gorgues, 1924
Radio Times Hulton Picture Library

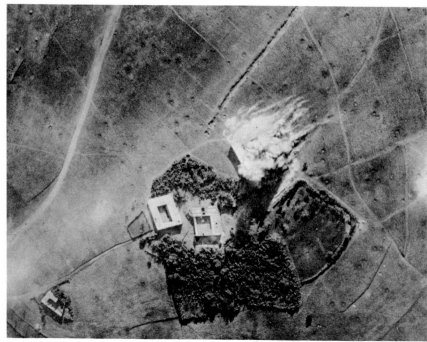

Spanish air raid on Abd el Krim's temporary headquarters at Tiguisas, 1924
Mansell Collection

Spanish machine gunners in the mountains near Chaouen, 1924
Radio Times Hulton Picture Library

Spanish blockhouses near Afrau, 1924.
Mansell Collection

Spanish military leaders at Alhucemas, September 1925. Left center: General Primo de Rivera. Behind Primo's right shoulder: General José Sanjurjo. Center: General Leopoldo Saro. Left center (facing Saro): Colonel Manuel Goded. Behind Goded's left shoulder (face only visible): Colonel Francisco Franco.
UPI Photo

The Spanish landing at Cebadilla Beach, near Alhucemas Bay, September 10, 1925
UPI Photo

Marshal Louis Hubert Lyautey
Radio Times Hulton Picture Library

Mohamed Abd el Krim (right) with
his children and his brother
Mhamed en route to exile on the
island of Réunion, aboard the
French steamship *Abda*, 1926
UPI Photo

Mohamed Abd el Krim
UPI Photo

the apparent failure of the parliamentary system in Spain were as important as the Moroccan problem in leading to the dictatorship. Deciding to risk his career to do something constructive about an intolerable situation both at home and in Morocco, Primo de Rivera issued a manifesto on September 12, 1923.[17] In it he swore to "liberate" the country from the leadership of those who were "responsible for the last twenty-five years of national misfortune and corruption." The King, who almost certainly knew of the Quadrilateral's plans, was conveniently "vacationing" in San Sebastián when the coup was announced. He returned to Madrid, and on September 15 "invited" Primo to take over the nation's guidance. The new Prime Minister promptly set aside the constitution under which the Spanish Government had functioned since 1875, and in place of it established a Military Directorate with himself at the helm.[18] It is almost certain that the Quadrilateral envisioned a military take-over as a temporary measure, and intended that the government be returned to civilian control as soon as the Moroccan problem had been settled. The new Directorate consisted of eight brigadier generals—one for each major garrison in Spain—and an admiral to represent the fleet. Although this sudden power grab had its opponents—among them, professional soldiers who were suspicious of a man who had long advocated withdrawal from Morocco, and professional politicians who were incensed at being superseded or summarily thrown out of office— Primo de Rivera had many more friends than enemies. Many generals, the Church, big business, and the majority of the common people were for him. Nevertheless, his advent was greeted with wary anticipation.

Fifty-three years old when he seized control of Spain, Primo de Rivera was an attractive man of medium height and robust physique, with white hair and a trim mustache. He was a grandee of Spain, the second Marquis of Estella, a title he had inherited from his uncle.[19] The first Marquis had been one of Spain's leading political generals, and many observers believed that his promotions in the Army were as much the result of family position as they were of his personal bravery in combat. In any case, the new dictator was courteous and honest, and possessed of an essentially simple nature. A popular rhyme had it that "A bottle, some cards, and a beautiful dame / Mark the coat of arms of our Primo's name."[20] He loved good food, drink, and conversation, and would often talk until three or four in the morning at some Madrid café. (In the opinion of Salvador de Madariaga, Primo de Rivera differed from the café politicians with whom he loved to talk only in quality; he was a genius of the species.)[21]

Sometimes he abandoned his work for sexual orgies. He disliked fanfare and ostentation, and even as dictator of Spain, he often walked along the streets or dined in the better restaurants unrecognized. He usually spoke in his native Andalusian dialect. According to Ernest Hemingway, when he attended a bullfight, he was wont to have the testicles of the bulls killed in early fights cooked and served to him in his box while he watched the remaining events of the day take place. On one occasion, when he lit a cigar in a Madrid theater, only to be reminded that smoking in theaters was forbidden, he stood up and announced to the audience, "Tonight, everybody may smoke!"[22] He had unlimited confidence in himself, and he was always sure of his own good intentions.[23] Although Primo de Rivera ruled Spain absolutely, in general he was a benevolent autocrat. His military policy changed from one of outright disengagement in Morocco to one of aggression. It became his greatest wish to extend Spanish control over the entire Moroccan Protectorate in order to compel respect not only from the Moroccans but from the other European powers.

To this end, he went to work with the energy and courage for which he had long been noted. The Directorate declared the country to be in a state of war. Strict censorship of the press was established, and public demonstrations of every kind were forbidden. A considerable pay raise was given to all noncommissioned officers of the Army, and a budget of 54 million pesetas—about $7,700,000 —was voted for roads, railroads, and other public works in Morocco. The new dictator promised "a quick, dignified, and sensible" solution to the Moroccan problem.

With the fall of constitutional government, High Commissioner Silvela was dismissed from his headquarters at Tetuan, and General Aizpuru—the seventh High Commissioner in the Protectorate's eleven-year history—was appointed to supersede him. Like most of his predecessors, Aizpuru was a respected veteran of the Moroccan wars. Acting under orders from the Directorate, he renewed friendly relations with Raisuli. The two met at Sidi Musa in October 1923. The mountain warriors put on a colorful show for Aizpuru, including musical entertainment and a huge banquet. Such amiability on Raisuli's part may have been prompted by his lingering ambition to become Khalifa of the Spanish Protectorate —after all, the Khalifa's annual subsidy from Spain was about $215,000, or only $71,000 less than that of the Spanish royal family itself. In any case Mulay el Mehdi, the original Khalifa, had died just a few days before the meeting, and his post was still vacant.[24] Raisuli persisted in claiming that his Sherifian blood and his long tenure as the real power in the Jibala qualified him above all others for the office. He had applauded Primo de Rivera's take-over in Spain, and had suggested to the new dictator that the Army could save men and money by leaving the Jibala to him and concentrating the Spanish military effort against the Beni Urriaguel in the east. The dictator liked the idea, but he knew Raisuli of old, and realized that the chieftain was both capricious and self-serving; treaties and promises meant little to him. Moreover, such an agreement would certainly not please the French, who kept a keen eye on Spanish Morocco, and were inimical to Raisuli because of his open cooperation with the Germans during the First World War. Raisuli himself must have regretted his ambitions now and then, for he once remarked to a group of Spanish officers, "You give a man safety, but you take away hope. In the old days, everything was possible. There was no limit to what a man might become. The slave might be a minister or a general; the scribe, a sultan. Now a man's life is safe, but he is forever chained to his labor and his poverty."[25] It was a moot point—one wonders how many Rifians or Jiblis would have preferred the challenge and exhilaration of their original way of life to the more regimented but comparatively more secure existence the Spaniards were trying to impose upon them. At any rate, in his amiable way, Primo de Rivera temporized and promised Raisuli nothing, meanwhile strengthening Spain's position.

On November 1, he authorized the creation of an African Army Reserve. This force was based on the southeast coast of Spain at the seaports of Almería and Alicante, and stood ready at all times to embark for Morocco should reinforcements be needed there. Soon afterward, in an effort to centralize the administration of Spanish Morocco, he established the Moroccan Office. Primo de Rivera was determined to save Spain's Moroccan venture.

Abd el Krim's rise to prominence had attracted the interest of numerous foreign groups, and the Rifian leader was approached with offers of assistance from idealists and businessmen, politicians and adventurers. To most of them, Abd el Krim lent a cautious ear, for he felt that in most cases their friendship was motivated more by the possibility of winning mining concessions than by any genuine interest in Rifian independence—and he was probably right. Among those who became involved with the Rif for one reason or another was Captain Robert Gordon-Canning, a wealthy Englishman who was intrigued by Islamic history as well as by the Rifian struggle.[26] He believed that England should respect the rights of the Rifians if only because the British Empire contained millions of Muslims whose reaction in favor of their co-religionists might be seriously detrimental to England. Gordon-Canning made two trips into the Rif, the first in November 1924 on behalf of the Red Cross, which had offered to care for the Rifian wounded. On his second trip, in late 1925, he went as an emissary of the French Government, which had decided to probe the possibility of negotiating peace terms with Abd el Krim. In the meantime, certain English corporations had expressed interest in buying up mining concessions in the Rif, and the German firms of Mannesmann and Stinnes were also hoping to cash in on Rifian minerals.* The Mannesmanns in particular were optimistic, because they had been strongly entrenched in northern Morocco in the past, and had established friendly relations with Abd el Krim's father. A certain Herr Hacklander was the representative of the German mining trusts, and he and an Englishman, Colonel Barry, proposed a solution to the Rifian struggle through the good services of the League of Nations, but nothing came of it.[27]

In general, the businessmen of Tangier were sympathetic to the Rifians, since Tangier was an entrepôt for all kinds of supplies destined for the Rif. French Communists saw in the Rif Rebellion a chance to discredit and weaken the government in Paris, and although it is improbable that they ever donated any direct aid to Abd el Krim's cause, they did advise him not to worry about possible Franco-Spanish joint action in the Rif. World opinion was strongly opposed to the Spanish point of view, and most of the for-

* Vincent Sheean thought the Germans had the lead in the Rif, and he thought that much of Abd el Krim's money came secretly from German sources. See Sheean, p. 148.

eign press acclaimed Abd el Krim as a hero—an underdog fighting against great odds out of love for his people and his country.

In June 1923, Abd el Krim authorized an Englishman, Sir Charles Gardiner, to establish a Rifian State Bank and to print money in any quantity that he deemed necessary.[28] In addition, Gardiner was to handle all mining and forest concessions in the Rif, and to dispose of all telegraph, telephone, docking, port, fishing, and railroad concessions in the Rif for a period of ninety-nine years. This agreement was to have gone into effect as soon as the English-French combine that Gardiner was to help organize deposited £300,000 to Abd el Krim's account in a French bank. Gardiner said that the money was never paid to Abd el Krim. The Rifian leader, in discussing the matter with Gordon-Canning, said he had actually received a bundle of paper franc notes from Gardiner during World War I, but that the notes turned out to be nonnegotiable. At all events, the combine was never organized. Meanwhile, various leaders of other colonized Islamic countries around the world gave the Rifians verbal encouragement, seeing in the Rifian struggle for freedom a capsulized replica of their own aspirations, and the Rifian chiefs remained convinced that a successful rebellion would, in the end, win them strong economic allies.

Although 1923 produced no outstanding changes in the military pattern in Spanish Morocco, it ended on a note of promise for the Spanish, for in Primo de Rivera, Spain at last had an aggressive, experienced general from whom much could be expected. On the other hand, an incident that had occurred in August demonstrated how insecure the Spanish position in Morocco really was.[29] At ten o'clock in the morning on August 22, a group of jellaba-clad tribesmen suddenly began firing into the crowds on one of Tetuan's main streets. Such was the ensuing confusion that not one of the raiders was captured, but eight Tetuanis were killed, more than twenty were wounded, and the Protectorate's capital city was thrown into panic. Evidently the tribesmen could move and strike wherever they pleased. It was into this atmosphere that the Spanish moved under their new leader.

9. THE YEAR OF CHAOUEN

Cold weather and driving rain reduced Spanish action considerably during the first few months of 1924. Meanwhile, the Rifians attacked the Spanish garrison at M'ter, on the Beni Buzra coast in the heart of the Gomara. Although reinforcements, including bombers, were brought in by sea from Ceuta, it took the Spanish more than a month to break up the attack. The rebels even succeeded in making trouble for the Spanish Navy: some of Abd el Krim's cannoneers, who were hidden in the coastal heights, made a direct hit on the Spanish warship *Cataluña*, killing a number of sailors and causing severe damage to the ship itself. In early March, the Rifians struck again, with simultaneous attacks at Afrau, Tizi Azza, and Midar on the Melilla front. Because of the rain and fog at Tizi Azza, air and artillery support were out of the question, and the Spanish were forced to defend their positions in hand-to-hand combat with bayonets, pistols, and knives.[1] In spite of the heavy casualties on both sides, the relative positions of the Rifians and the Spanish remained unchanged.

In the west, rebel pressure along the Wad Lau, north of Chaouen, increased. The local leader there was a fiery young man of twenty-five named Ahmed Heriro, who had once served with the Tetuan Regulares. Heriro, the son of a Beni Hozmar farmer, had been one of Raisuli's ablest protégés until 1923, when he and Raisuli fell out over the distribution of plunder taken by Heriro's harka. Incensed at Raisuli's arrogance and cupidity, and smarting over his refusal to make him Caid of Beni Hozmar, Heriro offered his services to Abd el Krim.[2] Because of his fighting reputation, Heriro was accepted. He worked openly with agents of Abd el Krim who were engaged in spreading the rebellion throughout Raisuli's domain. Raisuli's failure to take firm action against Heriro and these agents was to cost him his life, as well as Chaouen and the whole of the Gomara.*

In March, the Spanish Government received an interesting offer of assistance from Baron Peter Wrangel, late a general of the White Russian Army in the Crimea.[3] Wrangel and more than a hundred thousand soldiers under his command who had escaped from the Bolsheviks were looking for employment. The general proposed that Primo de Rivera send them as a Russian expeditionary force to the Rif. The dictator refused this unusual offer on the grounds that the Spanish Constitution (which he himself had suspended in other causes) prevented the presence of foreign troops on Spanish soil. It would seem that Spanish pride, among other considerations, forbade the acceptance of foreign aid.

Early in May, the Rifians stepped up their activity in both the east and the west, attacking Sidi Mesaud, not far from Anual, and hitting the Wad Lau line of blockhouses once again. The fighting near Sidi Mesaud was even fiercer than before. Although the Spaniards were using a few armored cars, the Rifians had long ago learned that they could halt and destroy them by trapping them in wide trenches, then attacking them with grenades from above. The Rifians could be driven away only at the point of the bayonet, a method usually more bloody and costly to the attackers than to the attacked. Meanwhile, the increased Spanish buildup along the Wad Lau line had alarmed the Beni Hozmar, Beni Said, and Beni Hassan. Encouraged by Heriro and other Rifian agents, these three tribes went over to Abd el Krim in June 1924. In retaliation, the Spaniards sent their planes over the escarpments of Beni Hozmar to bomb the dispersed communities there. Since most of the men were off fighting with the tribal harkas, it was mainly women, children, and very old men who were killed in these aerial attacks. The Spanish claimed that they usually dropped leaflets printed in Arabic and thamazighth to warn the population of bombing raids, but even if they had done so—and it seems that in most cases they did not bother—most of the tribesmen were illiterate.[4] Fortunately for the rebels, the Spanish air crews were poor marksmen, and as often as not they hit nothing but rock and cactus bushes. At all events, the bombing of defenseless communities made wonderful

---

* It is possible that Raisuli's laxness in hunting down Heriro was the result of ill health. Since 1911, the chieftain had suffered increasingly from dropsy.

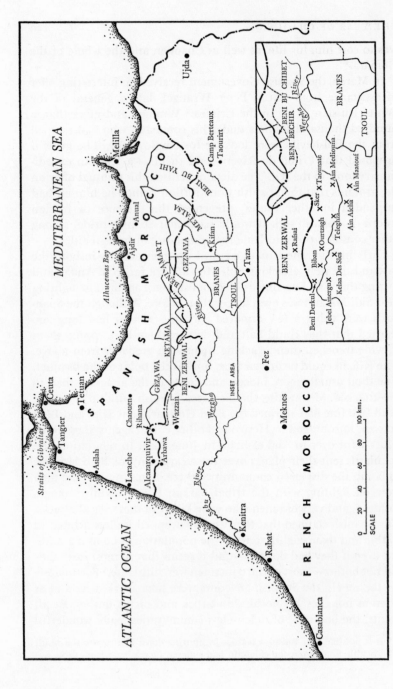

Map 3. Northern Morocco, 1924–25. The X's in the inset indicate French hill posts.

propaganda material for Abd el Krim, and the tribesmen soon learned that a few old men could keep the planes at a respectful distance merely by taking potshots at them with captured Spanish Mausers.

On July 24, Primo de Rivera visited Morocco and personally inspected the front lines.[5] For a week he toured Spanish positions all over the Protectorate, from Alcazar and Larache in the west to Ceuta and Tetuan in the north, and all along the Silvestre Line in the east. Before the trip, however, he had already decided to withdraw the Spanish troops from all positions in the local tribal areas. Spain would maintain her control of the hinterland through the governors appointed by the Khalifa—Abd el Krim in the east and Raisuli in the west—rather than by force. The flaws in this drastic policy were obvious. The Spanish Army, especially the *africanista* element, was certain to feel ashamed by withdrawal, and therefore would be dangerously resentful. The tribes that had remained faithful to Spain—or at least neutral—would now either rise against the Protectorate or be left to the sure vengeance of Abd el Krim and Raisuli. Moreover, there was little reason to believe that Abd el Krim would surrender the initiative at the height of his power in exchange for anything less than the full recognition of the Rifian State. Primo de Rivera must have understood the risks involved: in March, he had stated that it was impossible to remove troops from Moroccan interior posts because the natives would regard such a withdrawal as a major victory. Yet in July he chose what he conceived of as the lesser of two evils: not to keep the Army in a highly vulnerable position, but to order the men to retreat, regroup, and retrain, so that eventually they could return in full power. An American foreign correspondent, Webb Miller, who interviewed Primo de Rivera at this time, found the dictator's comments astonishingly candid: "Abd el Krim has defeated us. He has the immense advantages of the terrain and a fanatical following. Our troops are sick of war, and they have been for years. They don't see why they should fight and die for a strip of worthless territory. I am withdrawing to this line, and will hold only the tip of this territory. I personally am in favor of withdrawing entirely from Africa and letting Abd el Krim have it. We have spent untold millions of pesetas in this enterprise, and never made a céntimo from it. We have had tens of thousands of men killed for territory which is not worth having. But we cannot entirely withdraw, because England will not let us. England has great influence over the King and, as you know, the Queen was an English princess. England fears that if we withdraw, the territory will be taken by France, which might nullify the command the British have of the Strait of Gibraltar. . . . The Strait is vital to England's imperial interests; it is the gateway to her empire—India and Australia. England wants a weak power like Spain in possession of the territory opposite Gibraltar. They don't want a strong power like France there!"[6] In view of all these factors, Primo de Rivera decided to withdraw.

The Army, especially the *africanistas,* reacted violently to his tactic of *abandonismo.* When the dictator visited the Tercio post at Ben Tieb, in the foothills northeast of Tizi Azza, late in July, the officers gave him an unusual banquet at which nothing but eggs in various forms were served. Of course he remarked at this odd menu, and was quickly informed that those who wanted to get out of Morocco had no further need of "eggs," because "eggs" were needed only by those who were willing to stand and fight. Since in Spanish slang "eggs" means testicles or "guts," the implication was clear.[7] Surprisingly, the dictator took this shocking piece of insubordination in his stride. After dinner, Francisco Franco made a stirring speech, calling upon Primo de Rivera not to give up territory that had been taken at the cost of so many lives. "Morocco is Spanish earth," Franco said, "because it has been acquired at the highest price and paid for with the dearest coin—Spanish blood."[8] Not only could the present line be held indefinitely, claimed Franco, but with further reinforcements and coordinated assaults, the Army could go all the way to the heart of the rebellion around Alhucemas Bay. When Primo de Rivera himself rose to reply, his speech was both frank and full of the very "guts" his officers so admired. They listened attentively while he explained his plans for the Protectorate; but when he questioned the necessity for going on to Alhucemas, his audience actually booed. Furious as he must have been by this time, he nevertheless contained himself, and stated firmly that the Moroccan Question would be settled in due course, that the Army would only be required to surrender a minimum of territory, and that it was not the job of junior officers to decide upon the strategy necessary to succeed in Morocco. He could hardly afford to alienate the

Spanish Foreign Legion—the best troops he had—and therefore he chose to warn, rather than to punish, its officers. He took a stern tone: "Now I talk to you in an informal way, but on the day when your orders are given to you, you will have no choice but to obey them, whatever they may be."

The speech had a salutary effect, but Franco—perhaps worried about his part in the affair, or perhaps still in disagreement with the dictator—sent in his resignation. This placed Primo de Rivera in a bad position. Franco was one of the most capable and popular officers in the Army, and not only all of the Tercio's officers, but also most of the *africanistas* in other units were solidly behind him. After some thought, Primo de Rivera handled the serious situation deftly. He refused to accept Franco's resignation; and in view of *africanista* resentment, he modified his plans for withdrawal. The Army was ordered to withdraw in the Jibala, where it held no discernible line as it did in the Melilla *comandancia*, but only a scattering of small and isolated posts. Of these, Chaouen was the largest, most extended, and most exposed position. Should Abd el Krim ever rouse the Jiblis and invade the west, Chaouen might well become another Anual. In the final plan adopted, Primo de Rivera called for a strategic withdrawal from Chaouen and the Wad Lau area to a prepared line approximating that of 1918.[9] The "Primo Line," or "Estella Line," was to extend from the sea at Rio Martín, on the Mediterranean just outside Tetuan, continue west through Fondak Ain Jedida, and loop south, passing slightly east of Alcazar all the way to the French zonal border. Once safe behind the Primo Line, the soldiers would be trained by experts, and as many incompetent officers as possible would be replaced. Thus strengthened and reorganized, the Spanish would, at the proper moment, plunge resolutely back into the mountains to take up the difficult task of pacification with renewed force.

During the heat of July and August 1924, a succession of unseasonable cloudbursts reduced the Moroccan mountain trails to muddy slime. In spite of the fact that the Spanish had almost 100,000 men in the Jibala alone, the entire area was under constant pressure from the rebels. The sound of guns echoing in the mountains could be heard in Tangier and even in Gibraltar. A Rifian attack at Coba Darsa in Beni Said in July was beaten off,[10] although the garrison's water had to be supplied by low-flying planes, which dropped bags of ice to the defenders. Along the

crag-bound Wad Lau south of Coba Darsa, at Chentafa and So-
lano, the Spaniards held on under repeated attacks. They even
took hostages from among the local Beni Said now and then, and
they forced each warrior they caught to pay the heavy fine of one
rifle or one mule. Nevertheless, the rebels steadily increased their
attacks all over the Gomara, Lukus, and Jibala, until finally the
Spanish position in the west was all but untenable. At Chentafa,
when all hope was lost, the lieutenant in charge burned down the
post, and died with the remnant of his command in the final rebel
charge. In the southwest, the villages of Teffer and Buharash with-
stood wave after wave of assault by Sumata and Ahl Serif tribesmen for forty-one consecutive days, and the post at Seriya managed
to hold out for seventy-six days. In August, the Spanish lost their
staunchest native ally, Abd el Malek, who was killed while leading
a harka near Midar in the Melilla *comandancia*. Semiabandon-
ment of the Protectorate seemed more and more necessary. As
Primo de Rivera candidly admitted: "The reality was very sad.
From Tetuan to Chaouen, and from Tetuan to the International
Zone, not a single garrison or single detachment could be normally
provisioned. More than 25,000 men, with their cannon, machine
guns, rifles, and munitions, were the quarry which the enemy now
had for his own. There was no time to lose if the situation was to
be saved."[11]

Anual was still fresh in the minds of the Spanish people. In April
1922, the Picasso Commission had completed its investigations.[12]
Its report cited four major errors that led to the fiasco: the badly
planned and executed advance toward the Rif, the granting of too
many military leaves in the midst of such an all-important operation, the overconfidence of certain officers, and the gross inefficiency
of the Spanish air arm in Morocco. The Commission named thirty-
nine officers as directly responsible for the ignominious defeat—
Generals Berenguer, Silvestre, and Navarro, seven colonels, three
lieutenant colonels, seven majors, eight captains, ten first lieutenants, and a second lieutenant.[13] Silvestre's mistakes were said
to have been his excessive reliance on native auxiliaries, his failure
to note the enemy concentration, and his decision to evacuate
Anual instead of defending it at all costs. Minister of War Eza believed that Silvestre, more than anyone else, "engendered the
catastrophe"—an opinion shared by much of the Spanish nation.[14]

Yet even Silvestre had his apologists. At Melilla, six months after the debacle, General Cavalcanti, a loyal *africanista,* said: "Silvestre did not fail. The system failed, and Silvestre was the victim of it." Augusto Vivero thought Anual should be blamed on High Commissioner Berenguer and not General Silvestre. In Vivero's opinion, Berenguer had erred by conferring with Rifian notables at Alhucemas in March and April 1921 and thus confirming Abd el Krim's fear of an impending invasion of the Rif; by publishing his invasion plans in *El Telegrama del Rif*; by denying Silvestre the supporting military posts he asked for; by withholding reinforcements when Silvestre requested them; and, finally, by incautiously stating that the advance into the Rif could be accomplished with few casualties.[15]

In June, General Navarro, the commander at Monte Arruit, was tried by the Supreme War Council and absolved, as he probably deserved to be. But a General Tuero and a Colonel Sirvent were each given a year's imprisonment for cowardly behavior at Tizza (not Tizi Azza), near Melilla; and a Colonel Lacanal was given six months and a day in jail for his poor conduct in the same incident. General Berenguer resigned his commission and awaited prosecution. But in July 1924, the Military Directorate granted all these men a general amnesty, and shortly afterward it actually promoted Berenguer to the rank of lieutenant general.[16] This startling reversal of opinion by the military hierarchy was followed by a favor from the King himself, who appointed Berenguer to the post of Chief of the Royal Household—a plucky but hardly politic act. Since both the general and the King were popularly felt to have been implicated in the Anual disaster, people now said that Alfonso was protecting Berenguer and at the same time buying his continued loyalty. It was rumored also that the King had attempted to use the Army as a tool in gaining a personal control of the mineral wealth of the Rif.[17] At this juncture Berenguer, who disliked Primo de Rivera, had the temerity to make a derisive speech against the dictator at a Madrid dinner party. In spite of the King's favor, he was promptly sentenced to six months of detention in a fortress outside Madrid.

Blame for the fiasco of Anual was never officially established, for Primo de Rivera's coup and the subsequent dissolution of the Cortes occurred just twelve days before that body was to have discussed the Picasso Commission's findings. But the weight of evidence falls heaviest upon General Silvestre as the person most culpable. The public resented the King's alleged behind-the-scenes role in the disaster, and his popularity waned steadily afterward. Sir Charles Petrie[18] maintains that the King was never proved to have been involved—one might as well hold Victoria guilty of the death of General Gordon—but Arturo Barea claims that Alfonso lost public support because of Anual, and for good reason. According to Barea, fathers who had paid redemption so their sons would not be forced to serve in Morocco now found that their sons were being drafted just the same. These people naturally felt they had been swindled by their own government.[19] A large sector of the Spanish public would always feel that the Army, in the person of Primo de Rivera, had taken over the government to prevent further investigations into its own and the King's involvement in the Moroccan scandal. Had not Primo de Rivera openly stated in his manifesto of September 1923, "The country does not want to hear any more talk of 'responsibilities,' but wants to see justice carried out swiftly . . . against the political parties at fault"?[20] Those who blamed the King almost got their revenge when two Spanish leftists attempted unsuccessfully to assassinate Alfonso in Paris in 1924.

The long-awaited withdrawal order was finally issued in September 1924, and the retreat in the west began. Both M'ter and Wad Lau were evacuated on September 8, and the troops were sent back by sea to Ceuta. Spanish forces all the way from the Tangier Zone to Alcazarquivir were drawn back simultaneously. Only the grand operation of escorting the ten-thousand-man Chaouen garrison, and the soldiers in the smaller posts around it, safely back to Tetuan remained to be accomplished. For this undertaking, a rescue force was assembled in Tetuan under the direct command of High Commissioner Aizpuru. On September 19 the first phase of the relief of Chaouen was carried out by Generals Castro Girona and Federico Berenguer, who took the lightly defended heights of Gorgues easily. With the northeastern summits of the valley in Spanish hands, the main force moved south through the valley of the Beni Hassan on September 23. Another column was supposed to march from Larache under Colonel González Corrasco, but, like the 1920 Larache column, it never arrived. It had to fight its way over the hills, and at Zoco el Jemis, in Beni Aros, it turned back to avoid further heavy losses. While the Jibala tribesmen were not yet allied with Abd el Krim, they were against all Spaniards. Instead of joining the relief of Chaouen as planned, González Corrasco's men spent the winter fretting in Larache.[21]

The Tetuan force moving on Chaouen consisted of three columns. The left flank, under Castro Girona, moved over the mountains south of Gorgues; the center, under Colonel Ovila, marched up the rough, uneven valley floor; and the right flank, under General Serrano, ranged along the western slopes of the valley. General Federico Berenguer was in command of the reserve forces remaining at Ben Karrich. The men under Castro Girona spent a day trying to clamber over the peaks of the Beni Hassan heights on the left, but finding that progress was slow and difficult, even though there was no fighting, they descended and joined the main column in the valley. By September 28, the Army had arrived at Zoco el Arba, a post on a hill roughly halfway to Chaouen. There had been no real opposition, although there was constant harassment from snipers. Primo de Rivera, who had left Morocco in the summer but had returned to observe the development of his scheme, was ambushed with his staff far to the rear, near Ben Karrich, but escaped alive. General Serrano's column entered Chaouen on September 30, and troops led by Castro Girona and Ovila followed a short while later. In theory, communications were now safely established between Tetuan and Chaouen. The main body of relief troops rested while others went out as escorts for the garrisons of the smaller outposts. No large-scale attack ever occurred, but snipers were everywhere, making the Spanish pay in blood for every soldier they rescued. Frequently the relief detachments lost more men than they brought back from the blockhouses.[22] According to Arturo Barea, the Spanish were forced to ransom many of these garrisons by giving the rebels two rifles for every Spaniard.[23] Even the main road through the valley was unsafe; on October 1 a column of forty motortrucks driving back to Tetuan was fired upon, and a majority of the vehicles destroyed.

During the six weeks it took to accomplish the relief of Chaouen and its outposts, the Rifian snipers had a field day. The Chaouen operation was essentially a race against time, since the rainy season was approaching. Moreover, the Spanish could only guess how many Jiblis had thrown in their lot with Abd el Krim. General Aizpuru was relieved in October as High Commissioner, not because he was in any way lacking in proficiency, but because Primo de Rivera felt personally responsible for the withdrawal, and decided that he himself ought to take command of such a controversial operation.[24]

Many Spaniards, both in the Army and out, were dismayed and discouraged by Primo de Rivera's decision to give up Chaouen—the only large town between Tetuan and Melilla—as well as all the surrounding territory the Army had won in 1920 under Dámaso Berenguer. Political leaders at home felt that Spain was being disgraced in the eyes of the world. In spite of censorship, the Madrid newspaper *España Nueva* said: "In the past 60 days we counted 60 defeats. We are evacuating one by one all the positions acquired in sixteen years of bloody warfare. With 210,000 soldiers [sic] in the battle line, a call for 60,000 more troops has just been issued." The general mood of the Army became so depressed that Primo de Rivera felt it necessary to issue the following stern order on October 3, 1924: "It is regrettable that the troops should give way at this moment to pessimism, which is destroying the morale of the Army. In order to remedy this disgraceful weakness, I order all commanding officers, officers, and soldiers to refrain from all criticism or discussion of these questions; and they shall immediately put under arrest any military subordinate or civilian who disobeys me. They shall pass them over to me to be tried by court-martial. Should their guilt be proved, they will be executed. The High Command of the Army is hereby authorized to carry out this penalty upon the person of any who resist or show signs of disobedience in the field."[25] Indeed, opposition to Primo de Rivera was reaching a dangerous point: Francisco Franco and General Gonzalo Queipo de Llano headed a group of *africanistas* who actually were planning to arrest the dictator and his staff. But Queipo de Llano realized that the plotters had no political experience with which to bolster a coup, even if they succeeded; and while they had many junior officers with them, there was no assurance that a take-over would improve the military situation. Queipo talked Franco out of the idea, but he himself asked to be relieved of his command if he were not to be given a combat post. In reply, Primo de Rivera sent him back to Spain, and gave him a month's imprisonment as well. No action was taken against Franco. If the dictator knew of the plot against him, he apparently felt strong enough to ignore it.[26]

On the night of November 15, most of the Spanish occupation troops marched quietly out of Chaouen and down the hills into the valley without a shot being fired at them.[27] The advance guard under Castro Girona reached Zoco el Arba on the 18th, but the rest of the troops—more than 40,000 of them—were strung out between the *zoco* and Chaouen. The rear guard was composed of squadrons of the Tercio under Franco, which did not leave Chaouen until midnight on the 17th. As the Spanish left the town, the watchful Rifians sifted in quietly, with heads bowed and feet bare in celebration of their victory. Nothing happened until the 19th, and then everything exploded at once. Violent winter storms broke, with pelting rains, bogging down the Spaniards in what seemed to be endless quagmires of mud. The abrupt change of weather was just what the Rifians and the Jiblis, now 7,000 strong, were waiting for. Led by Mhamed Abd el Krim, they attacked all along the line of march with a fury that made the weather seem mild by comparison.[28]

Castro Girona's advance guard was lucky enough to reach the reserve stationed down the valley at Ben Karrich; however, most of the retreating troops were forced to fight every step of the way. The Spanish at Dar Coba were decimated by tribesmen who closed in from both sides of the valley. At Sheruta, General Serrano and more than a thousand of his men were struck down. The rest of the Army, exhausted, fled into Zoco el Arba and called a halt, for the troops were worn out with constant fighting and the effort of trying to drag the wounded and the cannon and other equipment through the mud. For almost three weeks the Chaouen forces were encircled at Zoco el Arba, praying for better weather and reorganizing for the final dash to Tetuan. Abd el Krim's rebels hit them relentlessly, day and night, and every soldier, from the officers of the High Command down to the lowest recruit, was haunted by the thought that the *zoco* might easily turn into another Anual. For, in spite of the years since the fiasco of 1921, Army leadership outside the Tercio tended to be incredibly poor, the supply situation was still very bad, training had been largely neglected, and morale was dangerously low. When Army units finally moved off the hill to the west

of the main road—which was really little more than a crude trail—
they tramped down slopes covered with abandoned equipment
and the bodies of the slain.

At Wad Nakla, three armored cars were left to cover the retreat.
The Rifian harkas easily bypassed them, but the fourteen Spanish
soldiers inside the cars held out for three days without food, water,
or hope of rescue. When they were too weary to fight any more, the
tribesmen allowed them to surrender and then were said to have
stood admiringly at attention while the four unscathed survivors
and the two seriously wounded ones were hauled out of the wrecked
machines and carried away as prisoners. Abd el Krim is supposed
to have been so impressed with the valor of these soldiers that he
placed them at the head of the prisoner-exchange list. These brave
men were lucky, for very few prisoners were taken by the rebels
during the Chaouen retreat; the Spanish wounded were more often
hacked and ripped to death as they lay helpless in the mud.

At the ford of the Wad Habana, the rebels hid among the low
hills and picked off the Spanish as they threw themselves down to
drink at the stream. It was all too evident that Spanish military
planning had not improved a whit since Anual. At Dar Coba and
Sheruta, the posts had been built below the surrounding hills instead of on top of them so that the troops would be closer to the
water supply. The first attacks on these places were also the last,
for the Spaniards were shot at from above as well as from all sides
by an enemy they could not even see. One Spanish officer said, half
admiringly, of the tribesmen, "We made war against shadows, and
we lost thirty men to their one!"[29]

Desperately fighting their way forward, and aided toward the
last by bombing planes and relief columns from Tetuan, the Spanish finally stumbled into Tetuan on December 13, almost a month
after they began their forty-mile retreat. The victorious Rifians
pursued them to the outskirts of the city, and on the last day alone
shot down more than 500 of Franco's rearguard Legionarios. It is
doubtful that the extent of the Rifian casualties will ever be known,
but according to Walter Harris, the withdrawal from Chaouen cost
the Spanish the lives of 800 officers, including the popular General
Serrano, and 17,000 men. Arturo Barea put the Spanish casualties
at 20,000, plus an immense amount of matériel, including a small
hospital left intact at Chaouen.[30] Even the Quadrilateral's General

Federico Berenguer was wounded at Zoco el Arba. The Army never officially announced its losses, but did admit that they were enormous.

Primo de Rivera was quick to hand out compliments. The worst was over. He promised his people revenge, and said that despite the fact that "a new trail of Spanish blood" marked the "track of civilization," punishment of the rebels would be "quick and severe."[31] Like it or not, Spain had to admit that the dictator had accomplished the first part of his plan. He and other military observers knew that the thankless job of withdrawal had been conducted by certain incompetents who could not be weeded out till now. A few Spanish observers began to realize the genuine courage and ability Primo de Rivera possessed. Said the newspaper *El Debate*: "An indefensible silence is maintained about all our victories. The relief of the Spanish garrison besieged at Chauen during two months is the work of a great military chief. We must by all means ask Primo de Rivera to continue directing us."

About 400 separate posts and blockhouses had been evacuated in the interior of Spanish Morocco, and now there was to be a period of recuperation. Primo de Rivera intended to take the military initiative in the spring with a new army—disciplined, well equipped, and competently led. Meanwhile, the Primo Line stood between Rifian and Spaniard. It was a series of typical blockhouses about a quarter of a mile apart, each built on dominating ground wherever possible and equipped with strong searchlights. The spaces between the blockhouses, particularly around Tangier, were usually mined. The Primo Line constituted a project of obvious magnitude—one designed in cooperation with a Spanish Naval blockade along the Mediterranean coast to cut Abd el Krim's supply lines as well as to furnish the Spaniards with base points for future offensives. Gradually the wisdom of Primo de Rivera's policies was borne in on the Army, and its morale and regard for the dictator rose accordingly.

It is interesting to read some of the local newspaper accounts for the year 1924. Most of the journalists, even those who admired Abd el Krim and perhaps believed in the justice of his rebellion, felt that Spain had the situation well under control. They could not, or would not, accept the possibility that a parcel of crude barbarians, however intelligently guided, could outmaneuver and outfight the soldiers of a European power. The *Tangier Gazette,* oldest paper in Morocco, whose English correspondents were closest to the fighting, gave scant space to the grave incidents occurring just beyond the Tangier zonal borders, and its writers assumed a patronizing attitude when the subject came up. Nobody seemed to remember Anual. For instance, in the April 5 issue, one Lieutenant Colonel Repington, a correspondent for the *London Daily Tele-graph,* described Abd el Krim as "that interesting bandit," and pointed out that far from being a romantic figure, the Rifian leader was instead an upstart and an ingrate whose cruelty was well known. Repington went on to report that Spain had not suffered a single reverse since 1921 (this was some months before Chaouen), and that the rebels could not last much longer. Accounts such as Repington's only demonstrated how little anyone except the combatants themselves knew about the true state of affairs in the mountains. Whereas it was fairly accurate to state at that time that Spain had not suffered a major defeat since Anual, it was likewise true that she had not won a single victory. It had taken her a year and a half to recapture and secure the area in the east. Where the forces of Abd el Krim chose to hold, they held; and it was the tribesmen, and not the Spaniards, who forced the fighting everywhere. Finally, on July 12, the *Tangier Gazette* began to see the light. It reported that several Spanish planes had been shot down near Dar Coba, and even conceded that a complete defeat of the elusive tribesmen would be most difficult to effect.

One of the outstanding apologists for Spain was Boyd Cable, correspondent for the *London Daily Chronicle.* He had come to Morocco in 1924 and had been permitted to visit some of the Spanish posts. Cable was angry with what he called the one-sided reporting of the Rif Rebellion, which he called "a little war." "It is a vain endeavor," Cable wrote on August 2, "to mislead the public into the idea that Spain can be ousted from North Africa by an enemy vastly inferior in numbers and resources of all kinds. Events prove that every time the unsubmitted natives endeavor to break the Spanish lines." On August 25, in an article called "As Others See Us," Cable wrote of the excellence of Spanish matériel, and the capabilities of the Spanish soldiers. The Spanish Army, so Cable reported, had modern trucks, tanks, and planes, the best

"75" cannon, and well-cared-for pack animals. Discipline had been greatly improved; officers could no longer strike their men! But Cable concluded by admitting that the troops had no relish for service in Morocco. He wrote these words, of course, before the costly evacuation of Chaouen, and his belittling term "unsubmitted natives" was a shallow description of the Rifian tribesmen, who had yet to be beaten in battle and who at the very time of his writing were successfully undermining Raisuli's and Spain's positions all over the Jibala. After all its applause for Spain, the *Tangier Gazette* announced on September 6 that the Tangier–Tetuan road was closed because of enemy raids. A week later, the paper admitted: "Unfortunately, it was impossible any longer to hope for a rapid and satisfactory cleaning-up of the situation in the west of the Spanish Zone." The tribes, it seemed, were going over to Abd el Krim. On September 27 there was a fresh outburst of reportorial optimism as "the great offensive" toward Chaouen drew closer (this despite the fact that Primo de Rivera had publicly explained his plan to withdraw to the Primo Line and to concentrate upon an offensive no sooner than the spring or summer of 1925). The somewhat pontifical *Illustrated London News* for November 22 told its readers that only six Spanish casualties had resulted from the fighting at Wad Lau and Chaouen.

According to the British papers, Primo de Rivera was upset over the fact that Dutch, British, and Portuguese capital was flowing into the Rif, and that Abd el Krim was supposed to have received at least £300,000 from these sources in return for mining concessions. The press reported that, whereas Abd el Krim denied ever receiving this money, Primo de Rivera claimed to have seen the funds himself. It was about this time, too, that the dictator was quoted as saying in answer to a foreign reporter's question concerning what good he expected of the Protectorate: "We want to do them [the Rifians] good, but they won't let us." Some weeks later this remark was repeated to Ahmed Budra, the Rifian Minister of War, and Budra answered simply, "They should conquer or get out."[32]

Boyd Cable visited some of the Spanish camps but he never lived or fought with the troops. Nevertheless, he reported that Spanish Army food was good—at least no worse than British Army food had been during World War I. On the other hand, a British youth serving with the Spanish Foreign Legion* stated in the columns of the *Tangier Gazette* that Spanish rations, which in the large camps consisted mainly of bread and stews, were awful, and that Spanish camps were unsanitary. He said further that the Spanish were peculiar in their conduct of battles, in that they frequently fought all one day and then slept all the next, regardless of the immediate situation; and that they never followed up a victorious action. He reported that the pay of privates in the Tercio was two pesetas per day, with one peseta deducted for food, and a bonus of 80 pesetas, or about $11.50, given each year. Another person who disagreed with Cable's picture of the Spanish Army was an unnamed British traveler in Morocco who summed up in a letter to the *Gazette* in 1924 his opinion of Spain's motives: "Spain fully realizes that she is fighting a battle which she can never win, and she would gladly retire from the country tomorrow if she could save her face with some show of peace with honor." This was vastly closer to the truth than anything Cable wrote.

The American correspondent and author Vincent Sheean was one of the very few persons to see the Rif and the Rifians during the war. Sheean interviewed both brothers Abd el Krim, and traveled over the mountains all the way from the French Zone to Alhucemas Bay.[33] He also interviewed Raisuli after his capture by the Rifians. Afterward, Sheean traveled with a rebel harka west toward Tangier, trudging down the valley of the Beni Hassan early in 1925 and observing at first hand evidence of the havoc wreaked by the Rifians on the Spanish Army during the retreat from Chaouen nine weeks before. At the end of his tour, he and a band of rebels sneaked through the Primo Line at night, past search-lights, mines, and guards, and held a celebration dinner at Tangier's Hotel Cecil.

No matter what the newspapers said, the retreat from Chaouen was a strategic victory for Spain, but a catastrophe as well. Almost the whole of the Gomara and the Jibala had enthusiastically gone over to Abd el Krim, and the Arab and Berber tribes of northern Morocco were now united for the first time in their entire history under a single, determined leadership. The prestige of the Rifian

* In 1922, the British Government, because of unsatisfactory conditions in the Tercio, had forbidden its nationals to serve in it.

leaders had never been higher, and the Rif Rebellion was running at full tide. The capture of Chaouen and the partial destruction of the Spanish relief force had given the Rifian State tremendous booty in supplies and arms. The Rifians had doubled their area of control and their fighting strength overnight. Muslims everywhere looked at Abd el Krim's experiment with speculative eyes; if the Rifians could win their freedom from a European power, perhaps underdog Muslims in other parts of the globe could do so too. The other tribes throughout Morocco, and also those in Algeria nearest the Rif, speculated restlessly, while the Spanish and French imperialists shivered in anticipation of unpleasant events to come.

10. ABD EL KRIM'S WARTIME GOVERNMENT

THE political and military machine that the brothers Abd el Krim forged in the Rif was the product of cogent planning. The Rifian leaders never lost sight of their limitations in manpower, food, and general supplies, but they also realized that they had two great military advantages—they understood their Spanish opponents thoroughly, and they were fighting on territory with which they were completely familiar. The brothers Abd el Krim were confident that they could force Spain into a formal recognition of the Rifian State within a comparatively short time.

Mohamed Abd el Krim was forty-three years old and at the very apex of his power in January 1925.[1] His army was unbeaten, his territorial gains had been astounding, and he had created a viable government. Abd el Krim, who called himself "Chief of State," or "Prince of the Rif," and was addressed as "Sidna"—"Our Lord"— was as much a dictator as Primo de Rivera. He was a despot. He had to be, in a land that had always known cruelty and the elimination of rivals by murder, and whose people understood power better than anything else.[2] Most of the tribes accepted him as a man of great learning, a brilliant soldier, and an unparalleled success as a leader. But although Abd el Krim was admired, respected, and feared, he was not loved. After several attempts had been made to assassinate him, his whereabouts were kept secret. The great mass of his subjects never saw him, for he seldom made public appearances.[3] As time went on, he became more and more a legendary figure to whom terrifying qualities were attributed.

Abd el Krim ran the Rifian State with the aid of a small group of henchmen.* The care of the Rifian organization was entrusted to a cabinet of *imgharen,* or counselors, selected by the Abd el

---

* The Rifian "capital" was the tiny community of Ajdir near the coast of Alhucemas Bay, where Abd el Krim was born.

Krims themselves. This body was made up of colorful personalities: Mulay Abdeslam el Khattabi, forty years old, Minister of Finance, the paternal uncle of the brothers Abd el Krim; Ahmed Budra, thirty-eight years old, Minister of War, in charge of levying troops and gathering war supplies; Mohamed Azerkan, thirty-six years old, Minister of Foreign Affairs, husband of Abd el Krim's favorite sister (though Azerkan was an able man, Abd el Krim never quite trusted him); Mohand n Amar of Temsaman, a cultivated, elderly man, Minister of Justice, faithful to Abd el Krim but ineffectual; Shaikh l-Yazid, forty-five years old, Minister of the Interior, a man of second rank concerned with perpetuating tribal unity; Mohamed Bu Jibar, thirty years old, Inspector General, an intimate friend of Abd el Krim and an expert on French and Spanish politics (he had been a pro-French delegate to Paris and London for sixteen months beginning in 1923); Mohamed Wuld Hadj Cheddi, twenty-five years old, second to Azerkan in Foreign Affairs, a favorite counselor of Abd el Krim; Mohamed Muhammadi, thirty years old, First Secretary, married to one of Abd el Krim's sisters (although he had served for eighteen months in 1923–24 as Rifian delegate to London and Paris, he was not a policymaker); "Severa" of Bucoya, Minister of Marine and chief of the Rifian small-boat squadrons; Hassan ben Abd el Aziz, Second Secretary, a middle-aged Algerian editor and journalist who understood European politics well, but who could never gain Abd el Krim's confidence, although he found both Azerkan and Bu Jibar approachable. The chief's brother, Mhamed Abd el Krim, was second in rank only to the Prince of the Rif; he was a man of education and enormous prestige, thought by many to be the most brilliant Moroccan in the country. As Commander in Chief of the Rifian Army, his was the key personality.

In addition, four young men who were all enthusiastically devoted to Abd el Krim served in lesser roles: Caid Hadidan, the chief of Abd el Krim's personal bodyguard; Mohamed Amgar, chief of protocol; Caid Seddik, Abd el Krim's personal secretary; and Hamou ben Hadj, Bu Jibar's cabinet chief. There was also Abd el Krim Haddu n Si Ziyan, the Army Chief of Staff. As political agent, the Abd el Krims employed Abd el Krim Hadj Ali Loh at Tangier; long afterward this man was friendly to the Spaniards, and actually became Pasha of Villa Sanjurjo, the town the invaders built at the northeast corner of Alhucemas Bay. Another agent was

Haddu el Kahal of Bucoya, who was intermediary with the French. Mohamed Gomari was the Rif's chief munitions buyer, and Caid Hammush, whom General Goded described as a "hateful character," was in charge of Rifian prisons.

The majority of these men were from Beni Urriaguel, and many were from the dispersed community of Ajdir. Abd el Krim placed members of his own family and close friends from his own Beni Urriaguel tribe in key positions, but he brought in experts and able leaders from other tribes as well. Domination by the Beni Urriaguel was resented by other tribes, especially the neighboring Temsaman, Bucoya, and Beni Tuzin. Tribes farther afield either refused to accept Urriagli leadership or were constantly on the verge of rising against Abd el Krim because of it, and only prompt and drastic action prevented serious schisms in the ranks of the rebels. When the Ahmas, around Chaouen, and one or two other tribes of the Gomara balked at joining Abd el Krim in late 1924, the Rifians killed forty-one of them. Some of the leaders were quietly poisoned; others were dragged away to jail, where they died of deliberate neglect. Rudyers Pryne says that houses, fields, and orchards were burned; that Caids who rejected the Rifians had their eyes burned out with hot irons, or were soaked in gasoline and burned alive; that still others had their genitals cut off in front of their horrified womenfolk—all very rare tactics for Rifians, who usually rid themselves of enemies by simple shooting and did not resort to torture.[4]

Abd el Krim either stamped out or cleverly manipulated the *liff* system of alliances as the particular circumstances dictated.[5] When two *liff* leaders refused to be reconciled to one another despite the threat from outside which the war with Spain posed, Abd el Krim would win their support by making them both *Caids-l-Miya*— giving them equal rank. The majority of the tribes remained loyal to Abd el Krim, but as the war went on and the sufferings of the people became more acute, many tried to evade his control. As a result, Abd el Krim turned more and more toward brutality and force. According to Sánchez Pérez, he sometimes killed in a rage; for example, he once had a Swiss mechanic and his assistant shot because they did not succeed in repairing an airplane that Abd el Krim had hoped to use to bomb Melilla.[6] Executions became commonplace. A number of Beni Tuzin, Tafersit, and even Beni Urria-

guel tribesmen were shot for collaborating with the Spaniards; and
Biqqish, the prominent Geznaya *amghar,* was poisoned at Abd el
Krim's order after evidence of his treachery came to light. Two
Urriagli traitors named Abd sram n Sidi Hamid Bu Rjila and
Hammu nj Hadj Aisa were executed along with five henchmen
at the Sunday market of Thisar. Apparently they were stoned to
death—a very unusual method of execution among the Rifians.[7]
The Caid Aqqa, of Beni Gmil, another leader who rebelled against
Abd el Krim, somehow managed to survive the Rebellion.

One of the most irritating problems Abd el Krim had to face
was the power of those saints and marabouts in his own mountains
who had become local political leaders—men such as Raisuli, and
Abderrahman Darkawi, who first helped Abd el Krim fight the
Spaniards, then later turned against him.[8] The Rifian leader per-
ceived these men as obstacles to the nationalism he envisioned, for
he knew that they had immense influence with the people. He tried
to avoid an open struggle with them, but attempted to discredit
them by means of propaganda, and to limit their power. When he
took their funds to buy war matériel, some of the marabouts became his outright enemies. Others he won over by giving them important positions in his government. The Pashas of Beni Hamid,
Beni Amart, and the Gomara and the Caids of Beni Smih and
Beni Akhamlish were among those whom he thus rewarded for
their cooperation.

General Goded estimated that at the peak of its strength, the
Rifian Army numbered approximately 80,000 men.[9] Monteil suggests that although Abd el Krim had a maximum of 75,000 parti-
sans, he was never able to arm more than 20,000 at a time. Yet the
French General Brémond thought that at the peak of their power,
the Rifians had at least 120,000 men under arms; Manuel and Ar-
miñan upped the estimate to 125,000. Léon Gabrielle's informants
told him that the Temsamanis and Beni Tuzin furnished between
5,000 and 6,000 men each, and the Bucoya and Geznaya about
5,000 between them. Almost half the Rifian Army was composed of
tribesmen from faraway areas—from the Anjera country in the
northwest to the Metalsa and Beni Bu Yahi in the southeast; but
the numerically small core of Beni Urriaguel fighters had the reputation of being the finest warriors in the Rifian Army, with the
Geznaya and Beni Amart rated next in ability.

General Goded has quoted Abd el Krim as saying that his Regulars, an elite corps of hand-picked, rigorously trained Ur-riaglis, never numbered more than 6,000 or 7,000; Gabrielli puts the figure at 2,500. All other Rifian forces were made up of con-scripts between the ages of sixteen and fifty. Conscripts were se-lected by their tribal Pashas and Caids, whom Abd el Krim ap-pointed. Thus each tribe had its own militia, which could organize quickly in case of attack or defense. There was a care-fully worked out roster system so that each warrior, who was also a farmer and therefore had his crops, flocks, and orchards to care for, served in an active harka about one week a month—never for more than fifteen consecutive days—and was free to farm the rest of the time. In every encounter, it was the tribes nearest the par-ticular objective, supported by elements of the Regulars, who did the fighting. Each front was under the jurisdiction of a military inspector, and by 1923 fixed trenches, with supports and strong points, had been established at vulnerable Alhucemas Bay.

Rifian Army officers were called Caids or Caids Kebir.* An army or a large division was called a *mehalla*; a *tabor,* consisting of three or four *miyas,* or smaller units, was the next largest unit; and smaller groups were called by number. A Kebir el Mehalla held a rank equivalent to that of brigadier general; and a Caid el Tabor could be likened to a colonel or a major. Other ranks included Caids el Miya, leaders of a hundred men; Caids el Hamsain, lead-ers of fifty men; and lesser leaders of Hamsains-u-ashreen (twenty-five men) and T'nash (only twelve men). According to General Goded, Caids el Tabor wore three red cords around their turbans as a badge of rank, and were paid 200 pesetas, or about $29, a month; and Caids el Miya wore two red cords, and were paid the equivalent of $18 monthly. (David Hart believes that the pay rates were actually somewhat lower.)

The most important generals in the Rifian Army were Haddu n-Muh Amzzyan, a Beni Urriaguel, the commander in the Kifan region of the southeast corner of the central Rif; Mohamed Cheddi, the young Urriagli already mentioned as a member of Azerkan's Foreign Affairs Staff; Ahmed Heriro, a Beni Hozmar, the youthful commander in the Jibala; Shaib el Yacoubi, of Temsaman, a very intelligent leader and commander of the entire eastern front; Shaib

* *Kebir* is the Arabic word for "big."

n-Muh of Temsaman, commander along the boundary between the French and Spanish Zones just north of the Wergha River; and Caid Buhut, a veteran of the Spanish Regulares, which he deserted in order to join the rebels during the Anual rout. Buhut was the principal training commander, greatly respected because he understood European methods of warfare and claimed that he knew how to counter them. The Rifians were generally supposed to be employing European officers on their General Staff, for the Spanish and many other Europeans were not able to believe that Rifians could outmaneuver them; but although it was true that Mhamed Abd el Krim's personal bodyguard was a snappy, precision-drilled outfit that could actually do the German goose step on occasion, the only Europeans in the Rifian Army were a handful of French and Spanish deserters and a few European renegades.[10] Among these last were Otto Noja, a German specialist in telephonic communications; a Serbian captain who served as an artillery instructor, who was eventually killed by a bomb; and Walter Heintgent, a Norwegian doctor. None of these people, however, had the least influence on Abd el Krim's policy or decisions. The Rifians ran their own show.

By far the most intriguing of the few foreigners in the service of Abd el Krim was a German named Joseph Klemms.[11] P. C. Wren, whose stories of Beau Geste and the French Foreign Legion were internationally popular, wrote a short story, "Odo Klemmens," about Klemms's career, and Sigmund Romberg's popular operetta "The Desert Song" is supposedly based on some of Klemms's exploits. Klemms seems to have been the son of a wealthy businessman in Dusseldorf. As a young man, he ran away to Paris with a dancer, taking with him funds obtained by forging checks on his father's bank account. For years he lived by his wits in Spain, the French Riviera, Turkey, and Morocco. He was strong, good-looking, intelligent, and unscrupulous. Before and during World War I, Klemms spent ten years as a German Secret Service agent in Morocco, where his linguistic accomplishments and his predilection for the perilous made him extremely valuable. He must have done something uncommonly foolish to have been suddenly discharged by the Germans: probably he was selling information to the French as well. In any event, he found refuge in the French Foreign Legion. While stationed at Fez, Klemms rose from the

rank of private to that of Commissary Sergeant. His career there
came to an abrupt end when the authorities discovered that
Klemms's commissary accounts were a maze of fabrications. He
was court-martialed, sentenced, and reduced to the ranks. Not
the man to accept just retribution, Klemms deserted the Legion
at the first opportunity, late in 1920, when he was stationed just
north of Fez. Picked up by members of the Beni Warain tribe,
south of Taza, he was somehow able to impress them, and they allowed him to become a Muslim and to join their tribe. Klemms
learned to speak thamazigth, married several Berber girls, and
soon was leading harkas in raids on the French. More than once
he donned his old Legion uniform, strode casually into a French
post, picked up whatever information he needed, and then led his
harka directly to the weakest link in the post's defenses. A romantic
as well as a dangerous enemy, Klemms would leave a scrap of
paper pinned to the corpse of his victim as a sort of signature. Each
scrap bore the name "El Hadj Aleman," or "The German Hadj."*
As El Hadj Aleman, Klemms gained a fearful reputation in the
Fez-Taza region. Impressed by the Rifian successes, he offered his
services to Abd el Krim early in 1924. He was accepted after proving his abilities, and became the Rif's leading topographer and
communications expert, as well as acting as an artillery instructor.
Abd el Krim referred to Klemms as "my grand artillerist," and assigned him to duty on the western front. Klemms mapped most of
the country between Tetuan and Chaouen, and it is certain that
his maps helped the tribesmen arrange ambush after ambush during the Spanish withdrawal from Chaouen.

The Rifian Army had only two important corps—the Infantry
and the Artillery—and the latter was staffed almost completely by
350 men of the Regulars. There was no cavalry, for horses were
impractical in the mountains, but the Metalsa and the Beni Bu
Yahi had a few horses, and a squadron of twenty-five mounted
tribesmen acted as messengers. Abd el Krim actually bought three
planes, which were flown into the Rif from Algeria by French
pilots. They were never used, and along with Abd el Krim's three
cars—a Renault, a Ford, and a Turcat-Méry—they were captured
intact by the French in 1926. Roger-Matthieu wrote that the Rifian

---

* *Hadj* is the honorary title given to any Muslim who has made a pilgrimage
to Mecca.

leader wanted planes to prove that the Rif, too, could obtain and use modern weapons.[12]

At Anual and afterward, Abd el Krim ordered his people to collect all the guns, cartridges, and gun parts they could find. Each warrior was his own source of supply; but if he had a surplus of arms or parts, he could sell them to the central government. French cartridges were worth four times as much as Spanish ones, presumably because French rifles were newer and better. By January 1925, the tribesmen were fully armed with French and Spanish Mausers, old Remingtons, Chassepots, Grass, St. Étiennes, a few 1886 Lebels, and some Bu Hafras from the Sultan's Royal Army. The Rifians soon learned how to dismantle Spanish 440-pound bombs, and to make grenades from the parts. One bomb would yield about 450 grenades. David Hart says that members of the Taghzat tribe in the Senhadja became experts in this procedure.[13]

The artillery had upward of 200 cannon of three calibers— 155 mm., 75 mm., and 65 mm.—the entire lot of them taken from the Spaniards. Practically all of them carried the Schneider trademark. They also had several hundred Hotchkiss machine guns gathered from the same source. Rifian artillery instructors included Bomoz, a Negro formerly with the Sultan's forces; a Serbian captain; and Mohamed Barnusi, known far and wide as "the man with the victorious cannon," who had gained valuable experience as a gunner in the army of Abd el Aziz. The exactness of Rifian artillery fire was disconcerting to the enemy. The tribesmen crept in as close as possible to their target, then opened up, often at point-blank range. Gunners serving cannon were paid about $11.50 a month, and machine gunners were paid about $2.50.*

Ammunition and various other kinds of war matériel were stored in caves near Chaouen, Targuist, and Ajdir. Abd el Krim is supposed to have had at least eight storage dumps, most of them located in the mountains of Beni Urriaguel. His telephone system was not a very good one, but it worked. It was installed under the direction of Mhamed Abd el Krim by Klemms and a Spanish captive named Antonio. Such Rifian fortifications as existed were expertly placed, especially after the early clashes, since many of the lesser Rifian officers had served with Spanish troops before the

---

* Or 77½ riffans and 17½ riffans, respectively. A riffan was roughly equal to a Spanish peseta.

Rebellion and therefore knew something about trench and redoubt construction. For target practice, the tribesmen would notch a branch of a nearby tree and place a small white stone about the size of an egg in the notch; at 30 paces, a Rifian could average five hits in six shots.[14] David Hart says that the now universal Rifian practice of carrying walking sticks began because the Rifians used the sticks as props on which to sight their rifles. The Rifian infantryman was paid 2 *riffans* a day by the particular tribe whose land he was defending. Rifian currency was printed in England for the "Banco del Estado del Rif," in green five-*riffan* notes worth 5 pesetas, or $.71, and red one-*riffan* notes, worth 1 peseta, or $.14. The tribesmen, however, were used to Spanish coins and preferred them to the new currency.

Discipline was never much of a problem in the Rifian Army, because punishment was meted out severely and on the spot, and warriors usually obeyed their officers without question. This obedience was merited, for in the Rifian system only the bravest men and the natural leaders rose to the top. Discipline did not, however, extend to such relatively unimportant items as clothing. The Army did not bother much about uniforms. Officers wore insignia on their turbans, and each corps wore turbans of a certain color. Artillerists wore black wool turbans, and members of the Cabinet and the Imperial Guard wore green wool ones. The Rifian flag was a vivid red, with a single white diamond in the middle surrounding a six-pointed green star and crescent.*

The Rifian warriors were generally tough, valiant, resourceful fighters, and superb shots, whose endurance gave them an amazing mobility. They could walk as much as thirty miles a night over mountain trails and yet be perfectly fit to attack at daybreak. Each man carried a gun, a long, straight dagger, cartridges, bread, and fruit. He slept wherever he happened to be, pulling the hood of his *jellaba* over his face, always ready to leap into action at the first strange sound. These men firmly believed one Rifian was the equal of six Spaniards, and their Islamic faith gave them a special, fatalistic strength that their opponents never had. According to a popular Rifian saying, it is better to die swiftly, in battle, than to

---

* The choice of a six-pointed star, or Star of David, instead of the five-pointed Moroccan star, seems odd at first. Abd el Krim seems to have been copying a Spanish flag that bore a six-pointed star.

die slowly under a foreign yoke. Death on the field was assurance of immortal life, for according to the Koran, all those who fought in a holy war went straight to heaven. Prince Aage of Denmark says that it was next to impossible to take Berber prisoners, because even the wounded would shoot or stab to the end.[15] An ex-Legionnaire who had fought in the Rif told Pierre van Paassen that the Legion's sentries often had their throats cut soundlessly during the night, and that attempts to place a field of buried grenades in front of blockhouses only resulted in having the grenades stolen and hurled back at the Legionnaires.[16]

Mhamed Abd el Krim's strategy and tactics were simple but effective. The Rifians were to surround each small enemy outpost and attempt to take it by sneak attack. If this failed, they were to wait for the garrison to run short of water or bullets, then kill the besieged men as they made a break for freedom. These tactics worked to perfection in eastern Spanish Morocco during the Anual rout, but by the next year, the Spaniards had become considerably more careful. By the time Primo de Rivera instituted his semi-abandonment policy, the Spanish Army generally could hold its own in battles with the Rifians. The tribesmen never offered battle in large formations if they could help it, and they usually attacked from the cover of boulders or trees or serried ridges. In retreat, it was almost impossible to pin them down or capture them, since they simply disappeared into the mountains from which they had come.

The big problem for the Rifians was always supply. But until the French got caught up in the Rebellion, even that problem was more theoretical than real. The coastal blockade by the Spanish Navy and the Primo Line of blockhouses could not stop the rebels from slipping into and out of Tangier almost at will. In spite of losing a few agents, Tangier remained throughout the war the chief source of supplies for Abd el Krim. According to Rudyers Pryne, in June 1924, even before the Spaniards had withdrawn from the Jibala and the Gomara, an English launch ran the Spanish blockade and landed 16,000 Lebel rifles on the Bucoya coast.[17] At Tangier, cartridges were sold openly in the streets. The poorly paid Moroccan Regulares serving with Spain often sold their own arms to Tangier businessmen, who then resold them directly to Abd el Krim's agents. Mhamed Abd el Krim once stated that Primo de

Rivera's withdrawal in the west had resulted in a sort of Hinden-
burg Line that not less than a million men could hope to hold successfully. The trend of events proved the Rifian general's statement
correct. Without mentioning other sources and kinds of supply,
Mhamed added, "The supply of arms will never cease so long as
Spanish soldiers have anything to lose."[18]

What were the sources of Abd el Krim's cash income? There was
little money in the Rif itself. The Rifian government had set up
a "*zoco* tax," that is, a small tax on foodstuffs bought in the local
markets, but this was said to have brought only 5,000 pesetas or
about $700 a day into the coffers of the Rifian State.[19] Yet the
Rifians seemed to have money enough to buy arms whenever they
could obtain them. The most likely source of Abd el Krim's money
was the group of German entrepreneurs whose longtime associa-
tions in Spanish Morocco made them financially interested in in-
vesting in the Rif Rebellion.* All the evidence points to the intercession of several optimistic cartels of European businessmen, who
believed in the economic future of the Rif and were willing to risk
large amounts of capital on the outcome of the Rebellion.[20]

Abd el Krim received foreign correspondents at Ajdir, but his
statements were often conflicting, and it was difficult to know what
he really meant to convey. Vincent Sheean and Paul Scott Mowrer
were among those correspondents who interviewed the Abd el
Krims at Ajdir. Mowrer reported in the spring of 1925 that Abd
el Krim thought that the Spaniards were finished in Morocco. Like
Sheean, Mowrer was impressed with the authority and intelligence
of the Abd el Krims, and left the Rif convinced that they were
sincere patriots.

Abd el Krim kept himself well informed about the outside world
and had large numbers of foreign newspapers and magazines, including fashion papers, sent to his headquarters at Ajdir. He continued to correspond with former Spanish colleagues, among them
Candido Lobera, with whom he had worked on *El Telegrama del
Rif* at Melilla. A constant flow of communiqués, most of them

---

* John Cooley, pp. 191–93, states that Abd el Krim's "republic" was supported
by European Communists, notably Jacques Doriot and the French Communist
Party; and the Blanco files name Sharif Mulay Hasanov and Namber Mahmudov
as Comintern delegates to Abd el Krim.

couched in majestic language, issued from the Ajdir headquarters. Abd el Krim claimed he had no political relationship with any other Arab country anywhere, that the war in the Rif was wholly nationalistic and not at all pan-Islamic, and that the sole enemy was Spain. "But this," he stated, "is through Spain's will, and not through ours. Nothing would be more suitable than peace with Spain and with the whole world. This peace can come whenever Spain wishes it, but Spain must [first] withdraw to Ceuta and Melilla, since the Protectorate has brought only misery and desolation, cruelty and inefficiency, to the Moroccan people."[21]

Having had himself proclaimed Amir, or Prince, of the Rif in February 1923, Abd el Krim claimed that his government was established from that date. Some of the available information indicates that Abd el Krim called his government Jumuriya Rifiya, the Rifian Republic. David Hart, however, points out that the word "Republik" in the Rif corresponded to the Blad s-Siba elsewhere in Morocco, and stood for the historic Rif *before* Abd el Krim.[22] Hart's informants, Foreign Affairs Minister Azerkan, War Minister Budra, and the Rifians' top general, Haddu n-Muh Amzzyan, claimed that Abd el Krim's government was called Jibha Rifiya, the Rifian Front, because of its provisional nature. In any case, Pessah Shinar states that, whereas Abd el Krim despised European imperialism, he thought that European countries provided the best examples of modern states. He hoped to found a modern nation in the Rif based upon the Koran and incorporating the best achievements of Western science and industry.[23]

Because of the complicated nature of the protectorate system in Morocco, Abd el Krim's rebellion threatened not only the Spaniards but the Sultanate and the French as well, for Spanish Morocco was the political child of the French-controlled Blad l-Makhzen. Given the strong and flourishing administration that Abd el Krim had installed in the Rif, the Spanish excuse for intervention on the grounds that Moroccans could not govern themselves was a weak one. Abd el Krim's nascent state flourished because he collected taxes, interpreted Koranic law for the area he governed, and maintained an effective army. He dealt with foreign envoys in the capacity of head of state. The Rifian tribes were therefore unified under a strong central authority, something that had never before happened in the entire history of the Rif. That Abd el Krim was able by conquest to increase the territory and the tribes he controlled, and that he was able to fend off the Spanish invaders and keep the French at bay, were further proof that he controlled an organization that worked well. And although Abd el Krim did not see himself as a direct threat to the Sultan, the Rifian Government could not recognize a Sultan who was such an obvious French puppet. As for the French, Abd el Krim constantly reiterated that he did not want a war with them, and he maintained cordial relations with them as long as possible. But the Protectorate boundary as delimited by the 1912 Treaty of Fez could not possibly be accepted by the Rifians because of the manner in which it divided some of the tribes, like the Metalsa and the Beni Bu Yahi, through whose country the boundary line passed. Abd el Krim kept reminding the Spaniards that when the indemnity money was paid over to Spain by the Moroccan Sultan after the war of 1860, one of the stipulations in the final agreement was that the Spaniards would retire forever from Tetuan. Since Spain had broken her word by reoccupying and holding Tetuan since 1913, the indemnity money should be refunded to Abd el Krim.[24] Why not to the Sultan? Because, said the Rifian leaders, Abd el Krim was performing the proper duty of the Sultan, who was doing nothing to repel the Christian invaders. All the Rifians wanted, said their leader, was to preserve their country's independence from foreign control. "We do not refuse to open our land to the industry and commerce of the Christians ... but this change must not affect our institutions, the free disposition of our lands, and the complete independence of the Rif." As a matter of fact, the Rifians intended to invite into the country a number of foreign administrators and technicians to assist them until they had learned how to handle their own affairs.[25] An American commercial organization had offered to take over the Rif from Melilla to Chaouen and to develop it for the Rifians on a concession basis, but Abd el Krim turned the offer down.

The Rifian hierarchy was at all times aware that the sooner the shooting stopped, the stronger in manpower, resources, and bargaining position the new Rifian State would be. In 1922, Abd el Krim's representatives at London had petitioned the Curzon government to invite Spain to stop the war in Spanish Morocco, and to recognize Rifian independence. Nothing came of the plea. Again, in April 1924, Abd el Krim approached the British Government by means of a letter delivered by Ward Price, special correspondent for the *London Daily Mail,* to Ramsay MacDonald.[26] Abd el Krim wrote in part: "If Spain desires an eternal war, she will have it. Our resolution is inflexible. Without having joined a single formal battle, 100 to 150 Spaniards die each week in Morocco. The Spanish Army does us very little harm except when they bomb villages full of defenseless women and children." Prime Minister MacDonald acknowledged receipt of this letter, but the British Government found itself unable to do anything constructive for the Rifians. Spain was European, and Spain was many times larger and stronger than the Rif. Therefore Spain was a better horse to back.

Although most of the foreigners who knew Abd el Krim encouraged him in his struggle for independence, they almost certainly had commercial and political rather than humanitarian motives for doing so. They were taking a gambler's chance—a side bet on a long-shot Rifian victory. But Abd el Krim was taking all the risks. He continued to receive just enough money, arms, and food to keep going, but he never had a surplus of weapons, and it was a moot question as to how long he would be able to replenish the losses incurred in his harkas.

One of the very few persons who pointed out to the Rifians the odds they were bucking was Walter Harris, the wealthy *London Times* correspondent in Tangier. It was plain to him that the rebels were being used as pawns by powerful European financial groups. Harris knew Abd el Krim slightly, and is supposed to have told him that time favored Spain, because of her superior resources and pool of available manpower. Harris's advice was for Abd el Krim to accept some sort of settlement while he still held a strong hand. But the Rifian chief felt that Spain was fed up with the war and that the Rifians themselves had never been stronger. (Roger-Matthieu says that Abd el Krim gave him quite a contrary version of his talks with Harris, in which Harris is supposed to have deceived Abd el Krim by predicting that neither France nor Spain would ever penetrate the Rif, and that Abd el Krim's best bet was to go on fighting.)[27] Whatever the truth of the matter was, in his letter to Ramsay MacDonald, Abd el Krim stated his hopes boldly: "The future of our country is unlimited. We have confidence in our industrial capacity and in our ability to distinguish ourselves in peace as well as in war, and we ask the outside world, in the name of justice, to give us that opportunity. If the world will not give us peace now, when we are ready for it, we shall fight until we have gained it by our swords and [by] the will of Allah![28]

11. THE FRENCH THREATEN

No sooner had the Rifians and their Jibala allies swept the Spaniards out of Chaouen and the interior of western Spanish Morocco than the Anjera, a tribe in the mountainous peninsula north of the Tangier–Tetuan road, revolted against Spain.[1] The tribesmen ran wild, plundering Alcazarseguir and attacking communications all along the Ceuta–Tetuan and Tetuan–Tangier lines. Within a matter of days, the Spaniards had sent columns west into the mountains from Ceuta under the command of Francisco Franco, and north from Tetuan under the leadership of General Saro. This was in December; yet it was not until April 1925 that the Anjeris were subdued. General Saro had established the usual chain of blockhouses from El Borj, where the road from Tetuan enters the Tangier Zone, north to Punta Altares, on the Straits of Gibraltar. Although the Spanish forces now completely encircled the Anjera Peninsula, they had to throw 10,000 troops against the tribesmen, who fought stubbornly. Even after Alcazarseguir was bombed, then retaken by a seaborne invasion in late March, remnants of the rebel forces continued to hold out in the hills.

Spanish bombing was notoriously inaccurate, and planes trying to bomb villages in the Anjera or Wad Ras country often hit sites inside the Tangier Zone instead. The Tangier administration indignantly complained, then organized a Committee of Inquiry to investigate the damage done by the Spanish flyers. Along with several Spanish officers, who scornfully denied the inefficiency of their aviators, the Commission made a sortie into the hills, and although they stayed well within the zonal borders, they were lucky to escape being blown to bits by Spanish planes, which unloaded bombs within yards of them.[2]

After the taking of Chaouen, the sole barrier between Abd el

Krim and total domination of the west was the tenacious Raisuli.
Now ill and unable to lead his men in person, Raisuli was virtually
isolated in his small palace at Tazrut. The Spaniards, who wanted
to save Raisuli for the sake of the political benefits they still believed would accrue to them through continued alliance with
him, had repeatedly urged him to leave the mountains and take
up residence behind the walls of Tetuan. Now it was too late. The
Spanish were as helpless as Raisuli to prevent the Rifian tide from
engulfing everything in its path.

From Abd el Krim's point of view, the capture of Raisuli was
a strategic necessity. There could be only one leader of the Rifian
State. Long before the Spanish withdrawal, Rifian agents had approached Raisuli and asked him to forgo his allegiance to Spain
and recognize Abd el Krim. Raisuli steadfastly refused to do so.
There was no choice but to eliminate him as soon as possible.

Ahmed Heriro, Raisuli's former lieutenant, was chosen to command the harka that would destroy the Sherif. Mhamed Abd el
Krim personally selected the attacking force with care. It consisted
of 1,200 Jiblis under Heriro's personal command, plus an additional 600 Rifians from Beni Urriaguel and Temsaman—300 of
them Rifian Regulars, armed with four machine guns—and a rear
guard of 2,500 tribesman from the Gomara.[3] The assault on Tazrut
was launched late on the night of January 23, 1925, and in a few
hours the Rifians had accomplished what the Spaniards had never
been able to do. Heriro's Jiblis got nowhere, and had to give way
to the Rifian hard core; the Gomaris seem to have stood around
in the rear, watching. There was no question of the outcome.
Raisuli stubbornly refused to flee, and outnumbered and devoid
of Spanish assistance (the Spaniards staged a brief and pointless
air raid on Tazrut hours after the battle), he was taken prisoner
at dawn. Si Muhand n-Si Hmid nj-Mqaddim of Temsaman,
whose uncle had been killed at Abarran, and who had himself
been wounded nine times before the attack on Raisuli, was the
first person to enter Raisuli's house. Abd el Krim, however, as a
political maneuver, announced that Heriro himself had captured
Raisuli.* The old brigand's Beni Aros cohorts defended him well,

* Evidently ashamed to face his old leader, Heriro did not enter the palace
until much later that day.

but they joined the Rifians as soon as the engagement was concluded, recognizing, as Moroccans are quick to do, that discretion
is the better part of valor. The captured Raisuli, who had behaved
calmly throughout the whole of the fighting, was treated with cold
deference. Swollen with dropsy and constantly in pain, the old
Eagle of Zinat was transported in a litter all the way over the
mountains, first to Chaouen, then to Targuist in the Rif, where he
was held prisoner in a Rifian house. Raisuli's anguish over his
downfall was extreme. He refused to eat, and begged to be allowed
to die. At Targuist he said, "Raisuli wishes to forget the outside
world. I have asked to die and I want to die. Why do they not kill
me at once? Raisuli will never be a prisoner and a slave to dogs in
the place where Raisuli reigned as lord. They have taken my horse
and saddle. Let them take the rest. The Prophet will receive me
in Heaven."[4] In April 1925 Raisuli died at Tamasint, in central
Beni Urriaguel, and was buried without fanfare in the Tamasint
community cemetery. As David Hart expresses it, Abd el Krim had
written *finis* to the life of a classical master of bet-hedging.

In the fighting at Tazrut, the Caid of Jebel Habib had been captured along with Raisuli, and now he and such tribes as had not
been previously committed passed over to Abd el Krim. The military stores taken at Tazrut proved a valuable acquisition. According to Fernández Almagro, they included 100,000 Spanish Mausers,
ammunition, and various other types of equipment.[5] The Pasha
of Targhzuit, who was there with the Rifians, told Vincent Sheean
that the treasure taken from Raisuli amounted to 16 million pesetas (about $2,300,000). But Si Muhand says that his Rifians, who
behaved correctly and did no looting, listed everything. They
found horses, saddles, guns, books, papers, and sacks containing
a total of 31,000 duros.[6] The Spaniards had paid Raisuli the huge
stipend of 80,000 pesetas per month—almost $12,000!

An incident that serves to show not only the hatred with which
many Jiblis regarded Raisuli but also the prompt severity of Rifian
justice, has to do with the Caid of Beni Lait.[7] This notable had
been instructed to deliver a message from Abd el Krim asking
Raisuli for the last time to join forces with the Rifians or take the
consequences. Out for revenge, and either knowing or guessing the
contents of the letter, the Caid purposely withheld the note in
the hope that Raisuli would be destroyed in the ensuing battle.

Raisuli fell, but so did the Caid. His complicity was discovered, and he was shot to death on the spot for having caused so much unnecessary killing.

It was during the winter of 1924–25 that Abd el Krim and the Rifian Government first faced the problem of the French Army in Morocco. War with France was the last thing in the world the Rifians wanted. Abd el Krim said so often enough. Their enemy was Spain; the Rifs had no historic quarrel with France. The tribes of the Rif were different in language, in customs, and in certain important features of social structure from the Arabic or Arabicized tribes of French Morocco. Moreover, the Rifian Government fully understood the odds involved in any hostile undertaking against a nation much richer, much more efficient, and far more capable in every way than Spain. Yet trouble between the Rifians and the French was unavoidable. One difficulty was the boundary line between French and Spanish Morocco as set down in the 1912 Treaty of Fez. As we have seen, this boundary existed only on maps; it had never been surveyed, and it had no meaning to the tribes involved until the arrival of French officers in certain sectors. Abd el Krim asserted that he had been no party to the 1912 accord, and that the entire fabric of the French and Spanish Protectorate system constituted an unwarranted interference in the affairs of the Moroccan people.[8] In fact, he considered all the territory north of the Wergha River, an east-to-west-flowing stream south of the zonal border in French Morocco, the domain of the Rifian Government. Abd el Krim had logical reasons for this contention. For one thing, the ineptly drawn border line ran directly through such unquestionably Rifian tribes as Metalsa and Geznaya to the east of the Wergha Basin, through Beni Amart, through the Senhadja Srir tribes of Beni Bechir, Beni Bu Chibet, and Ketama, and through the Lukus tribe of Gezawa within the basin itself, thereby splitting all these tribes between French and Spanish administration. For another, the Wergha River had long been considered a natural boundary by these tribes. Much more important, the fertile lands drained by the Wergha and its tributaries to the north provided the Rif with a great percentage of its grain.[9] Furthermore, until 1924, neither the Spanish nor the French had set foot in this land that they now claimed belonged to them. In 1923, Abd el Krim had sent his emissaries to the tribes north of the Wergha; and these tribes agreed to accept his leadership. It will be recalled that the Spanish mercenary Abd el Malek, who had successfully led some of these very tribes against the French during World War I, had found the same tribesmen very cool to the French when he tried to stir them up against Abd el Krim during the early years of the Rebellion. It is clear that Abd el Krim was not encroaching upon French-controlled territory or dealing with tribes sympathetic to France.

The crucial confrontation between Abd el Krim and the French occurred within the tribal area of the Beni Zerwal, a fairly large tribe of perhaps 24,000 people living in the very center of the Wergha Basin between Ketama on the east and Gezawa on the west. The boundary of 1912 had placed the whole tribe within the Spanish Zone, but the French, for strategic purposes, had persuaded the Spaniards to allow them to administer to all those tribes who watered their cattle at the Wergha or at streams tributary to it.[10] Thus Beni Zerwal passed under the nominal control of the French, but remained technically a part of the Spanish Zone. Spain later relented and suggested that she take over the northern two-thirds of the tribe while France retained administration of the southern third, but France objected, and the matter was dropped. France's refusal to split the tribe had a logical basis. What influence she had among the Beni Zerwal derived almost completely from an alliance with the Sherif of the Darkawa. The Darkawa, a powerful religious group in the heart of Beni Zerwal, which had many adherents both there and in the Rif, represented a classic example of the religious groups that so plagued Abd el Krim's attempts to unify northern Morocco. To have returned to Spain two-thirds of this tribe would have complicated matters that were already complicated enough, and would probably have nullified French influence there altogether. The French, therefore, while not actually in Beni Zerwal, worked through the Darkawa Sherif, and the Sherif in turn persuaded Caid Bu Monala, an important Beni Zerwal chief, that friendship with the French meant valuable trade for the tribe.[11] The French also bribed some of the shaikhs to sell the concept of cooperation with France to their fellow tribesmen. Had not God given the French many victories in the past? Was it not, then, certain that Allah intended France to rule the country?[12] Thus the

Beni Zerwal were pulled toward France by the advantages of commerce, while at the same time they were drawn toward Abd el Krim by territorial and religious ties. The end product of all these conflicting considerations was that the Beni Zerwal became restless and undecided in their loyalties.

The struggle for control of these tribesmen precipitated the almost inevitable clash between France and the Rifian State. For his part, Abd el Krim needed to create a solid block of allies on the southern flank of the Rif, and needed in addition to preserve his access to the rich harvests of the Beni Zerwal, which were so vital to the expanding power of the Rifians. The French, on the other hand, were bound by the Treaty of Fez and their own ambition to maintain the Sultan's authority over all Morocco, that is, to move against the Blad s-Siba, wherever it was. Although the Spaniards had been given a token slice of the country, their mismanagement of it only increased France's "responsibilities." France dared not allow Abd el Krim's influence to spread, or even to continue, since his every triumph was a threat to French suzerainty in Morocco, and might conceivably undermine the French position not only in the Protectorate but in Algeria and Tunis and even farther afield. Colored lithographs showing Abd el Krim defeating the Christians were already being distributed in the Near East.[13] In Morocco, the French were especially fearful that the Beni Warian tribesmen—difficult people from the Middle Atlas Mountains below Taza, who inhabited a wild, rugged area that the French had designated "the Taza spot"—might declare for Abd el Krim. (The French had lost more than 100 officers and 3,000 men to the Beni Warain in 1923.) In view of these serious possibilities, it is more than likely that the French Army wanted a showdown with Abd el Krim, and that they wanted it at a time when Spain was still able to cooperate with them in some sort of joint pincer movement that would crush the rebellion forever. It was therefore hardly surprising that Primo de Rivera's decision to abandon most of western Spanish Morocco horrified the French even more than it did the *africanistas*.

Perhaps the only high-ranking Frenchman in Morocco who did not want war in the Protectorate was the veteran soldier Marshal Hubert Lyautey, the first and only Resident-General. French President Poincaré said of Lyautey, "He meant to make the

[French] Army the quartermaster of civilization [in Morocco], and
the soldier the forerunner of the engineer, the trader, and the
teacher."[14] Lyautey, who was the most distinguished of all French
colonial administrators and an able general as well, was the architect of French colonial policy and the builder of French Morocco.
In a mere dozen years, Lyautey had a prosperous, peaceful land of
great potential. French Morocco was over twenty times larger than
the Spanish Zone—a fact that only made Lyautey's accomplishments the more remarkable. The Marshal had enjoyed a successful military career from the time of his late adolescence. Born at
Nancy, France, in 1854, he attended the French Military Academy
at St. Cyr, then served as a cavalry officer for many years. In 1894,
at the age of forty, he had been posted to Indochina on the staff of
General Gallieni, who was himself an outstanding colonial officer.
A few years later, when Gallieni was transferred to the island of
Madagascar, Lyautey accompanied him, and it was here that
Lyautey's genius for colonial administration was first demonstrated. As a lieutenant colonel, he was given command of the
whole south of Madagascar—an area as large as all of France and
full of hostile natives. Combining tact with a minimum of force,
Lyautey convinced the Madagascar tribes that the French Army
was on their island to bring them the benefits of modern technology. Gradually his soldiers taught the local people to cultivate
their fields scientifically, to build roads and telegraph installations, and to use many machine-made tools. When Lyautey left
Madagascar, the island was more tranquil and materially better
off than at any previous era in its entire history.

At nearly sixty, Lyautey was sent to serve in Algeria, first as
commander of the Ain Sefra District in the desert, and afterward
as chief of the important Oran Sector, next to the Moroccan frontier. The general's greatest achievements still lay ahead. Sent to
Morocco in 1912 to become the Protectorate's first Resident-General, he arrived in the midst of a typical Moroccan uprising. Fez
and Taza were in the throes of mutinies because of Mulay Hafid's
signing away the country as a French Protectorate; more than a
hundred Frenchmen had been killed within two weeks of the pro-
mulgation of the Treaty of Fez. The French situation was perilous.
Although it was suggested that he withdraw from the area, Lyautey
set up headquarters at Fez, and within two months had restored

quiet and a degree of order in the surrounding region. During the
First World War, German-inspired forays by the surrounding
tribes seriously threatened French control. At one point, the military position in Morocco seemed so perilous that the French High
Command ordered Lyautey to abandon the interior. He refused
to budge from Fez and Taza. Lyautey's tenacity paid off; for, in
addition to holding out against Abd el Malek's raids in the Wergha
area, he succeeded in increasing the area of French control. In
recognition of this achievement, the French Government made
him a Marshal of France in 1921—the first such promotion in twen-
ty-eight years.

The Lyautey formula called for handling the natives of an occupied territory through the authority of their own chiefs. As expressed in one of the Marshal's pet formulas: "Govern with the
Mandarins, not against them. Do not offend a single tradition; do
not change a single habit."[15] The authority of tribal leaders was
carefully upheld, and all local customs and local religious practices were preserved intact. Wherever French troops went under
Lyautey, they immediately taught the local people better methods
of agriculture, showed them how to grow more and better crops,
dug better water holes, built hospitals, and set up marketplaces
where prices were low and where the items offered for sale were
diversified as never before. In this manner, the unsubmitted tribes
and the out-groups did not have to be conquered with guns, for
they had visible, tangible proof of the value of cooperation with
the French, and this was sufficient for the majority of tribes.
Lyautey sought to prove that both France and the tribesmen
gained from this peaceful, practical, progressive program. He
applied most of the methods he had used in Madagascar to Morocco, creating his constructive program around the slogan "le
Maroc utile," and as in Madagascar, he was able to persuade many
of the Arab and Berber tribes that the French were in Morocco to
promote peace and prosperity for all.[16] Lyautey built railroads,
highways, and schools. He improved the land, put people to work,
and opened mines. Both the modern metropolis of Casablanca,
one of Africa's largest and finest cities, and the busy town of
Kenitra were Lyautey's creations. At Kenitra, the Marshal transformed a primitive settlement on the coast above Rabat into a
commercially valuable and bustling seaport (called Port Lyautey,
in his honor).

In the field, Lyautey shared hardships with his men and lived in an ordinary tent like one of his soldiers. He was always approachable, vigorous and firm but just and respectful of Arab and Islamic rights when he dealt with Moroccans. Paradoxically, Lyautey was an aristocrat; he was in favor of private investment in Morocco aided by government loans. Little wonder, then, that Lyautey was a favorite of the French conservatives. Although there was not much actual disposition of land in Morocco, most of it was bought at very low prices by rich colons.[17] That the French would be liked was too much to expect, but Lyautey did determine to make them respected. The French anthropologist Montagne, who had served as a junior officer during Lyautey's time, felt that the partial French conquest of Morocco had won the notables of the large cities. He sympathized with the Marshal's problem—how to reconcile two peoples so completely different socially and religiously, separated politically and economically by a thousand years—and agreed that there should be a strong central government in Morocco working with and through the Sultan.[18]

When the results of Lyautey's policies were put to the test, and when the tribes of French Morocco felt the strain of Abd el Krim's rebellion, Lyautey's soundness was proved; very few tribesmen defected to Abd el Krim, and most remained faithful to France. Since 1912, Spain and France had been on trial in Morocco, and surely there could be no doubt that the Spanish had failed as surely as the French had succeeded. There was simply no comparison between what the French had achieved in Morocco and what the Spanish had accomplished.

The evidence tends to show that French militarists deliberately provoked a war with Abd el Krim. From a long-range point of view, this move was probably a sound one. No one could say where Abd el Krim's victories might lead, and his ever-increasing influence made him the focal point for every dissident or hitherto tranquil Muslim element in North Africa. Even Lyautey, who had no part in this provocation, had stated in a letter to the French Government in December 1924, in which he predicted an attack on French Morocco by the Rifians by May 1925: "Nothing would be so bad for our régime [in North Africa] as the installation near Fez of an independent Musulman State, modernized and supported by the most warlike tribes, with a morale exalted by success against Spain . . . in short, the most serious kind of menace, which should be dealt with at the earliest possible moment."[19] On another occasion he said, "A maggot-breeding spot in the Rif would be a grave threat to civilization and the peace of the West."[20] Yet Lyautey certainly did not want to attack Abd el Krim and thereby make the Rifian cause a rallying point for other Moroccans. The Marshal suspected that Abd el Krim's Rifian State was not as well organized as it seemed.[21] In his view, the Beni Zerwal should be organized through political, not military, action. On the other hand, France should maintain enough of an army in Morocco to compel obedience to the Sultan, for the Sultanate must be upheld at all costs. The Marshal always considered his adversaries of today, not as enemies to destroy, but as opponents who could be persuaded to be friends tomorrow, and he hoped that Abd el Krim could be won over as a vassal to the Sultan much as Thami el Glaoui, a rebel shaikh in the region of Marrakech, had been won over.

Meanwhile, Abd el Krim continued to reiterate his contention that French and Spanish attempts to invade the Rif or the lands of allied tribes were unjustifiable. "I recognize," Abd el Krim said, "that the French have given Morocco order, security, and economic prosperity; but I shall bring the same benefits, with the further advantage that I am a Muslim, and so it will be from a leader of their own faith, and not from an infidel, that the Moroccans shall receive these blessings."[22] Abd el Krim accused the French of deliberately introducing anarchy among the Beni Zerwal, where he himself was trying to establish order. "Still," he said, "to me, war with France is inconceivable—unless we are attacked."

On March 28, 1924, the Rifian State asked the French to appoint a commission to help the Rifians define the limits of the French and Spanish Zones with greater accuracy and satisfaction. It was a shrewd ploy on the part of the Rifians, because if France had agreed, it would have meant that the French recognized the Rifian State.[23] The French rejected the proposal, and suggested that instead some sort of informal agreement might be reached, but this was not at all what the Rifians wanted.

Early in 1924, the French Minister of War, acting upon special reports from French Morocco, declared that the Rifians had pillaged Beni Zerwal and robbed the tribe of its food stocks, and he therefore authorized the French Army to march in and occupy the disputed tribal area north of the Wergha.[24] In May 1924, in an interview with Major Chastenet, a French representative, the Rifians' Caid Haddu ben Ali asked that the French delay their Wergha advance in order to allow Abd el Krim to explain to the Beni Zerwal why the Rifians were retreating.[25] But the French moved across the river and forward into the range of hills bordering the Wergha Valley on the north. There was no opposition, and the French, employing a preponderance of Senegalese and Algerian troops, proceeded to construct numerous small forts and blockhouses. These posts dotted a 75-mile front extending roughly from Biban, in the west above Fez, to Kifan, in the east above Taza. General Chambrun was made Commander in Chief, and French headquarters were established at Ain Aicha, on the south bank of the Wergha near the geographical center of this front. At an airdrome just east of Ain Aicha, at Ain Mediouna, the French maintained five air squadrons. Most of the new posts were fairly well placed and well constructed, often in such a way that one post could assist another with cross fire in case of attack, but in spite of this, the French faced a familiar problem in supplying these small garrisons, since there were no roads at first and everything had to be carried over rough mountain trails. The French, however, remained confident that the tribesmen would never be able to break the French line as they had the Spanish one. In fact, the French said, Abd el Krim could never have got started in the French Zone, for the surveillance exercised over the tribes in their zone was far superior to that exercised by the Spanish in theirs.

From the Rif, the brothers Abd el Krim surveyed the French activity with a concern bordering on apprehension. They were sure they had beaten Spain, but France was an altogether different matter. Better to come to some sort of arrangement than to fight. Yet the Rifians could hardly dismiss an advance which, sooner or later, not only would alienate or contain allied tribes, but also would effectively shut the Rif off from its bread basket. Some of the Beni Zerwal had helped Abd el Krim against Spain; now he owed them support if they wanted it. Moreover, the Rifians' prestige was at stake—they dared not refuse to accept combat at the zenith of their power. Abd el Krim nevertheless sent a deputation to the French requesting a conference, but the French refused to discuss the issue and went ahead strengthening their defenses in the Wergha hills. Rifian propagandists, working hard to counter-act the influence of the Darkawa Sherif among the Beni Zerwal, apparently gained some ground: while a few members of the Darkawa order remained suspicious of Abd el Krim and rejected his offers of assistance, the great mass of the tribe was impressed with the rebel movement, and they became increasingly inimical to France. When the French moved across the Wergha, the Beni Zerwal were thoroughly alarmed. One of their Sherifs had already been beaten by a French intelligence officer, and thirteen Caids who were alleged to have plotted with Abd el Krim were shot by the French.[26] The Beni Zerwal organized a harka and petitioned Abd el Krim to lead them in a holy war against France.

While the preoccupation with French intentions was claiming more and more of the Rifians' time, Abd el Krim was by no means allowing the Spaniards to relax. His men kept up a constant sniping and raiding against posts in the Tizi Azza sector in the east, and they annoyed the garrisons in the Primo Line all the way from Tetuan south to the Alcazar region in the Lukus.

It must have been sometime during the early months of 1925 that the Rifians finally decided to fight the French. Provoked by French depredations, worried about his food supply, goaded by questions of honor and prestige, and lured on by his own over-confident advisers, Abd el Krim was drawn into the fatal decision to attack the French. One wonders what he hoped to gain by it. War with France meant a three-front war against the armies of two European powers. The Rifians were far too realistic to expect to defeat France entirely. Rather, they must have hoped to punish the French so drastically that they would willingly negotiate some sort of treaty that would leave the Rifians free in their own country. His plan for war was simply and clearly to cut off French communications by taking Taza, and to rally all Moroccans by taking the cultural capital of Fez.[27] The Rif had neither the man-power nor the resources to occupy captured cities like Fez or large areas of land, and the possibility of amalgamating with other tribes in French Morocco little known to the Rifians and probably jealous of them was remote. Fear and desperation must have been the deciding factors. From the moment the French actively entered the picture, the Rifian State was on the defensive, and any attack on or by the French Army meant a calculated risk, with the odds heavily against the Rifians; yet to stand by doing nothing while France consolidated her position north of the Wergha was impossible. A fighting chance was better than none.

All the while, the Abd el Krims ceaselessly informed one and all that their only real enemy was Spain, and that if they were ever forced to fight the French, it would be in sheer self-defense. Statesmanlike bulletins continued to issue from the Rif. Responding to an invitation proffered by a club of university students in Buenos Aires, Abd el Krim wrote an article directed to all Latin American republics that were then celebrating the centennial of the Battle of Ayacucho, where the patriot General Sucre had defeated the Spanish Army under Viceroy La Serna in Peru in 1824 and then broke the power of Spain in South America:[28] "The heroic people of Morocco are fighting for the same ideals that Miranda, Moreno, Bolívar, and San Martín vindicated. We possess racial, cultural, and religious qualities that forbid our tolerating dependence upon any European power. We, today, are offering our lives and fortunes on the altar of our national liberty."

In Spanish Morocco, sporadic fighting continued. In March 1925, Primo de Rivera journeyed back to Morocco, and until the middle of April he inspected the Spanish lines and drew up projects for the future. At this point, the Jibala lost one of their braver leaders when El Mudden was killed while attacking a Spanish blockhouse near Larache.[29] Soon afterward, Caid Bu Monala, France's best friend in Beni Zerwal, was assassinated—almost surely through the machinations of the Rifians—and the greatest obstacle to an outright alliance between Abd el Krim and the Beni Zerwal was removed.

12. WAR WITH FRANCE

ON APRIL 13, 1925, Abd el Krim launched a carefully planned attack against the French positions along the Wergha.[1] Five harkas consisting of tribesmen from Gezawa (Jibala), Beni Yahmed (Senhadja Srir), and Beni Mestara (who were actually in the French Zone, bordering the Beni Zerwal on the west), each with a selected cadre of Urriaglis and the whole led and directed by Mhamed Abd el Krim in person, enveloped the Beni Zerwal on three sides and struck all the French posts in the west. Those who resisted were massacred, and their villages were sacked and put to the torch. Other raiders hit the French in the Kifan sector above Taza, in the east. Although these initial attack waves were estimated to include no more than 4,000 warriors, with another 4,000 in reserve, the Rifians were able to pour through the French lines without hindrance and reach a point twenty miles north of Fez within a few days. During the onslaught, the Rifians displayed their characteristic mobility. This was a strange war—a series of violent skirmishes and desperate sieges between small groups of men at widely separated points among hills and ravines rather than a meeting of armies.

After the initial attack, the reaction among both the tribes lukewarm to Abd el Krim and among the French military was unprecedented. The zonal border tribes who had demurred came over to Abd el Krim almost to a man, while the French were thrown into pandemonium. Before April 13, it would have been difficult to find a French soldier who believed the tribesmen capable of such deft maneuvering. This myopic underestimate of the Rifians cost the French dearly in casualties. Previously they had sneered at the Spanish, and considered their own position impregnable: catastrophes like the disgraceful routs at Anual and Chaouen could not possibly happen in French Morocco. The French had always considered the Spanish Army incredibly inefficient, corrupt, and blundering—a sad excuse for a military machine, and one that really deserved to be beaten by the Rifian guerrillas. Most Frenchmen felt that the Rifians despised the Spaniards as a people once conquered and ruled by their own forebears, and now humbled again. Any cooperation between France and Spain could only result in the loss of French prestige in Morocco. Meanwhile, the French had enjoyed the comforting conviction that they were superior soldiers—that their own Wergha Line would hold off anything Abd el Krim was likely to throw against it. Foreign Affairs Minister Aristide Briand told the American correspondent Paul Scott Mowrer: "You have seen the great Abd el Krim. These native chiefs . . . we know them well. They are really simple fellows. Properly handled, they respond to kindness. There is, of course, not the slightest chance that this one will ever attack us."[2] Now the French found themselves caught up in the bloodiest fighting they had ever faced in North Africa.

Marshal Lyautey had never been completely sure that the Wergha forts would hold in case of attack. He had predicted just such an attack and had asked for reinforcements, only to be refused (French forces in Morocco had actually been reduced over the years from 95,000 in 1921 to 64,000 in 1923). Now he acted with his usual efficiency, calling in the nearest reinforcements he could find, from Algeria; but these forces were numerically insufficient to repel the Rifian thrusts. The Marshal then organized the French command into three fronts, under the direct charge of General Colombat on the west at Wazzan, Colonel Freydenberg in the center, and Colonel Combay on the east at Taza. The whole front remained under the direction of General Chambrun at Ain Aicha.[3]

Meanwhile, post after post was being overwhelmed by the rebels or evacuated by the French. While the major Rifian pressure was directed against the center of the French lines, aimed at the historic capital city of Fez, the French policy of concealing events at the front from the public was so well enforced that no one knew what was happening in the north, or what might happen around Fez if the tribes south of the Wergha raised the flag for Abd el Krim. In fact, the Rifians' main hope lay in this possibility. Fez had enormous significance as a seat of Muslim orthodoxy and as the archetype of the Muslim city, dear to the hearts of every Moroccan. The rumor spread that Abd el Krim himself had sworn to enter Fez on or before the great Muslim feast of l'Aid el Kebir—"the big feast"—in order to supersede the Sultan at the religious ceremonies connected with the Aid. The local Moroccan significance of l'Aid el Kebir, which celebrates the Biblical and Koranic story of Abraham's sacrifice, is that the Sultan of Morocco himself traditionally comes to Fez for the ceremonies and cuts the throat of the first sheep to be ritually slaughtered. Abd el Krim, so it was rumored, intended to be in Fez and to perform this rite himself, thus demonstrating dramatically that he, and not the puppet Sultan, was the true leader of Moroccan Islam.* The residents of Fez —the Fasis—are generally considered the urban aristocrats of Morocco, an extraordinarily self-centered, self-contained, and conspiratorial people. It is hard to believe that they would have accepted the leadership of a man whom they looked upon as a barbarian from the mountains, an adventurer and usurper. According to some observers, the citizens of Fez greatly feared that Abd el Krim was going to overwhelm and conquer them,[4] and they implored the French to defend them.† On the other hand, Abd el Krim was a Muslim and a Moroccan, and he might be, in the long run, just barely preferable to the French. A few young Fasis of good family, feeling that France was an oppressor, were openly in favor of Abd el Krim.[5] As for the French garrison, López Rienda reports that the gardens of Fez rang with the laughter of cocottes and the tempo of jazz bands and dancing.[6] Abd el Krim's entrance

---

* Paul Scott Mowrer, who helped give currency to this rumor, claimed he had heard it first from Joseph Klemms. Léon Gabrielli tells us, however, that Abd el Krim was very angry with Mowrer for having said that the Rifian leader would essay such a thing, for Abd el Krim never, as far as is known, made any claims to the Sultanate (quoted by Furneaux, p. 161). Just the same, Robert Montagne (Revolution and Maroc, p. 160) suggests that the ulemas at Fez, in good bet-hedging fashion, had secretly recognized the future conqueror of Morocco. And Monteil (p. 157) claims that the Rifian secession "was directed as much against the throne as against foreign powers," and that Abd el Krim admitted this in Cairo in 1953. During the attack on French Morocco, when Abd el Krim was asked "Where is your frontier?" he replied, "War will decide it."

† When Lyautey asked a Fasi student of advanced ideas what he thought about Abd el Krim, the young man replied, "The modernism of Abd el Krim is a joke. Our fathers knew a while ago another type of 'modern' Sultan; it was Abdul Aziz and his entourage of adventurers. We know what he cost us. He ruined Morocco." (Maurois, p. 233.)

into Fez at this juncture might well have changed the whole history of modern Morocco. His son, Idris, is quoted as saying, "My
father believed that if he had ordered his troops to advance, he
would have taken Fez and Taza and occupied all Morocco [in May
1925]."[7] Why, then, did Abd el Krim not take Fez and Taza, in
May or at any other time? The answer is probably that he knew he
could not take these two cities and hold them successfully. Nor
would his Rifian mountaineers be adept at holding a city, or doing
anything else of a defensive nature. Occupied, the cities would have
presented a compact target that French artillery and aerial bombs
could have reduced to a shambles. Abd el Krim was too intelligent
for that. He hoped to hold the Rif, and to hurt France so badly that
she would let him retain it.

What actually happened was that Sultan Mulay Yussef marched
to Fez, surrounded by troops, and enacted the ancient ceremonies
of l'Aid el Kebir unmolested.[8] The Sultan, in addition, published
a plea for peace among the Moroccan tribes, and followed this
with a heavily guarded tour to several tribal strongholds, where
he asked for and obtained numerous recruits for the French native
units. Some 5,000 tribesmen from the Cheraga, Hayaina, and Ulad
Aisa joined the French forces in July 1925 at his request.[9] It was at
this point that Marshal Lyautey's policies toward the indigenous
population were vindicated. Far from rising against the French,
most of the tribes of northern French Morocco remained loyal.
(Those few tribes, or those fragments of tribes, that did revolt
were, strangely enough, the very ones thought to be most depend-
ably pro-French.) It was this loyalty that brought about France's
final victory over Abd el Krim. Furthermore, the fact that Abd el
Krim was attacking the French "protectors" of the Sultanate made
the French position as its defenders legitimate in the eyes of many
Moroccans.

Meanwhile, in May, Lyautey's headquarters issued a communiqué stating simply that the situation was neither grave nor dis-
quieting. In point of fact, it could hardly have been worse. The
largest French post in the west, Biban, north of Fez in Beni Zerwal, had been invested since the first day of the Rifian offensive.
There were four bloody battles there in May alone, as the post was
taken and retaken, and the last of these, distinguished by a grenade
charge led by Major Delandes of the French Foreign Legion, cost
the French 103 dead and more than 300 wounded.[10] On June 5 the

French garrison was wiped out, and the fort at Biban remained in
Rifian hands until late in September. Everywhere the Rifians and
their allies met with success. They burned the headquarters of the
Sherif of the Darkawa in Beni Zerwal, and the Sherif fled to Fez.
They attacked fixed positions everywhere with cannon, grenades,
and charges. To make matters worse for the French, the summer of
1925 was a long and torrid one, with temperatures as high as 130
degrees.[11] The logistic weaknesses of the French were apparent
from the first, and food and water in the form of ice bags had to be
dropped by planes to the garrisons cut off by the rebel drive. This
airlift was organized in part by young Captain de Lattre de Tas-
signy, who much later became one of France's leading generals in
the Vietnam campaigns of the 1950's. In an attempt to keep the
morale of the defenders at a high pitch, he saw to it that supplies,
mail, and even decorations were dropped to French soldiers.

The assaults at Aulai and Blockhouse Number 7 furnish good
examples of how the tribesmen operated and how the French
troops responded. At Aulai the rebel invaders subjected the
French garrison to sustained mortar fire, day and night, for three
weeks. They threw the horribly mangled bodies of the French
dead close to the French barricades—where they lay decomposing
under the eyes of the defendants. The survivors at Aulai were
rescued on the 22d day of the fighting, but the post was abandoned
to the enemy, who completely razed it. Blockhouse Number 7, a
small outpost perched on a rock and held by fewer than thirty
soldiers, held out for fifteen days; then it was rushed and the survivors were slashed to death by their besiegers. The story was much
the same at Beni Derkul, a few miles from Biban. The post's complement, composed of Senegalese troopers and a French lieutenant, held out valiantly for over two months, waiting for relief that
never came. Its commander, Lieutenant Pol Lapeyre, was a young
and inexperienced officer, but his gallant defense of Beni Derkul
became a legend. On June 15, exhausted beyond endurance, Lapeyre ignited the powder stores, blowing up Beni Derkul and killing himself and his few remaining comrades.[12] Other small posts
like Bab Wender, Ain Jenan, and Bu Azzin in the center of the
French lines, Aoudour and Achirkan in the west, and Anizer and
Ain Leuh in the east, were abandoned. In the Sker-Taounate sector north of Ain Aicha, the battle kept up at a deadly pace. Lieu-

tenant Berthélemy kept his defenders at Taounate alive on dried
meat; unable to reach the bags of ice dropped by the airlift outside
the walls of their fort, they were saved from death by thirst by an
unexpected rainstorm.[13]

Sher was taken and retaken several times. The town of Wazzan,
in the west, was so seriously threatened that by the end of May, all
Europeans had been evacuated and sent down to Meknes or over
to the coastal cities. Nevertheless, by the end of June, the situation
was stabilizing. There had been no large-scale French victories,
and enemy raiders still roamed behind the French lines. But the
Rifians were never defensive fighters, and seldom bothered to hold
what they had taken. Slowly, the French contained the Rifian
drive and turned it, but they were not able to mount an offensive
against the enemy. Although some 60,000 French troops, mostly
Legionnaires with Algerian and Senegalese levies, held a line extending from Wazzan, 200 miles east, almost to the Algerian
border, they were discovering that even this number of soldiers
was insufficient. For one thing, French technological advantages
were not so great as the troops expected them to be, and artillery
made little impression on guerrilla fighters individually scattered
among the ravines and boulders. Aerial bombs and armored equipment proved relatively ineffective. It became increasingly clear
that some degree of cooperation with Spain would be necessary if
the Rifians were to be crushed. This was not a novel concept; in
1913 Marshal Lyautey and General Marina had discussed such a
possibility. Now the possibility had become a necessity, in spite of
the reluctance of the French to involve themselves with a military
organization they considered vastly inferior to their own.

The Rifian whirlwind strike in French Morocco in the spring
of 1925 changed all this in the space of a few weeks and pushed
France into Spain's arms.

Foreign Minister Briand met at Paris in May with Spanish Ambassador Quinones de Leon to discuss joint Franco-Spanish military operations against the Rifian State. Primo de Rivera, now
firmly in control of the Spanish Government, welcomed the French
proposals. Representatives from both countries met in Madrid in
June 1925.[14] Led by Louis Malvy and Gómez Jordana Souza, the
conference debated for more than a month before deciding on a
plan of action. France and Spain were to participate in simulta-

neous but not necessarily combined attacks on the Rif. Both France and Spain would have the temporary right to send troops in pursuit of the enemy into one another's zones. The boundary between the two Protectorates would be carefully and fully defined.* Peace terms satisfactory to both France and Spain would be arrived at jointly.

As a result of the Conference of Madrid, another attempt was made to treat with Abd el Krim. The Rifian chief of state, for all his bravado in striking at the French, was desirous of peace. In an interview with Léon Gabrielli at the N'Teghza *zawia,* near the Mediterranean in Temsaman, on June 28, 1925, Abd el Krim said that he regretted being forced to fight the French, but felt obliged to defend the Rif.[15] He reiterated that his involvement had been solely with the Spanish until the French had provoked trouble with the Beni Zerwal. The majority of the people in that tribe, he said, had asked him to intervene. Both he and they were convinced that France wanted to conquer the Rif, and that the French Colonial Party wanted to dominate the Rif without regard for the Rifians. After this meeting, Gabrielli was convinced that treating with the Rifian State would be a hopeless task, because of Abd el Krim's perception of the situation. Nevertheless, plans for approaching the Rifian leader were developed. The eternally complicating factor of prestige entered the picture here, and each side proceeded with caution so as not to seem too eager to be the party asking for peace. The new allies were afraid that if they sent peace terms directly to Abd el Krim, they would seem to be suing for a cessation of hostilities. For his part, Abd el Krim felt that if he publicly requested to see the Franco-Spanish terms, he would be considered to have submitted to the European powers. For these reasons, Franco-Spanish terms were sent to Abd el Krim unofficially sometime during the summer of 1925. According to Walter Harris, the terms read as follows:

"The French and Spanish Governments agree to guarantee to the

---

* Significantly, every time France and Spain discussed zonal boundaries in Morocco, Spain lost. In 1902 the French secret offer to Spain included a region extending some miles south of Fez. In 1904 the offer still included land south of the Wergha. By the 1912 Treaty of Fez, the zonal borders ran north of the Wergha. In 1924 the French moved still farther north, when they seized two-thirds of the Beni Zerwal.

Rifian and Jibala tribes such autonomy as is compatible with the existing international treaties. Further, the two European governments agree conjointly to open negotiations at once in order to reestablish peace and to put into effect the new regime. The salient points to be observed in these negotiations are (1) the release by France and Spain and the Rifians of all prisoners; (2) reciprocal and complete amnesty dating from January 1921; (3) the definition of districts falling within the new regime; (4) agreement upon the geographical limits of the above districts; (5) agreement upon the formation and number of police required to maintain order in the new districts; (6) recognition of commercial liberty in the territories in question, under the terms of International Customs and other treaties; (7) recognition of the illegality of all trade in arms and ammunition; and (8) the choice of a position on the Rif coast to be occupied by Spanish forces, agreed to by common consent, upon the cessation of hostilities."

After studying these terms briefly, Abd el Krim tentatively opened negotiations through his agents in Tangier and Tetuan. The agents let it be known that any binding negotiations must be made in full conference in the Tangier International Zone, and that the full independence of the Rif would be an unalterable condition of any peace agreement. Because of the double meetings at Tangier and Tetuan, some observers thought that Spain was secretly trying for a separate peace. But in July, Primo de Rivera met with Rifian agents at Tetuan, where he courteously but clearly explained that any sort of peace must be a three-way affair. In the same month, Abd el Krim asked Walter Harris to intervene for him with the British Government, saying that he admired "the British sense of humanity and justice,"[16] and stated that he would accept any French or Spanish terms to which England would agree. But the British, wishing to avoid involvement, replied that they could not intervene in a Franco-Spanish matter.

On August 14, 1925, Paul Painlevé, Prime Minister and Minister of War for France, made public the Franco-Spanish terms. He stated that the French Government would guarantee the Rifian and Jibala tribes administrative, economic, and political autonomy, under the sovereignty of the Sultan and subject to the delegation of the Khalifa, then added that Rifian independence was internationally impossible, because it would run contrary to existing treaties. The Spaniards topped the French guarantee in a communiqué they published on August 16, stating that, in the future, the Sultan's authority over "the Rifian State" would be merely "nominal." Despite such conflicting guarantees, the Rifian agents urged Abd el Krim to consider the Franco-Spanish terms. Under them, the Rif would have most of the practical advantages its leaders wanted, with little diminishing of their military power, except for the outright recognition of the Rifian State itself. The terms represented a genuine opportunity for the leaders of the Rif Rebellion. Any degree of recognition was a big step forward. However, the Abd el Krims refused the terms, believing that they could keep on fighting until they obtained even more concessions. Besides, they were advised by various European factions, undoubtedly self-interested, not to trust either France or Spain but to continue their struggle. Thus Abd el Krim held out for total recognition of the Rifian State, occupied himself further with the strategy of war, and waited optimistically. By this decision, the Rifians lost their best chance for autonomy, for the Spanish landing at Alhucemas in September changed the whole picture in the Rif overnight.

Nevertheless, in June 1925, no one could foresee the end of the fighting. Although the Rifians had been forced to pull back north of the Wergha, they had swung the important Tsoul and Branes tribes near Taza to their side, and they now seriously threatened the city of Taza itself. All European civilians were evacuated from Taza, but Marshal Lyautey once again dug in and held. Yet France's position was far from encouraging. There was grave dissatisfaction among the Wergha tribes, who blamed the French for the destruction of their villages. Although they had contained the Rifians' drive southward, the French could hardly claim any great achievement thus far in the war, since almost all of the newer French posts north of the Wergha were either ruined or in the hands of the enemy. With Abd el Krim's harkas constantly making sneak attacks on posts south of the river, the French were in circumstances almost as perilous as those of April and May. The airport at Ain Mediouna, with its buildings and storage tanks, had been knocked out of commission by the rebels, and many French troops had been killed there. Captain Merzegues, France's most famous air ace of the war, had been shot down and killed near Sidi

Mesaud.[17] Ain Maatouf was heavily invested, and the French were in retreat everywhere. At Mzoua, on the Lukus River, a shrewd sergeant strapped his dead commanding officer, Lieutenant Latour, in an upright position on his horse, so that the evacuating garrison would not realize he was dead and lose heart. By the end of June, the Rifians had taken forty-three of sixty-six French posts.[18] They had captured an estimated 51 cannon, 200 machine guns, 5,000 rifles, millions of cartridges, 16,000 shells for cannon, 60,000 grenades, and 35 mortars with 10,000 shells. They had carried off at least seventy Frenchmen and 2,000 mercenaries as prisoners, and no one cared to report publicly how many French troops had been killed and wounded.

The Paris Government blamed Marshal Lyautey for failing to contain the Rifians. In July, the aging Marshal was replaced as commander of all French forces in the field by General Naulin (Lyautey was retained, however, as Resident-General).[19] At the same time, Marshal Pétain was dispatched from Paris to Morocco to make a thorough inspection of French forces there. All the while, the Rifians continued their attacks on the French lines. On July 12 they surrounded Kelaa des Sles, and the same day they took the steep fortified heights of Jebel Amergu, a seventeenth-century Portuguese castle, both posts being south of the Wergha and northwest of Fez.

The Pétain Report was the first honest news to reach the French public, and it did not minimize the seriousness of the French position. Both Pétain and Lyautey repeatedly asked for reinforcements, especially dependable white French troops, and Lyautey estimated that the French forces in Morocco would have to be doubled to cope with Abd el Krim.[20] Impressed at last with the gravity of the situation, the French Government rushed 100,000 fresh troops to Morocco. Marshal Pétain was placed in complete charge of operations and gradually, throughout the remainder of July and August, the French advantage in numbers and equipment began to tell. But whatever his inner thoughts may have been, Abd el Krim gave a brave answer to the problem of French superiority. Late in April, he had granted an interview to a Spanish businessman, and when the latter quite candidly asked the Rifian chief how he hoped to measure up to the French, who had, or soon would have, ten times as many soldiers in the field,

Abd el Krim replied without hesitation. One Rifian, he explained, had the advantage over any ten Frenchmen, for out of every ten, two or three were sure to be sick or exhausted from the effects of the climate, and four would be busy guarding the military convoys. That left only three fighting men out of ten—each more heavily equipped and therefore far less mobile and far less knowledgeable about the country in which he was fighting than his Rifian counterpart.[21]

Another Spaniard, Enrique de Menses, who had once fought against the Rifians and had great respect for them, reported: "When a Moor fights, he is brave, or rather, he forgets fear.[22] The Moor who sees his companion fall does not run away; he takes his place. Abd el Krim's characteristic fighting tactics are to withdraw or retreat while the enemy advances, but at the first halt of the latter, to start sniping, at which the Moroccans are experts. And it is very difficult to shoot them down as they never collect in large groups, but in isolated bevies which are continually on the move; whereas the French and Spanish troops, moving in concentrated masses, are easy targets." And a French officer, a veteran in Morocco, averred: "They are magnificent fellows, these Berbers. They do not know the word 'surrender.' One of them will engage a whole patrol. They never run away. I admire them and love them but I kill them on sight."[23]

The Rifians displayed such capable maneuvering that once again the stories that they were European-led cropped up. Some of the Rifian artillery in the skirmishes along the Wergha were serviced, as we have noted, by a few European renegades and deserters, but only Joseph Klemms held a position of even minor importance with the Rifians.* But it must be reiterated that the Rifians owed their remarkable battle record to their own leaders and their own resources. One of the most harrowing aspects of the war for the

---

* It was partially due to Klemms that the myth of European officers in the Rifian service took root and grew, since during the Wergha offensive Klemms distributed written pleas addressed to all Germans in the French Foreign Legion, urging them to desert. A sample note read: "Why do you fight with the French? Abd el Krim means freedom. Come into the Rif with your arms, and if you do not want to continue fighting, you will be repatriated through Tangier. Lt. Klemms will help you. At Ajdir, we make war the modern way, and you, Germans, will understand. You have been with the French for adventure.... Abd el Krim fights for an ideal, to defend his native land." (Pryne, p. 217.)

French was the extraordinary ability of the Rifian tribesmen to slip in among them undetected. Rifians frequently knifed sentries and stole guns from open encampments, and even though the French habitually slept with their rifles strapped to their wrists and their rifle butts buried in the ground beside them, naked, oiled Rifians often managed to squirm silently into field camps, cut throats, appropriate the rifles, and steal out again.* Men who fought with the French Foreign Legion during the Rif Rebellion have stated that Legion losses from this sort of attack were so drastic that the authorities never dared publish the truth. Prince Aage said that the Legion, tough as it was, had met its equal in the Rifians.[24]

At Ourtzagh, near Taounate, the garrison had all been killed and thrown off the surrounding rocks by the time French relief columns arrived. The bodies had been mutilated by having their toenails and eyes torn out or their fingers hacked off, and their gutted stomachs filled with stones and straw.[25] At Telaghza, west of Taounate, the small fort was built on a craggy height covered with tangled undergrowth. When the garrison was ordered to retire, the French soldiers were almost all shot down by Rifian snipers. Although the Rifians had held the important position of Biban, in the west, since early June, the French never relented in their efforts to get it back. There were actually two posts on the crown of a roughly horseshoe-shaped hill at Biban—one at the northern apex, where the horseshoe opened toward the west, and

---

* It was established that Abd el Krim's main supply base was at Targuist, and that it was from this point that ammunition for the Rifians was distributed on muleback all along the front. The tribesmen were observed to have developed something like a medical corps, too, which picked up and cared for their wounded after each engagement. It was claimed that the Rifians treated their wounded according to traditional remedies. For example, to stop bleeding they applied hot cinders or spiders' webs to wounds. To extract a bullet, they would place another bullet over the point of entrance, because they were convinced that lead attracts lead and that the second bullet would, like a magnet, draw out the first. Rupert Furneaux (p. 89) says that the Rifians claimed to rely upon "healers"—members of families who specialized in medicine—who could cure rabies and smallpox before Pasteur, but who were powerless against typhus. David Hart, in commenting upon Furneaux's claim, says that there are no "hereditary families" specializing in medicine, although there might be "specialists"—"dentists"—in the zocos of the Rif. And Dr. Ruiz Albéniz (*España en el Rif*, pp. 51–52) says that the Rifians often put mud, sour milk, and honey on wounds before opening them to sunlight; they burned themselves to let pus out, and they cut without anesthetic to remove gunshot.

one back on the concavity of the central section. According to French reports, the casualties at Biban in May alone amounted to over 400 Frenchmen and 1,000 Rifians killed.

In spite of the accuracy of Abd el Krim's analysis of the French soldier's fitness to fight in Morocco, he must have known that the Rifians had little hope of triumphing over the military machine now being thrown against them. The French had 160,000 troops in northern Morocco alone, and the Spanish had increased their Moroccan forces to 200,000. Now and then the Moroccans, almost surely Rifian allies and not the experienced Rifians themselves, abandoned their shrewd guerrilla tactics and concentrated their forces inside captured forts. They did this notably at Biban and Jebel Amergu, thus giving French pilots, at last, the rare opportunity to bomb and strafe them. Worse, the Rifians were suddenly faced with poor harvests. In many places there were no crops at all because either the Rifians themselves or the French had burned the fields. In addition to this, a typhus epidemic had begun among the northern tribes, who completely lacked the means to control it.

In the Taza area, the French owed their victories to the leadership of Captain Henri de Bournazel, a colorful character known as "the Red Man" because of his habit of wearing a flaming-red tunic into battle.[26] The man seemed to live a charmed life, especially when one considers the accuracy with which Rifian marksmen brought down their quarry. De Bournazel was not killed until the battle of Bu Gafar, near Marrakech, in 1933—the last stand of the fierce Ait Atta tribe against the French. He was largely responsible for the fact that the Tsoul and Branes tribes were rapidly overcome, and that by July 1925 Taza was out of danger.

Wazzan was relieved in August by Freydenberg (then a general), who used strong detachments of troops supported by tanks and armored cars to break through. On August 10, French and Spanish troops joined forces for the first time at Arbawa, far to the west.[27] But the opposition had been considerable in this region, too. The post of Rihana, in the hills above the Lukus River, had been saved once by air support, but it had eventually surrendered.[28] (In this instance, survivors were well treated.) At Beni Ruten, after the tribesmen had rushed the position, the ammunition stores accidentally blew up, killing more than a hundred rebels. The greatest loss to the Rifians was the fall of Biban, in the latter part of September, for that stronghold had been a focal point of Rifian strength and had stood as a beacon of supremacy over the French during the brief period when the tribesmen held the fortifications there. A strong September drive all along the French line pushed the Rifians out of the French Protectorate and won back practically all the ground north of the Wergha that the French had first occupied in 1924. There was no concentrated Rifian opposition to this drive, which lasted only from September 11 to 15, and Marshal Pétain was severely criticized for halting it.[29] While Abd el Krim's major effort during 1925 was directed southward, his harkas struck constantly all along the Spanish line. In May, for example, General Sanjurjo, commanding the Melilla front, had to deal with a serious insurrection behind his lines in Beni Said. The Spanish, gathering strength for the joint attacks to come, remained on the defensive most of the summer.

One of the matters discussed between the delegates at Madrid was a plan for an amphibious landing in the neighborhood of Alhucemas Bay. The idea of landing a large body of troops on the Rif coast and then proceeding to invade the mountains of Beni Urriaguel was an old one, and had long been considered an absolute necessity for successful control of the Rif. Only a leader with the will to do it, the military knowledge, and the operational ability was lacking. Primo de Rivera now provided that leadership. The energetic dictator, when he was finally convinced that the risks of such a landing should be taken, gave all his attention to the task. He took full responsibility for the project, and personally investigated every detail of it. Alhucemas Bay had wide, flat beaches, and fair protection from the wind. Abd el Krim's capital of Ajdir stood nearby, and could be bombarded from the sea once the shores of the bay were in Spanish hands. Under an able leader, the Spanish were developing a precise military formula for their first positive move of the war.

Initially the French were against the proposed landing, for they feared that the Spanish lacked the organization to bring it off. But Primo de Rivera was a competent soldier. He planned well, and knew how to implement his plans. When the French examined the Alhucemas project and noted that it was as complete and as practicable as any that could be devised, they agreed to back it. French troops took no part in the Alhucemas action, but the French Government furnished a few ships for the flotilla. In preparation for this all-important operation, Spanish troops practiced landing techniques from small ships on various beaches near Ceuta and Melilla, and were given special training in attacking trenches and throwing grenades. The hard-fighting Tercio was to furnish the shock troops, and the landing was slated to commence on the morning of September 7, 1925. Troops would board their ships at Ceuta and at Melilla; both fleets would make diversionary attacks en route to the rendezvous at Alhucemas; and the first landings would be made by the Ceuta contingent, with the Melilla troops acting as reserves. General José Sanjurjo would be in charge of operations, but Primo de Rivera would be on hand to supervise.

On August 20, General Sanjurjo had personally flown over the western part of the bay in order to scout enemy fortifications. On September 1, with everything finally ready for the great attempt at Alhucemas—warships and troop carriers, seaplanes, land-based bombing planes, and an observation dirigible—Primo de Rivera issued an ultimatum to the tribes, printed in Arabic and scattered over the mountains by planes.[30] The gist of the message was that the Rif was about to be invaded by the combined Spanish and French armies, that Abd el Krim was to be seized and punished, and that the tribesmen had just three days in which to surrender. As far as is known, not a single Rifian heeded this ultimatum. On the contrary, the rebels of the Rif merely consigned themselves to the will of Allah, and checked their rifles.

Abd el Krim had been informed of the Spanish buildup and the Spanish ultimatum came as no surprise; the sole question was when and where the Spanish would strike. The Rifian leader decided that the attack would be delivered across the flat sands where the Guis River ran into Alhucemas Bay. To meet the challenge, the Rifians strengthened their entrenchment all the way from Cala Quemada to the vicinity of Ajdir. To divert the Spanish from the main push, the Rifians moved against Tetuan. The first step was the elimination of the strong Spanish fort at Cudia Tahar, in the mountains of Gorgues.[31] For this effort, the Rifians chose their staunchest veterans in the west, and Cudia Tahar was cut off

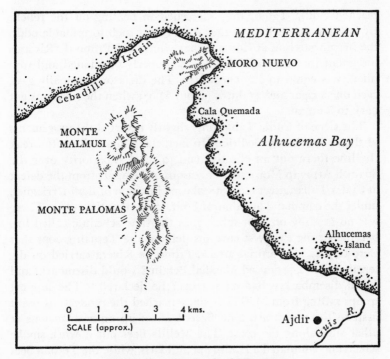

Map 4. Site of the Battle of Alhucemas

from Tetuan on September 3. On the 6th, the rebels, who had placed nine cannon in hidden positions directly fronting the fort and who had surrounded the Spaniards with machine guns as well, opened up with an intense barrage at almost point-blank range. By the 12th, the original garrison of 200 men had been reduced to thirty-four, of whom twenty-two were wounded, and all the officers had been killed or wounded. But the survivors held on stubbornly, and planes managed to drop them food and ice. The Spanish flotilla was already steaming toward Alhucemas when Primo de Rivera received news of the attack on Cudia Tahar. He immediately ordered part of the Spanish Foreign Legion back to Tetuan to act as relief troops, and 4,000 men then set out from the capital city toward Cudia Tahar.

From Ben Karrich onward, these troops had to fight every inch of the way with costly bayonet charges. When they finally reached Cudia Tahar, they succeeded in beating off the rebels. By holding out as long as they did against such formidable odds, the heroic garrison at Cudia Tahar vindicated Primo de Rivera's judgment that the Spanish soldier, properly positioned and supplied, was equal to any encounter. The dictator personally gave each one a cigar and 25 duros (about $4.07) when the survivors got back to Tetuan.

The siege of Cudia Tahar only slightly diverted the movements of the Alhucemas expedition. In fact, the Rifian failure to break the line there put an effective end to rebel superiority over the Spanish Army in Morocco. For reasons quite apart from the defeat at Cudia Tahar, however, the seaborne invasion of Beni Urriaguel, under the command of Admiral Yolif, faltered at the outset. There was no landing on September 7, as the time schedule called for, because strong east-west currents delayed the Tetuan troops that were to make the initial attack. Primo de Rivera carried on determinedly. "I promised Marshal Pétain I would disembark, and I will disembark, whatever it costs," he declared.[32] The support troops sailing from Melilla actually reached the rendezvous point first. In the meantime, both fleets had set up noisy diversions at other sites along the coast. The Melilla fleet put down a smoke screen and simulated a landing at Sidi Dris, while the Tetuan fleet shelled Wad Lau—but neither maneuver fooled the Rifians. Finally the troops were united and arranged in proper assault order, and on September 8 the main effort got under way. There were sixty-three ships of from 900 to 4,000 tons each, borrowed from the Spanish Compañía Transmediterránea and transformed into troop transports, and thirty-six Spanish Navy ships as well.[33] There were eighty-eight land-based aircraft of Bristol, Hispaño, and Breguet make, and twelve hydroplanes of Rolls, Dornier, and Junkers make. Each Spanish soldier was fully equipped with rations, ammunition, grenades, and a gas mask, and the ships carried large supplies of bombs and poison gas. Drinking water was brought along in casks and barrels. Last, there were special floating docks built specifically for use during the Alhucemas operations. Admiral Yolif directed the Spanish fleet from the deck of his flagship, the *Alfonso XIII*, watched by Primo de Rivera and General Sanjurjo. Admiral Hallier, on the *Paris*, had charge of such French forces as were present.

The fleet began a heavy bombardment of the dunes along the shores of Alhucemas Bay at six o'clock on the morning of September 8. Planes continued to support this attack all day with bombing and strafing. Meanwhile, the ships landed, not at Alhucemas itself, but to the northwest, on two narrow strips of beach called Ixdain and Cebadilla. Some writers say that Abd el Krim was duped by the diversionary barrage. This may have been true, yet with many miles of coastline to watch—Alhucemas Bay curves like a half-moon for about nine or ten miles—and with too few men to watch them with, Abd el Krim was forced to take the obvious stand. The western approaches at Ixdain and Cebadilla were defended too, but only lightly, and there is some evidence that the Bucoya tribesmen posted there left their positions soon after the Spanish landing.* The beaches are actually in the Bucoya tribal area, and Abd el Krim had never wholly trusted his Bucoya neighbors. It was 11:40 in the morning before elements of the Tercio under Colonel Franco moved in toward the beaches on landing boats under cover of the bombardment. When the boats grounded on shoals and sand, Franco and the Legionarios went overboard, wading through water up to their necks until they reached Cebadilla. In less than two hours, Franco's men had stormed across the narrow beach and up the low cliffs, and by nightfall they had taken possession of the heights of Moro Nuevo. Their announced losses of only seven officers and 117 men, some of whom were said to have been killed by gunfire from their own ships, were light, considering the position the Spanish now occupied.[34] More than 8,000 troops and three batteries were ashore, and the surprise landing could be counted a success.

The Rifians counterattacked heavily all through the nights of September 11 and 12, but the Spaniards hung on, and continued to land more troops. The combat developed from the west, where the Tercio had first waded ashore, toward the east and the southeast, where the Rifian capital of Ajdir lay. All the land from Cebadilla and Ixdain beaches to Ajdir is rough and rocky, with several wide, steep coves on the north, and many peaks and caves. The

---

* More than that, it seems that Rifian Marine Minister "Severa," secretly in Spanish pay, actually planted mines near Rifian gun emplacements. "Severa" was later killed by a fellow Bucoya tribesman under mysterious circumstances (Hart, letter, June 2, 1967).

Rifians used this excellent defensive terrain as only trained guerrillas can, and fired their cannon only at night so that Spanish
planes had a much harder time finding the gun emplacements.
It took the powerful, well-equipped Spanish force fifteen days to
advance one and a half miles. By September 23, General Goded,
Sanjurjo's chief of staff, had fought his way to the sands of Cala
Quemada. This sheer-walled cove on the northwest horn of Alhucemas Bay held caves that had to be taken one by one. Goded
tells of stumbling over the body of a huge Caid who had just been
killed on the Quemada slope, his rifle beside him, and a copy of
the Koran in one dead hand; the general retained both as me-
mentos of the battle.[35] The Spanish, who now had 12,000 men
engaged, surged forward and took Monte Malmusi on the same
day. The struggle for this salient point was so bitter that when the
heights were finally taken, only a single Rifian defender remained
alive, and he kept firing until stabbed to death by troopers of the
Tercio. On that day alone, the Spanish lost 700 men.[36] By September 30 they had charged over the rocks and ravines to Bujibar and
Monte Palomas, and on October 2 they swept into the dispersed
community of Ajdir, seven miles from Cebadilla Beach. Rifian resistance had been as ferocious and obstinate as anything the Spanish had ever faced, and the fighting was carried on literally from
boulder to boulder every step of the way, with sudden charges
and countercharges and numerous hand-to-hand encounters. Even
with their planes, poison gas, and cannon, the Spanish had aver-
aged only about 400 yards a day in their advance on Ajdir. But in
the long run, Spanish numbers simply overwhelmed the Rifians,
and they were reduced to making the inevitable Spanish victory a
costly one. The cost notwithstanding, Alhucemas was a great victory for Spain—the only definitive one they were to achieve during
the whole of the Rif Rebellion. On October 3, the battle was
broken off, the Tercio burned most of Ajdir, and a garrison of
13,000 men was encamped in the Alhucemas area.

There was rejoicing all over Spain when the news of the outcome of the fighting at Alhucemas was given to the public. Generals Sanjurjo, Saro, and Fernandez Pérez—the commanding officers, respectively, of the overall operations, the Ceuta forces,
and the Melilla forces—were all promoted, and Primo de Rivera
received various decorations from the King. It was in the fighting

at Alhucemas that Colonel Franco outdid himself.[37] He had long ago established a reputation for icy courage in battle, and though for a while given to riding a white horse in the murderous battles around Tizi Azza, he was never hit, although several horses were killed under him, and bullets tore through his sleeves and his cap On one occasion, as he was talking with Millán Astray on the Tizi Azza front, the latter was suddenly struck down and badly wounded, while his two aides and his standard-bearer were killed outright. Franco was not even touched. General Sanjurjo once half-seriously told Franco that he would club him if he did not stop riding white horses near the enemy. In any case, having been the first high-ranking Spanish officer to land at Alhucemas, Franco was nearly lost when he was completely buried by debris from a bursting shell; but his Legionarios quickly dug him out, unhurt as usual. Franco always knew what he wanted and where he was going, which was up. A demanding officer, he was not liked, but he was greatly admired and respected. Marshal Lyautey once said, "Spain has only one man in Africa—Franco." After Alhucemas, Franco was promoted to the rank of brigadier. At thirty-three, he was the youngest general in all Europe.

The invasion of their homeland may have shocked the Beni Urriaguel, but it in no way diminished their will to fight. One Urriagli, when he first heard the news of the Alhucemas landing, said, "Let them come, and if I'm the only one here, that's all that will be needed to cut off their heads."[38] Abd el Krim had telephoned to his brother Mhamed, who was still in the Jibala directing operations there, when the landings began. Mhamed called a conference of thirty of his top lieutenants at his headquarters in Beni Hassan and told them the bad news. Most of the Rifians wanted to get back to the Rif to fight and to look after their families. But Mhamed promised them that the Spanish would be repelled, and decreed that none of those present must discuss the affair or show their worry; failure to comply with these orders meant having one's tongue cut out.[39]

On September 10 the French had launched an offensive of their own along the Wergha line—an overland drive aimed northward at the heart of the Rif. The French and Spanish met when a Spanish column under Colonel Dolla advanced south from Dar Drius to meet a French detachment at Zoco el Telata, in Metalsa, on October 8. A week later, Marshal Pétain and General Sanjurjo met at Zoco el Sebt de Ain Mar in Beni Bu Yahi, farther south-east.[40]

Marshal Lyautey, who had been ill for some time and had asked to be retired, was finally relieved of all duties by the French Government on September 24, 1925. The Marshal was not popular in Paris because many of the bankers, the corporations, and the colons had wanted to exploit Morocco, and Lyautey refused to allow this.[41] He was also unpopular with the left wing, who wanted to settle Morocco with large numbers of French World War I veterans, who would be assisted with public aid.[42] Lyautey was caught in the middle; he was an aristocrat, but he did not want the Moroccans exploited. The French Government, liberal since the elections of 1924, wanted disarmament, partly in order to combat inflation. It was markedly hostile to the military services, and had already withdrawn the French Army from the Ruhr. The very last thing the French Government wanted was another expensive war. There had been much criticism in France of Lyautey's "misjudging" the Rifian whirlwind attack along the Wergha in April, and the feeling in many influential French circles was that the Marshal, for all his past greatness, was now too old to be relied upon any more. The facts were all on the side of Lyautey. Far from being unprepared for the Rifians, not only had he repeatedly requested reinforcements from a parsimonious government, even before the rebellion involved France, but he had also predicted the Rifian onslaught almost to the day. If there was any error in French thinking in matters concerning the Rif, it was a broadly shared underestimation of the Rifian guerrilla warrior. When Marshal Pétain reported on the situation in French Morocco, he stated truthfully: "The brutal fact is that we have been suddenly attacked by the most powerful and best-armed enemy that we have ever had to encounter in the course of our colonial operations." Pétain went on to give Lyautey the full credit he deserved: "One can but render homage to the great Chief, who, in spite of his age and the burden of his rough colonial career, has been the soul of this defense and has known how to preserve against the overwhelming rush of the barbarians his work of civilization, which all the world admires."[43] Pétain then relieved Lyautey as commander in chief of the French forces in Morocco. According to Hubert

Jaques, Pétain is supposed to have said, "But certainly you don't suppose, my dear friend, that I have played a role in this affair?" To which Lyautey is said to have replied, "No, my dear friend, I know you are too straight and loyal for that, but . . . are you sure that the role was not forced on you?"[44]

The manner of Marshal Lyautey's leaving was sad. This greatest of French colonizers deserved every honor that France could give him, and he received practically nothing. He sailed back to France from the port at Casablanca, bidden goodbye by a host of personal friends. When the ship that was carrying him home passed through the Straits of Gibraltar, a squadron of British warships gave the Marshal a respectful salute. But his own government treated him shoddily.[45] Nobody met him officially at Marseilles. There were no troops, no parades, no fanfare to greet the man who, far more than any other Frenchman, had established Morocco as part of the French colonial empire. It remained for a group of Arab *shaikhs* to give Marshal Lyautey the true accolade. When he left Morocco, they wept. "We thought," they said, "when the French first invaded the country, that everything was finished—our families, our world, our religion—and then he came, this man whom Allah himself has sent to us. . . . Our sons will date their history from Lyautey."[46] Theodore Steeg replaced Lyautey as Resident-General. Steeg, a civilian, had distinguished himself as Governor-General of Algeria. It was left to him to harvest the fruits of the French victory over Abd el Krim.[47]

On November 2, Primo de Rivera, who was as elated as anyone in Spain over the events at Alhucemas, resigned his position as High Commissioner.[48] The office was turned over to the capable General José Sanjurjo. Meanwhile, the Spanish had appointed a new Khalifa for Spanish Morocco, a choice made the more simple for them by the capture and subsequent death of the perennially irksome Raisuli. They chose the first Khalifa's son, Mulay Hassan ben el Mehdi, who was installed at Tetuan in colorful ceremonies on November 8–10, 1925.[49] The youthful Hassan was proclaimed Khalifa at the grand mosque in the presence of Primo de Rivera and others of the Spanish hierarchy.

On November 25, Primo de Rivera met with Resident-General Steeg and French General Naulin, the new commander in chief in French Morocco, at Alcazarquivir. After mutual congratulations and expressions of confidence, the leaders put their heads together over their military maps. Spanish losses, while substantial, were not as harrowing as had been expected, and in the heady climate of victory, few Spanish were inquiring about them. But the 1925 fighting had cost France an estimated 12,000 casualties and 45 million dollars, and the French were maintaining over 300,000 troops in Morocco. There was still much to be done.

Together with the French advance from the south, the epic landing at Alhucemas Bay forecast the doom of the Rifian State. The brothers Abd el Krim had few illusions left. With their tribesmen weary after more than four years of constant struggle, their most productive land lost to the enemy, their homes battered by Spanish bombings, their people half-starved and typhus-ridden, and their mountains now entirely surrounded by more than half a million victorious French and Spanish soldiers, the Rifians could never hope to win.* Mingled pride, patriotism, and fear, plus the faint possibility that they could yet salvage some sort of arrangement beneficial to the Rif and to themselves, kept the Abd el Krims and their loyal tribes fighting. Pétain thought that Abd el Krim was counting on a rift between the Franco-Spanish allies to get him out of his all-but-hopeless situation.[50] And thousands of well-organized tribesmen were still in possession of the greater part of Spanish Morocco. After Alhucemas, the Rifian Government had retired to Tamasint, in central Beni Urriaguel, and its functionaries operated either from there or from Abd el Krim's military headquarters farther west at Targuist. As winter came on, giving the Rifians a measure of respite from the advancing enemy, they discussed the future. As for the jubilant European allies, they thought that, one way or another, by next spring the struggle should be over.

* Monteil, *Morocco*, p. 154. The French Army fighting Abd el Krim in Morocco numbered 325,000, with 400,000 reinforcements, plus 140,000 Spanish (revealed to the tribune of the French Chamber on June 1, 1956).

13. THE END OF THE RIF REBELLION

IT WAS obvious at the beginning of 1926 that the European allies were eventually going to conquer the whole of Spanish Morocco. The Spanish Army was in a vengeful mood, for it felt that it had never achieved the necessary retaliation for Anual. In a sense, this was true. The Army held far more—and more important—territory than it had ever before controlled in Morocco, yet the Rifians had still to be routed and flayed as the Spaniards had been during those frightful days at Anual and Chaouen. After almost five years of fighting, the rebels still showed amazing stamina, clinging tenaciously to their positions at every encounter. The successful landing and take-over at Alhucemas had helped to reduce Spanish resentment of Primo de Rivera's semi-abandonment policy, but the Spanish Army still had the onerous task of invading and subduing the Blad s-Siba. To its credit, the Army was eager to get on with the job. Somewhere among those bleak pinnacles were the Abd el Krims, whom the Spaniards were determined to conquer once and for all.

France's position was a much simpler one. The French needed only to sweep the rebels out of their own zone, after which they had the alternative of marching to the support of Spain, or of containing Abd el Krim's warriors along the zonal borders. The French chose to help Spain because they realized that unless Abd el Krim were disposed of, he would continue as a threat to the peace of all Morocco. Marshal Pétain met with Primo de Rivera in Madrid in February 1926, and the two leaders planned further joint action.[1]

Meanwhile, in Spanish Morocco the rebels continued to harass the invaders. In February, Ahmed Heriro began cannonading Tetuan itself from the mountain of Gorgues (despite the Spanish relief of Cudia Tahar, he had managed to hide several guns in caves among the peaks).[2] When Spanish planes zoomed overhead in search of the emplacements, Heriro's gunners simply dragged their cannon back into the caves, out of sight. Though the practical effect of the shelling of Tetuan was negligible, the Spanish decided to put an end to it. In an effort to separate Heriro's Beni Hozmar tribe from the rebels in neighboring Beni Said, they landed troops on the Mediterranean coast near the community of Emsa. In a three-day attack beginning on March 4, 1926, the Spanish succeeded in pushing back the local tribesmen, and most of the Beni Said submitted to the invaders. (Millán Astray, who had been promoted to the rank of colonel and commander of the Spanish Foreign Legion after the battle at Alhucemas and Franco's promotion to general, was wounded yet again during this battle.) At the same time, Lieutenant Colonel Asensio led a Spanish column in the Lukus against the Ahl Serif and Beni Isef,[3] where rebel resistance rapidly dwindled away.

Throughout the rebellion in the Rif, peace factions in Spain and France kept up an incessant demand that Abd el Krim be treated fairly. Many people saw the Rifians as a gallant group fighting for their families and homes exactly as millions of Europeans had done during the First World War. It seemed to many people that the very Europeans who had cried loudest over the German invasion of France were now deliberately inflicting the same sort of suffering upon a people overwhelmingly outnumbered and overmatched, and for the most venal of motives. When Abd el Krim took the initiative in the spring of 1926 and asked for another conference to discuss peace terms, France and Spain were practically forced to accept the request because of the weight of worldwide opinion.

However, the Spanish Army was far from willing to give up the idea of crushing Abd el Krim. If peace were made, the Army would suffer the ignominy of the technical loss of a war against half-civilized tribesmen. Moreover, most of the Spanish Army would be sent back to the mainland: there would be no more chances for action, foreign service pay, rapid promotion, or easy profiteering, and above all, no opportunities for earning the "glory" that military pride demanded. In view of this attitude, which may have been shared by certain elements within the French military organization, there was little likelihood that a peace conference would bear fruit. The French and Spanish had the rebels trapped between them. They were willing to endure the formality of a discussion, but they had no intention of loosing their military hold on the Protectorate until Abd el Krim had been humbled and the Moroccan conflict had yielded all it could of graft and glory.

It was agreed that the conference would take place at Ujda, near the Moroccan-Algerian frontier, in early April.[4] The Rifians were to be represented by Foreign Affairs Minister Mohamed Azerkan, Haddu el Kahal, and Mohamed Cheddi. Although Cheddi was an Urriagli, he and Haddu el Kahal were supposed to represent the interests of all the tribes, not just those of the Beni Urriaguel oligarchy. The two men had been chosen by a council of Rifians, and not by the Abd el Krims alone—a clear indication, said some, that Abd el Krim's leadership was being challenged within the Rif itself. General Simon, Director of the French Moroccan Intelligence Service, headed the French delegation, and Señor López Olivan, Director of the Moroccan Department at Madrid, led the Spanish. As agreed upon beforehand, the agenda was to include four topics: Rifian recognition of the Moroccan Sultan as sovereign over the whole country, the disarmament of the Rifian tribes, the release of French and Spanish prisoners, and the expatriation of Abd el Krim. But in a preliminary meeting at the French position of Camp Berteaux, seven miles to the north of the village of Taourirt and about sixty miles west of Ujda, the Europeans began the talks by stating forcefully that there would be no conference at Ujda unless the prisoners held by Abd el Krim were set free at once. In addition, they demanded that the French and Spanish forces be allowed to advance unopposed at specially designated points along the front, in order to assure the "strategic security" of the armies while the Ujda conference was in progress. The Rifians were angry and suspicious, and Haddu el Kahal was flown back into the Rif to discuss these arrogant demands with Abd el Krim. The Rifian leader refused to consider them, and the French and Spanish were forced to carry through their agreement to meet at Ujda and reach a peaceful settlement of the items on the original agenda.

As a result of these delays, it was not until April 27 that the Ujda Conference began in earnest. In spite of their resentment at the Franco-Spanish ploy at Camp Berteaux, the Rifians proved reasonable. They agreed to accept the theocratic authority of the Sultan. Further, they agreed to accept the disarmament of the tribes, with the proviso that Abd el Krim be allowed to handle the operation. It was he who had given the Rifians most of their guns; let him take them away; if European troops tried to collect them, the tribesmen would be sure to hide as many as they could, or else to attack the French and Spanish troops outright. Once Abd el Krim had accomplished the disarmament and had turned over the administration to Spanish authorities, he would allow himself to be deported. Evidently the Spaniards did not openly contest the idea of deporting Abd el Krim, but they almost surely intended to imprison or execute him when they had the opportunity; such a powerful figure could not be left at liberty. Regarding the prisoners held in the Rif, Mohamed Azerkan said that they would be exchanged only after the declaration of peace. Meanwhile, French and Spanish medical units would be allowed to enter the Rif and minister to the wounded until the fighting stopped and the prisoners could be returned to European bases. The truth was that Abd el Krim was fearful that the French and Spanish would discover the condition of the prisoners before reasonable peace terms could be arranged, and that they might then be more vindictive. Approximately half the prisoners taken by the Rifians were dead, and the survivors were either too ill or too weak to work. There had been much criticism in European newspapers of the way in which the Rifians allegedly treated their captives. Historians disagree on the matter. According to Walter Harris, Rifian prisoners were often mistreated, tortured, or killed. Andres Sánchez Pérez states that Abd el Krim did mistreat them, against the wishes of his mother and his brother[5] (Prince Aage erroneously believed that the Berbers always killed their prisoners).[6] Carleton Coon says that sometimes Abd el Krim's jailers tormented the prisoners by giving them bread in which dirt had been mixed, but that otherwise they did not treat them badly. Emilio Blanco Izaga's files on Hammush n-Ziyan, who was in charge of Rifian prisoners, relate that Hammush stole money from the prisoners' mail, burned their letters, and possibly killed now and then, but that he was not the sadistic ogre the Spanish believed him to be.[7] (Although the Blanco Izago files also reveal that one of Abd el Krim's secretaries, who had something to do with the management of the Rifian prison camp at Tamasint, behaved pretty badly to his charges, we are led to believe that this was not typical.) Vincent Sheean wrote that

European prisoners were treated no better and no worse than the Arab and Berber captives.[8] Sheean described the prisoners he saw at Ait Kamara, a few miles inland from Ajdir in Beni Urriaguel, as working lazily; they were better off than they would have been fighting. It will be remembered, too, that the Rifians never had large stores of food, even for themselves, much less medicine, doctors, or nurses, and that the very Spaniards who criticized the Rifians for their treatment of prisoners refused to allow the Red Cross or private parties to bring medical supplies into the Rif.

The Rifian people were capable of cruelty and savagery. But most people can be cruel and savage under heavy pressure, and the pressure in the Rif was that of wartime. Life was always hard in these mountains; it still is. A friend was a friend; an enemy was an enemy, whether he was Spanish, French, Arab, or Berber. A Rifian enemy expected and received short shrift. If the Rifians were barbarous, they had always been barbarous; they had never known any other way of life. Contacts between Christians and Muslims throughout Moroccan history had characteristically been violent. Given this background, the Rifian treatment of the Spanish prisoners does not appear to have been unusually vicious. In the case of prisoners who were wounded, for example, their treatment was no worse than that given their own wounded. With practically no medical supplies available for their own people, the Rifians were hardly likely to go to great lengths to preserve the lives of their enemies.

In any discussion of barbarism or cruelty in Morocco, one must consider the underplayed truth that the Spanish and French could be more cruel than the Rifians when they chose to be. For example, in September 1925, when the columns that had gone to the relief of Cudia Tahar paraded in review before Primo de Rivera at Tetuan, the much-lauded Tercio carried aloft on their bayonets a hideous collection of mutilated human parts—severed arms, bunches of ears skewered together, hearts, and so on.[9] Primo de Rivera subsequently issued orders prohibiting such barbarism; but a Captain Hernández of the Tercio told Patrick Turnbull at Tetuan some years afterward: "Later, after battle, we sent the heads and genitals of those we killed to our reserve companies here in Tetuan. They made a public bonfire of them out there in the Plaza de España."[10] As for the French, the troops under General

Drude at Casablanca in 1907 tied groups of captives together and killed them all with shots in the back.[11] More than one group of Legionnaires was photographed carrying the bloody heads of Rifians killed in combat; and the photograph in Roger-Matthieu's book showing ragged Spanish soldiers carrying strings of Rifian ears is famous.[12]

Bombers were used by both the French and the Spanish, who seemed to have no qualms about bombing villages from which all the men were absent.[13] The Franco-Spanish forces regularly used artillery barrages against tribal communities that stood in the way of their advance, and on more than one occasion they used poison gas. During the retreat from Chaouen, a Spanish officer ordered the bombing of a dispersed community precisely at sundown so that the guns would be sure to kill the maximum number of tribesmen, who would be gathered in their mosque for evening prayers.[14] The *Illustrated London News* for November 29, 1924, contains aerial photographs of Spanish planes dropping gasoline bombs on the Moroccans. The French even set up a special squadron of volunteer flyers called the Escadrille Chérifienne, composed mainly of Americans.[15] The commanding officer was Colonel Charles Sweeny, an American soldier of fortune, whom the French had hired to organize the unit. After attending college at Notre Dame, Sweeny had spent several years at West Point. He had joined the French Foreign Legion during the First World War and had afterward fought against the Russian Bolsheviks as an artilleryman with the Polish Army. With his Legion record, Sweeny made an excellent contact for the French. The Escadrille Chérifienne, formed in Paris in July 1925, contained seventeen Americans— twelve of them pilots—and four or five French aviators, including the celebrated Sadi Lecointe, the captain who had at one time held the world altitude and speed records for aircraft. The ground personnel was entirely French. Several of the Americans, including Lieutenant Colonels Charles Kerwood and Austin Parker, had flown with the famed Lafayette Escadrille. Once in French Morocco, the Escadrille Chérifienne flew 470 missions and logged 653 air hours in observation and bombing operations. The squadron flew ten World War I vintage French Breguet planes powered by 300-horsepower Renault engines. Curt Day, once a lieutenant with the group, reports that the whole thing was handled most informally. There were no formal enlistments, no oaths of allegiance, and no formal discharges. Day was paid the equivalent of $40 a month, which included flight pay and foreign service pay. Out of this, he had to buy his own meals. There were rumors that Abd el Krim had hired German and English flyers, and the Escadrille Chérifienne was always on the alert for dogfights. Although the Escadrille encountered no enemy planes, they were harassed by rifle fire from ground emplacements. The Rifian marksmen were able to inflict a surprising amount of damage on low-flying aircraft.

As one might expect, the United States was widely criticized for the activities of the Escadrille Chérifienne, even though the squadron's American pilots were volunteers who in no way represented the nation. After the 1925 bombing of Chaouen, which had been declared an open city, public opinion turned even more strongly against the flying group.[16] In view of the plans of Marshal Pétain to launch an offensive against the Rifians in the spring of 1926, and the assignment of various squadrons of the regular French Air Corps to northern Morocco, the Escadrille Chérifienne was finally disbanded in November 1925.

The major issue in the negotiations at Camp Berteaux and at Ujda was the matter of Rifian autonomy. The European allies pointed out that the Rif was just as much a part of Morocco as the plain around Casablanca was, and they reminded the tribal delegates that the Sultan was still the legal ruler of all Moroccans. Regardless of the amount of "home rule" the Rif might be allowed, final governmental control must rest in the hands of the Sultan, or whatever person or government agency he might designate in his place. For this reason, said the allies, the Rifians would be obliged to recognize the Franco-Spanish Treaty of 1904, which was the whole basis for the French and Spanish Protectorates in Morocco, as well as the Act of Algeciras, which awarded commercial equality in Morocco to all signatory nations. Finally, they would be required to recognize the 1914 Mining Law, which extended the rights of foreign powers on Moroccan soil. Unless the Rifians were willing to abide by these treaties, there could be no discussion of autonomy. But what sort of self-government would the Rifians be left with if innumerable treaties and documents to which they were not privy allowed foreigners to exercise a decisive degree of influence in the Rif? In spite of this contradiction, the Rifian delegates agreed to consider the allied proposals, but they continued to insist that control of the Rif be left in the hands

of the Rifian Government. Aware of their deficiencies as states-
men, the Rifians planned to hire foreigners of intelligence, experience, and organizational ability to help them learn the techniques
of statecraft. With this in mind, they declined autonomy and held
out for complete independence. They promised that Abd el Krim
would be retired to private life once he had carried out the disarmament of the Rifian forces, and they agreed to turn the arms
over to the French and Spanish authorities for final counting and
disposition. The Rif would accept the Sultan's religious authority.
All female, ailing, and juvenile prisoners would be handed over
at once to the allies, but male prisoners and the bodies of prisoners
who had died would be retained in the Rif. Under these conditions, the Rifians would bring their resistance to a halt.

In answer, Spain and France issued an ultimatum on May 1,
1926, giving the Rifians a week in which to comply with their
terms and to release all prisoners. Abd el Krim, now at Targuist,
refused the Franco-Spanish demands. It is estimated that the Rifians still had 12,000 men under arms, mostly tough Beni Urriaguel
and central Rifian tribesmen, whereas the French and Spanish
troops, including native mercenaries, now numbered almost half
a million, giving the Europeans an advantage of 40 to 1, but by
this time Abd el Krim seems to have grown reckless. While the
Ujda–Camp Berteaux talks were progressing, he was holding his
own conference in the cedar forests of Ketama with three hundred
tribal notables, urging them to reorganize their depleted harkas
and resist the invaders to the last man.[17]

The French had previously agreed with their Spanish allies that
in case the Rifians refused their terms, they would launch a joint
offensive. The French were to drive northward on April 15, 1926,
and the Spanish were to start south on May 1. Both armies made
slight advances, in spite of the truce that was supposed to be in
force during the peace talks. With three French divisions sweeping
north and west, and large Spanish concentrations rolling south and
west, the Rifians were forced to draw back into the mountains.

Time was running out for the rebels.* The last important battle
of the Rif Rebellion took place from May 8 to May 10 at Aith

---

* They had lost most of their key men by this time and were using whoever
was available: the chief of Abd el Krim's telephone system was a fourteen-year-
old boy.

Hishim (Hill of the Saints), in the neighborhood of Ain Zoren, to the southeast of Ajdir. In it, the Spaniards lost seventy-six officers and 1,200 men, but they broke the power of the Beni Urriaguel, whose losses were estimated at 1,000 men.[18] This Spanish drive into the Rif was organized by General Castro Girona at Ajdir, and by Colonel Pozas at the small port of Afrau, in Beni Said (Kert). Both forces pushed inland and slightly westward. Although the best of the Beni Urriaguel had perished in the combat at Aith Hishim, the survivors made a final stand on the slopes of Jebel Hammam, in central Beni Urriaguel, on May 28. In a skirmish on the left bank of the Guis River at the Thisar market on May 29, the Urriaglis were decisively defeated for the first time.

Meanwhile, two French columns headed north into the Rif from the Wergha Valley. Led by Generals Ibos and Dosse, they were soon joined by a small division under General Vernois. A Spanish column commanded by General González Corrasco moved from Midar, at the foot of the Rif Range, southwest to Zoco el Telata de Ain Amar. Castro Girona's troops in the north encountered stiff resistance, but nevertheless they carried south and east across the Nekor River. González Corrasco's troops swept directly west, then north, through Zoco de Telata de Azlef in Beni Tuzin. On May 20, they reached the Nekor at a point a few miles east of Targuist. During these operations a few houses were burned, but there was no pillaging. The allied forces taking part in this five-pronged drive into and through the central Rif included about 12,000 infantry, eight squadrons of Spanish planes, and ten squadrons of the French Flying Corps. On May 22, General Sanjurjo and his staff rode on horseback from Ajdir all the way over the heights to a point on the River Kert, and from there took an automobile across the Plain of Garet to Melilla. When Colonel Pozas's men finally stood among the charred ruins of Silvestre's last stand at Anual, almost five years after the fall of that post, they felt that, at last, they had made up for the terrible rout of Spanish troops that began there.

Abd el Krim, cornered at last, had few choices open to him. His government was barely functioning, and the cause of independence was hopeless. Many of Abd el Krim's people had become resentful of him because of his increasingly tyrannical attitude. When the emissaries returned from Camp Berteaux without the guarantee of Rifian independence that many had optimistically expected, there was keen disappointment. During this crisis, the Rifian leaders pondered the possibility of escape. There was a slight chance that they could flee west to Tangier, but that was finally considered too risky. Abd el Krim is said to have contemplated hiding near Mt. Tidiguin with a few dependable Urriagli henchmen, but he abandoned this idea in the knowledge that his enemies would sooner or later ferret him out. The safest thing was to surrender to the French, for the Spanish would be almost certain to execute him. On May 23, when the Spanish entered Targuist, Abd el Krim and his staff had already fled north to the little village of Snada in Beni Iteft, where they sought refuge with the Sherif Hamido el Wazzani.[19] They waited tensely there, realizing that as more and more of their territory was overrun by Europeans, the tribesmen might turn against them.

Abd el Krim wrote two letters, one to French Resident-General Steeg, and the other to High Commissioner Sanjurjo, asking that hostilities cease and that further negotiations be reopened at Ujda. The danger of assassination by his own men or capture by the Spanish was increasing almost hourly. On May 18, Mohamed Meknasi, reputedly one of Abd el Krim's secretaries, revealed his leader's hiding place to the French, who bombed the village at once.[20] Abd el Krim realized that only swift action would save the lives of his family and staff. The closest French column was one led by Colonel Corap; Abd el Krim hurriedly dispatched a surrender note to him, and Corap promptly sent several of his officers to Snada to discuss terms with the rebel chief.[21] After a meeting at the house of Hamido el Wazzani, Abd el Krim sent another note to Colonel Corap requesting security for himself and his family, and promising that he would release all European prisoners on May 26, and give himself up the following day. The terms were immediately accepted by the French.

The European prisoners were in terrible condition when they straggled into Targuist the next day. None of the Spanish officers taken prisoner had lived through the ordeal of captivity, but 105 soldiers, two women, and four children had somehow managed to survive. The French prisoners included fourteen officers and non-coms, twenty-seven soldiers, and nineteen civilians, as well as 112 Algerian and Senegalese mercenaries. All told, less than half of those captured by the tribesmen survived. Lieutenant Clerget, one of the French survivors, said that he thought the French prisoners were better treated than the Spanish, but that the best treatment was reserved for those prisoners whom the Rifians considered to be valuable. All Spanish prisoners who could not walk had been shot. Dr. Mosnier, who treated the survivors, added that many prisoners had died because of poor food, typhus, or bad treatment.

On May 27, 1926, Abd el Krim and his family stole away from Snada before dawn, and at sunrise they rode quietly into Targuist and presented themselves to General Ibos and Colonel Corap. The Rifian leader was then received courteously by French General Boichut "as only France knows how to welcome a conquered enemy who has given proof of military qualities."

Abd el Krim's party numbered twenty-seven altogether, and included his brother, Mohamed Azerkan, Cheddi, and the leaders' uncle, Finance Minister Abdeslam el Khattabi. With them were Abd el Krim's mother, his two wives Thaimunt and Fatima, his three small sons, and a daughter. Mhamed's wife and two children were also in the party. Sánchez Pérez says it took a train of 270 mules to carry the family possessions, including money; he believes that Abd el Krim got safely away with a quarter of a million dollars.[22]

The French treated their captives well. They were held first at Taza and then at Fez. General Brémond comments that at least Abd el Krim had the satisfaction of being captured at his own request, thereby saving himself from both Spain and his erstwhile supporters, some of whom were ready to make him pay for forcing them to serve him.[23] Abd el Krim appears to have made the best of his defeat; Robert Montagne says he accepted his position realistically and with good humor.[24] The French decided to send Abd el Krim and the most dangerous among the Rifians into exile on the island of Réunion, in the Indian Ocean. Those whom the French considered less important were allowed to live on in Morocco.*

On September 2, the Abd el Krim party, which included forty Rifians, was placed aboard a French warship to start the long voyage to exile. Abd el Krim optimistically announced that he

---

* Some of this latter group, Mohamed Azerkan, for example, are still alive.

would count on the French to safeguard his property and interests until he returned.[25] Once on Réunion, he was given a large country estate not far from the island's capital city of St. Denis, and an annual stipend of 100,000 francs. According to the French, Réunion was chosen for the Abd el Krims' exile because the countryside and the climate were similar to those of the Rif. In all, about 150 Rifians were exiled, most of them to French islands in the southern Indian Ocean.

Meanwhile, Abd el Krim's property in Spanish Morocco was ordered confiscated. His former headquarters at Ajdir was used for years afterward as the headquarters for the local Spanish Interventor Comarcal. The portion of his property that had been taken by force from various tribes and individuals was redistributed.

Resident-General Steeg wanted Abd el Krim to be "neither exalted nor humiliated, but in time forgotten." Not unexpectedly, the Spanish Army was furious when it discovered that Abd el Krim had been taken by the French. Spain, General Goded tells us, could never forget or forgive Abd el Krim's "treachery, ingratitude, hatred and inhumanity," even though the Spanish military admired his strength and organizational ability.[26] The Spanish Government vehemently insisted that the Rifian chiefs and their more important lieutenants be handed over as the rightful prizes of Spain, and that Abd el Krim stand trial for his alleged brutality to prisoners.[27] The Rifians, Spain claimed, were natives of the Spanish Zone, and rebels against the Spanish Protectorate; by holding them, France was infringing Article I of the July 13, 1925, agreement, in which France and Spain had promised one another to deal jointly with Abd el Krim. To these demands the French replied that Abd el Krim had chosen to surrender to them, that they had guaranteed his security, and that they would stand by their agreement.

Spain seems to have considered France's refusal to give up Abd el Krim as a black mark against France, an action that spoiled the cooperation between them. Indeed, Spain never seemed to have found exactly the glory she was searching for in Morocco. Her troops had never been able to rout the Rifians unaided, and she had been forced to give up the ultimate prize in the person of Abd el Krim. Furthermore, the French quietly refused to retire from the Geznaya, the Beni Zerwal, and part of the Gezawa tribal areas, all of which had once been included in the Spanish Zone. Spain, who lost territory every time she dealt with France, was apparently so exhilarated by the Alhucemas victory that the French take-over in these areas was allowed to go unchallenged.

The work of occupying the Rif went slowly ahead, for now that the French had gone, the Spaniards were left with a series of tedious mopping-up expeditions. Some of the tribes refused to believe that Abd el Krim had surrendered. Others felt that whether he had or not, they must fight on for their villages. But a few of the tribesmen thought that Abd el Krim's defeat was God's will, and they accepted the termination of the Rifian State with fatalism and without question. Primo de Rivera had the Spanish Army well under control. Discipline was comparatively good, and the dictator's orders were explicit: the Spanish occupation was to be as bloodless as possible. From each captured rebel the Spaniards demanded a rifle in token of submission. There was to be no pillaging, no cruelty, and no reprisals of any kind. As the Spanish moved farther into the interior, a few Rifians, far from resisting, actually joined the Spanish native harkas that they had been battling so fiercely for the last five years.* The Rifians defected to the Spanish for various causes. Some of them hated Abd el Krim and the clique he represented, and saw an opportunity to revenge themselves upon him. Others may have thought that service with Spain was a convenient way to settle long-standing intertribal feuds. Still others may have joined the Spanish for the good that it would do them after peace was declared. It would be interesting to trace the careers of these turncoats and see if they became victims of Rifian retribution.

Most of Abd el Krim's cabinet had surrendered with him, but the

---

* David Hart tells us that the number of Rifians joining the Spaniards was extremely small, that Walter Harris's estimate of 1,500 is too high, and that Rupert Furneaux's statement that 15,000 Urriaglis burned their homes and came to Targuist to surrender is sheer fantasy. There would have been no reason at all for a Rifian to burn his own home, nor was there any point for the Beni Urriaguel to go all the way to a neighboring tribal area to surrender to the Spanish. The Beni Urriaguel stopped fighting where they were, on their own ground. What is more, they pointedly omitted sacrificing a bull in token of submission to the Spaniards, an omission emphasized by the fact that the Geznaya performed this ceremony for the French. Walter Harris goes on to say that the turncoats, whatever their number, proved to be as exceptionally fine combatants on one side as they had been on the other; and he claims that they were particularly valuable in leading the Spanish against hitherto secret rebel lairs in the mountains.

leading Rifian generals, including Ahmed Budra, Haddu n-Muh Amzzyan, and Shaib n-Hammadi, stayed in the Rif. They were eventually offered high offices by the Spanish.[28] Mohamed Wuld Hadj Cheddi, one of Abd el Krim's trusted secretaries, who had been responsible for much of the mistreatment of prisoners at the Tamasint camp in Beni Urriaguel, succeeded in stealing a bag of banknotes from the Abd el Krims during their hectic preparations for surrender at Snada. But such treachery as Cheddi's was rare. Most of the turncoats were simply cutting their risks in the best Moroccan tradition.

Even after Abd el Krim's exile, pockets of resistance remained. In the west, the Jibala dissidents, now without the support of Rifian cadres, fought on under Ahmed Heriro. On May 19, Spanish columns under Lieutenant Colonel Sáez de Larín crossed the River Martín southeast of Tetuan and surrounded Heriro's harka in the mountains near Bu Dara. More than a hundred tribesmen died in the subsequent battle, and every rebel cannon was lost—a rare defeat for the rebels.[29]

In the center of Spanish Morocco, among the cedar trees and the high peaks of Senhadja Srir, a band of diehards fought on under an Akhamlish marabout named Slitan. Some marabouts, who had been despised by Abd el Krim as troublemakers, were now rallying points for those who had decided to continue the struggle. In the southwest, in the Lukus, Lieutenant Colonel Asensio organized a drive through the mountains, the objective of which was to link up with Spanish forces from Tetuan in an effort to retake Chaouen. But the mountains were difficult to maneuver and the Spaniards had to contend with the familiar but formidable problems of summer heat, inadequate supplies, and snipers. It took Asensio more than three months to establish contact with Chaouen. His men fought from June 26 to September 29 through the villages of Taatof, Mexerah, and Draa el Asef before breaking into the Ahmas tribal territory around the target city. By that time, Chaouen had already been bloodlessly repossessed by a special force that struck over the mountains and through the Gomara in what has ever since been termed the Capaz Raid.[30] Major Capaz, a young and able junior officer, had made a surprise landing from the sea in the Wad Lau area at Cala Mestaza. Since he was known and liked by certain Caids of the Gomara tribes, Capaz hoped to capture the Gomara by persuasion rather than by force. He and his detachment of a thousand men started inland from Wad Lau on June 12, and after zigzagging through the rough country of Beni Said, Beni Hassan, and Beni Zeyel, they entered Chaouen on August 10. Not a shot had been fired. Capaz was able to disarm most of the Gomara, collect considerable war matériel, take Chaouen, and demonstrate to the tribesmen that the Spanish could deal fairly. In recognition of his achievement, he was promoted immediately to the rank of lieutenant colonel. After the Capaz Raid, the arrival of the main Spanish force at Chaouen under General Federico Berenguer in mid-September turned out to be an anticlimax.

But in Spain itself, where Primo de Rivera shared in the general jubilation over the course of events in Morocco, a paradox developed. A dictator is seldom popular, and Primo de Rivera was no exception. Although he possessed many excellent qualities, and although he had solved the Moroccan problem, strengthened the Army, promoted the construction of roads and public works, helped labor, and established what he called the Patriotic Union, through which he appealed to all men of good will to band together in order to realize a happier way of life in Spain, he was becoming more and more unpopular. Primo de Rivera meant well for Spain. He was genuinely patriotic, and he had given his proud people more glory than any Spaniard since the Napoleonic Wars. But his government insisted on absolute control of the country's affairs, and this aroused resentment at all levels. Workers' organizations, for example, that were not willing to participate in organized arbitration were ruthlessly suppressed. The press was so badly muzzled that newspapers sometimes appeared spattered with black patches where government censors had ordered words suppressed. Primo de Rivera took such tyrannical measures in the name of Alfonso XIII that the King was contemptuously referred to as "Segundo de Rivera." Finally, feeling the need of a public endorsement, the dictator ordered a sort of plebiscite in an attempt to demonstrate that the Spanish people were still with him.[31] Between September 10 and 13, 1926, his managers succeeded in accumulating 6,700,000 signatures as a vote of confidence, even though, as some critics suggested, it is highly doubtful that that many adults in the whole of Spain knew how to write.

In June, the Government had unearthed a plot against Primo de Rivera led by Lieutenant Generals Valeriano Weyler and Fran-

cisco Aguilera and the Conde de Romanones, who felt that the
dictator was using the Army to support a régime that was becoming
less and less liberal. So as not to make martyrs of the plotters, Primo
de Rivera let the three leaders off with heavy fines; the lesser fry
received prison sentences.[32] He conducted a running fight against
the Spanish Artillery Corps from June through December 1926.[33]
Their complaint was that he had broken his word to them by pro-
moting officers for merit rather than by strict seniority. The dictator, whose own career had been built upon promotions for meritorious conduct, felt that exceptional officers should be promoted
to ranks consistent with their abilities. Nevertheless, as a guarantee
against favoritism, he had agreed to promote only by seniority.
Now he claimed never to have made such a promise. He went
ahead with plans to fill certain vacancies in the various corps by
special selection. The Artillery Corps decided to resist, but Primo
dissolved the Corps entirely before they could carry out their
threats. Some 1,800 Artillerists were suspended from active duty,
and Primo de Rivera retained his role as strong man.

Meanwhile, the mopping-up in Morocco continued. In a two-
pronged invasion late in September, General Castro Girona's columns had passed through Beni Urriaguel and had entered the
Ketama country well to the west. Colonel Pozas led the northern
advance, proceeding due west from Targuist, and Captain Ostariz
led the southern into Senhadja Srir from the southeast. Another
command under Lieutenant Colonel Capaz came on from the
Chaouen area, intending to link up with the other two somewhere
in the Ketama region. In this campaign one of the few high-ranking
rebel turncoats, Caid Dris Mimoun Joya, formerly an aide to Abd
el Krim, personally assisted the Pozas column.[34] By October 1926,
fifty-five of the sixty-six tribes in Spanish Morocco had submitted
entirely, and seven of the remaining eleven had been partially
subdued. Only the Sumata in the Lukus, the Beni Lait in the
Jibala, the Gezawa, and the Beni Ahmed still resisted. Setting
out from Tetuan in November against the Beni Lait, Beni Gorfet,
Beni Aros, and Beni Ider, the Spanish reached Tazrut before
the winter rains set in. In this brief and successful campaign
they bagged Ahmed Heriro, the most impressive leader in the west.
He was shot down in an engagement near the Beni Ider community of Serrama on November 3, and died a few hours later of

a wound in the left kidney.[35] Heriro, who was still under thirty when he died, had been one of Abd el Krim's most imaginative and intelligent lieutenants, and the Spanish had hoped to capture him and perhaps induce him to hold office under the Protectorate. Knowing his own value, and consciously or unconsciously emulating the late Raisuli, Heriro aspired to be nothing less than Caid of the Jibala, and to have a Spanish-paid army at his command. He might have made it, although the days when racketeering chiefs could bluff and outthink the Spanish were gone. The tribesmen carried the dead Heriro off to the mountains of Beni Aros, where he was buried with honor.

By the end of 1926, the Spanish had collected 58,000 rifles, 175 machine guns, 119 cannon of various types, more than 5,000 hand grenades, and much other matériel.[36] Almost all the tribes had submitted, and consequently the Spanish reduced their force in Morocco to less than 90,000 men. The winter passed uneventfully, but on March 26, 1927, the garrison at the small post near Tagsut, in the mountains of Ketama, was suddenly attacked by Slitan's rebels. It took Slitan's Ahmas, Beni Yahmed, and Beni Kalid tribesmen six hours of fighting to do it, but they finally rushed the post and massacred the defending Regulares, leaving only one trooper alive.[37] When Captain Ostariz led a command of 245 men to the relief of Tagsut the next day, he was ambushed near the community of Admam, and he and his entire command were killed. Electrified by this grim news, the Spanish sent columns under Colonel Pozas, Colonel Mola, and Lieutenant Colonel Solans—a total of 7,000 troops—to comb the woods and the valleys for Slitan. A freak blizzard on April 11 stopped all searching operations, and for several days the Spaniards suffered far more casualties from snow, wind, and rain than they did from the rebels, who took advantage of the weather to get in some sniping. This foray by Slitan was his last. Rather than face almost certain capture and probable execution, he and the seven hundred to eight hundred people with him slipped over the zonal borders into French Morocco. The French either could not find him or did not want to, and he and his men disappeared from sight.

There were no more battles and practically no more fighting. All through May and June, Spanish troops crisscrossed the Jibala, the Lukus, and the Senhadja Srir tribal areas, and in the first week of July, the Blad l-Makhzen, for the first time in history, included all of northern Morocco. Spanish Morocco, at last, existed in fact as it had for so long on paper. July 10, 1927, marked the official end of the Rif Rebellion. During the first week of October, the King and Queen of Spain, accompanied by Primo de Rivera, Generals Dámaso Berenguer, Burguete, Franco, and others, made a triumphant tour of the Spanish Protectorate.[38] They arrived at Ceuta on October 5, continued on to Tetuan on the 6th, and arrived at Villa Sanjurjo, the new name of the port above Cala Quemada in the northwest corner of Alhucemas Bay, where the great landing had taken place, on the 7th. With a small party, the King visited Anual and walked among its ruins. On October 9, the royal party was welcomed at Melilla, and on the 10th it returned to Spain. By royal decree, on November 21, 1927, a Moroccan Peace Medal was created.[39] Its inscription read: "Spain, always disposed to every enterprise of universal civilization, contributed to that of Morocco with the precious blood of her sons and the gold of her coffers. The triumph of her arms and the culture of her methods are the foundation of this great work of humanity."

14. ABD EL KRIM'S LEGACY

THE rebellion in the Rif had failed, but only in a military sense. The victory for the allies, on the other hand, while complete, had been a particularly inglorious one. The Spanish were never able to stampede the Rifians into anything like the stinging setbacks which they themselves had suffered at Anual and Chaouen, and the French method of military attrition, although it proved to be excellent strategy against the tribesmen, produced nothing so sensational or spirited as the Rifian assault on the Wergha lines. In spite of Primo de Rivera's capable leadership, a plausible case against the probability of unaided Spanish victory in Morocco could be presented. So long as Spain, largely disorganized and corrupt,* had been the sole opponent of the Rifians, the rebels had had a good chance of winning the war.[1] Had Abd el Krim not joined battle with France, an enemy far more powerful than Spain, it is probable that Spain would have had to settle for an independent Rifian State after all. In the end, victory forged by the European allies was largely a triumph of numbers and technology over courage and stamina.

The motives behind Abd el Krim's assumption of leadership in the Rif were mixed. He himself emerges as a complex and elusive personality. At first, perhaps, the Rifian leader had in mind nothing more than simple vengeance against a country for which he had developed an intense personal hatred. He almost certainly had plans for cooperating with the German financiers interested in utilizing the supposed mineral deposits of the Rifian hinterland. But the expulsion of the Germans after World War I and the en-

* Spain had thirty-nine ministries in the twenty-one years between Alfonso's coming to the throne in May 1902 and Primo de Rivera's seizure of power in September 1923.

croachment of the Spanish Army combined to reduce his chances for personal aggrandizement. Unless the Rif won free of all foreign control, Abd el Krim would gain nothing. But the economy of the Rif was also a motivating factor. When a *Chicago Tribune* reporter asked one of Abd el Krim's Caids why he fought, the Rifian replied simply: "The Rif is poor; we fight to get rich."[2]

Walter Harris felt that the underlying motive for Abd el Krim's rebellion was revenge; but such a sustained, complicated, and intelligently directed undertaking as the Rif Rebellion must surely have been based upon a variety of motives more compelling than mere revenge. Even before Anual, Abd el Krim's ambition had included the formation of an independent state with himself as head. He and his brother were shrewd planners. They may or may not have preferred to attack the Spanish, as they actually did at Abarran and Anual, but it seems certain that sooner or later they would have come into conflict with the Spanish imperialists: General Silvestre's rapid advance toward the central Rif only hastened the inevitable Rifian-Spanish confrontation.

Abd el Krim allegedly said several times that in the event of the Rifians' winning their independence, he would step down and let someone else take over leadership of the government. On the other hand, he seems never to have named a successor. Did Abd el Krim want to become Sultan of Morocco? Almost certainly not. The problems of managing a newly independent state would have been wearing enough without the additional task of subduing and governing an area twenty times larger than the whole Spanish Protectorate.

While Abd el Krim, through force of arms, might have won his way to the governorship of a large part of Morocco, it seems probable that France, with the help of Spain, would have provoked a war with him and brought him to ruin sooner or later. This is precisely what did happen, except that Abd el Krim's government was never formally or officially recognized. Under the Protectorate treaties, the Act of Algeciras, the Mining Law of 1914, and other international treaties—contrived and grossly unfair to the Moroccan people as they were—neither France nor Spain, much less the Sultan, would have dared award the Rifians their independence. Had they won it anyway, the victory would have been temporary. Premier Painlevé of France expressed this idea clearly just after the 1925 peace conference with Abd el Krim had failed. "It is very lucky for France, and also for Spain, that, drunk with victory, he [Abd el Krim] should show himself so arrogant, so intransigent. If peace had been made on the proposed terms, everything indicates that the peace would have proved only a truce."[3] Painlevé went on to point out that France would have been obliged to leave thousands of troops strung out along a lengthy and difficult frontier for an indefinite period. As Douglas Ashford notes, the history of Berber resistance to firm central control, or even to supervision, suggests that coercion would have been used in any case.[4]

An obvious question is whether the Rifians could have maintained or profited from independence if they had achieved it. The dearth of education, the infertility of the land, the extreme poverty of most tribesmen, the persistence of feuds and tribal rivalries, the influence of the marabouts, the manifold details of administration and tax collection necessary to run the government—all these factors lead the observer to doubt that the Rifians could have managed their own affairs. But who can rightly say when a people are ready for self-government? A beginning must be made sometime. If those who want autonomy are willing to fight for it, surely they are entitled to a chance to deal with the problems that accompany freedom. Good government, one of the boons that all imperial powers claim to bring to the peoples of their colonies, is no substitute for self-government. What imperialists and colonialists everywhere cannot admit is that almost anyone would rather be ruled badly by his own kind than well and wisely ruled by outsiders. This held true in the Rif. What else could have furnished the incentive for the Rifians' struggle against their own Moroccan tribal neighbors as well as two modern European nations whose combined populations outnumbered their own a hundred to one, and whose resources were astronomical compared with their own? In Morocco, it was winner-take-all, and the more reckless the game, the more disastrous it was for the loser, who, from the time of the Rogui and long before, through Silvestre and Raisuli, usually paid with his life. Abd el Krim was a fortunate exception. He gambled and lost, and if the Spanish had been able to get their hands on him, he would have been tried and executed.

Abd el Krim blamed his defeat, somewhat surprisingly, on the marabouts, who had a powerful religious influence over the Moroccan people.[5] As a strong believer in orthodox Islam, he considered the worship of saints a destructive and divisive element. "The truth is," Abd el Krim said, "that Islam is an enemy of fanaticisms and superstitions. . . . Islam is furthest removed from sanctifying persons because it enjoins brotherly love and unity before the enemy and encourages men to die for the sake of freedom and independence. . . . The intrigues of these ignorant fanatics [the marabouts] have convinced me that no country where their influence is strong can develop quickly or without resorting to coercion and violence." Abd el Krim claimed too that his own Rifians never understood him. "The upshot of it all is that I have come before my time. . . . I am convinced that all my hopes will come true sooner or later by the force of events and the vicissitudes of the times."

Precisely what did Abd el Krim accomplish? His first effort at unification was necessarily made within his own tribe. To use David Hart's simile, "Like an accordion, the Aith Waryaghar [Beni Urriaguel] could and did squeeze together to play in harmony, but more often than not the keys were damp, the stops pulled out full blast, the instrument was pulled and wrenched apart, and the music ended in a discordant screech. . . . Abd el Krim knew how to play this accordion [and indeed all other local tribal accordions as well]—but nobody else did."[6] Thus the unification of Beni Urriaguel was followed by the gradual inclusion of more and more northern Moroccan tribes into a Rifian State, with a cabinet, an army, and a tax system. Once in control of the Rifian State, Abd el Krim, whose training as a cadi was probably the most important influence in his whole life, meant to bring the 'urf, or total corpus of Rifian customary law, into line with the Sharia, or orthodox Islamic law. The 'urf represented tribal traditionalism. As part of his attempt to model his own government on that of the Sultan's Makhzen, Abd el Krim made the Maliki Islamic legal system official in the Rifian State and appointed new Caids for each tribal faction.

Abd el Krim was as great a reformer as he was a military leader. Among the various reforms that he instituted in the Rif and elsewhere was the obligation to pray five times a day.[7] Any man who did not do this had to serve fifteen to twenty extra days at the front; a woman was fined a chicken. Men had to cut off their traditional scalp locks, to wear some sort of foot covering, and to cut

or trim their beards. Wedding ceremonies were cut from seven to
three days (for the duration of the war only) so that the money
saved could be spent on war matériel. Tribesmen were forced to
give up smoking *kif,* or marijuana; this was no trial for the Rifians,
who hardly touched it, but it hit some of the Jiblis and Gomaris
hard. Even such major institutions as the *liff* system and feuding
were eliminated by Abd el Krim; feuding pillboxes, common to
every Rifian house, had to be torn down. These and other reforms
resulted in a uniformity and a discipline that the northern Moroccans had never before known. Moreover, the Rifian Government indirectly helped the Blad l-Makhzen by doing its work for
it, so that instead of having to conquer the Rif piecemeal, the
Blad l-Makhzen could take over *en bloc.* As a result, until 1956
Spain governed her Moroccan Zone on a pattern laid down not by
her own administrators but by Abd el Krim. The Spanish merely
substituted their own authority for that of the Rifian leader.

A military failure, the Rif Rebellion nevertheless gave the Moroccan tribesmen a feeling of affinity and a first taste of nationalism. The rebellion was also a powerful inspiration to young urban
Moroccan intellectuals in their search for national unity.[8]

An indirect but important result of the rebellion was the destruction of the constitutional government in Spain because of its
inability to deal with Abd el Krim, and the substitution of military for civilian power. Neither Alfonso XIII nor any of his min-
isters or favorite generals were equal to the challenge posed by
Morocco. It remained for a powerful military clique, using Primo
de Rivera as a front, to take over the government of Spain and accomplish the pacification of the Protectorate. Military dictatorship persists in Spain to this day under the leadership of a general
whose character and career were formed during his participation
in the Rif Rebellion.

Abd el Krim's position in history is assured as an indigenous
leader who united and led the tribes of Spanish Morocco where
the Spanish themselves could not, as a reformer who replaced Berber customary law with Koranic law, and as one of Morocco's first
nationalists.

IT IS interesting to trace the lives of prominent figures on both sides of the Rif Rebellion, and to see how closely some of them are linked with events today.

The ex-Sultan Mulay Abd el Aziz died at his villa on the Mountain at Tangier in 1943.

The ex-Sultan Mulay Hafid, who signed the Treaty of Fez with France in 1912, thereby giving France a perpetual protectorate in Morocco, fled the country and lived for awhile at Málaga, on Spain's Costa del Sol. Eventually he moved to Paris, and died at suburban Enghien-les-Bains in 1937.

Sultan Mulay Yussef, who succeeded Hafid, and was the reigning monarch throughout the Rif Rebellion, died in 1927.

The Spanish dictator Primo de Rivera, the man who conquered the rebels in the Rif, resigned at the urging of his associates, and left a nation grown tired of dictatorship. He fled to Paris early in 1930, and died there in March of that year—ill, impoverished, and disillusioned.

Alfonso XIII, the last King of Spain, walked out on a Republic-minded country in 1931. There was no formal abdication: he simply stepped out of his Madrid palace into a waiting car, and drove himself to the southeastern port of Cartagena, just below Valencia. From there a cruiser took him to Marseilles. Queen Eugenia and the royal children departed the day afterward.[1] A Republican Cortes found the king guilty of treason, confiscated his lands, and outlawed him forever. Although Francisco Franco later restored the King's Spanish citizenship and upwards of $8 million in funds and property, and invited him back to Spain, Alfonso never returned. He died at the Grand Hotel in Rome of a heart attack in

February 1941, and is buried outside Madrid at the Escorial. At the time of this writing, Queen Eugenia is still living, in Lausanne, Switzerland.

General Dámaso Berenguer, former High Commissioner, and the soldier who, after Primo de Rivera, achieved more than anyone else in the Protectorate, survived several political fights to emerge as head of the King's Military Household. He was made Conde de Chaouen and finally head of the Spanish Government as Primo de Rivera's successor. After the King's abdication, Berenguer lived quietly until his death in 1953.

General José Sanjurjo tried to lead an insurrection against the government in 1932. Sentenced to be shot for treason, he was later let off with life imprisonment, then released in 1934. En route to General Mola's headquarters to take over as titular leader of the rebel movement in Spain, Sanjurjo was killed when the small plane in which he was riding crashed at the Lisbon airport.

General Francisco Franco, the present Spanish chief of state, followed up his brilliant record during the Rif Rebellion by holding increasingly important positions, until he became Chief of Staff of the Spanish Army in 1935. In the summer of 1936, he and his various associates launched the rebellion that became the Spanish Civil War. Franco emerged as Spain's strong man in 1939. He managed to keep Spain neutral during the Second World War and to entrench himself in the destinies, if not in the hearts, of his people. Opposition to his one-man regime has been vigorous from time to time.

Marshal Hubert Lyautey, the architect of French Morocco, died peacefully at the age of 80 on his estate at Thorey, in the province of Lorraine, France, in July 1934. His ashes were brought back to his beloved Morocco, where they lay in state in a beautiful mausoleum in the Chellah, at Rabat, under the soil of the land he served so well. After Morocco became independent in 1956, his remains were returned to France and interred in Les Invalides in 1961.

Si Mohamed Azerkan, Abd el Krim's Minister of Foreign Affairs, now lives in Tangier. Almost any afternoon he can be seen taking Arab mint tea or coffee at Café de Paris on Tangier's main plaza. Most people are totally unaware of who he is, or was.

Ahmed Budra, Abd el Krim's Minister of War, became Caid of

the lowland Beni Urriaguel under the Spanish. He was still living in the Rif in 1967.

Slitan of Senhadja Srir, the chief who fought the last battles for the Rifians and escaped to the French Zone, came back into the Rif at the end of 1927. Although the Spanish never really trusted him, Slitan was made Caid of Targuist and Beni Mezdui in 1940. He held this post for at least twelve years.

Nobody seems to know exactly what has happened to Joseph Klemms, the picaresque German deserter who fought for Abd el Krim. The Rifians swear that the French killed him, but another story has it that although he was a deserter from the Legion, who had murdered dozens of Frenchmen, he was punished with nothing more than exile from North Africa. Yet a third story says that Klemms was betrayed by a jealous Arab girl and taken in irons to Meknes, where he was court-martialed and sentenced to death, but for some reason this sentence was reduced to eight years' service in the Legion's penal battalion. General Goded says that Klemms tried to get out of the Rif dressed as a tribesman, but that the French caught him.[2] Klemms, who was only about forty-five years old at the time the war ended, may well be alive today.

The Khalifa of Spanish Morocco at Tetuan, Mulay Hassan el Mehdi, held that office from 1925 until the Spanish Protectorate was dissolved in 1956. Always an obliging friend of Spain, he never possessed any real power, either with the Spaniards or with Moroccan nationalists, but he has recently served as Moroccan ambassador to England.

Mohamed ben Abd el Krim el Khattabi, the leader of the Rebellion, died during the night of February 5, 1963, in Cairo. He and his brother and their retinue had lived tranquilly on the island of Réunion for twenty-one years. On several occasions, Abd el Krim made public protestations of friendship for France; he repeatedly asked to be released from his island prison, and he offered his sons to fight for General de Gaulle during World War II. Finally, during the winter of 1947, the French suddenly announced that they were going to allow Abd el Krim, his brother, and some of their retainers to leave Réunion and take up residence on the French Riviera. This announcement was greeted with anger and alarm in Spain, for it was feared that his release would encourage the mounting nationalism in Morocco. The French paid no attention, however, and proceeded with their plans. Abd el Krim was to be lodged on a large estate at Villeneuve, and he was to be free to travel in France, to give interviews, and to receive anyone he pleased. He was to be accompanied by forty-two members of his entourage, and would receive 300,000 francs a month for expenses. In May 1947, Abd el Krim's party left Réunion aboard the *Katoomba*, an Australian ship. On May 31, while the *Katoomba* was held up at Port Said in the Suez Canal, Abd el Krim somehow passed through Egyptian customs, took a taxi to the governor's palace, and requested sanctuary in Egypt. Egyptian Prime Minister Nokrashy Pasha was willing to grant Abd el Krim's request, provided that he would refrain from engaging in political activity while in Egypt. Abd el Krim agreed, and that same day buses and lorries arrived to transport to Cairo the Abd el Krims and their entourage, including the Rifian leader's two wives, his eleven children, and his uncle, together with their baggage and the coffin in which rested the body of Abd el Krim's mother (he hoped, eventually, to give her a Moroccan burial).³ They became guests at the Maghrib House, which had been founded, ironically, by General Franco for the use of Spanish Moroccan students who might be studying in Cairo. For a long time, the Maghrib House had been the center of the Moroccan nationalist movement abroad, and in it such leaders as Allal el Fassi, Abdelhalek Torres, and others talked and planned with other Moroccans as well as with members of the Arab League. Far from staying out of politics, Abd el Krim took charge of the Maghrib House group, while the Egyptians looked the other way.⁴ How and why Abd el Krim and his people were allowed to leave the *Katoomba* has never been satisfactorily explained. The ensuing investigations of the *Katoomba*'s crew at Marseilles revealed nothing. However, one Sidi Mehdi Bennuna, a nationalist from Spanish Morocco, later asserted that Cairo nationalists had engineered the coup.

King Farouk gave Abd el Krim two choice villas in the resort city of Alexandria, a rumored $8,000 a month, and security so long as the Rifians chose to live under the protection of Egypt. Nasser apparently honored Farouk's guarantee. From time to time, Abd el Krim threw verbal thunderbolts at both the French and the Spanish, warning his compatriots not to heed "honeyed promises," but to continue the fight to wrest the Maghrib—not only Morocco,

but all of North Africa as well—entirely out of the hands of foreigners, and never to cease their efforts until they had defeated the
imperialists.

Mhamed Abd el Krim went back to Morocco in September
of 1967 with the intention of spending his last years in the Rif.
While he and his family were waiting at Rabat for their possessions to be transported from Cairo, the Rifian leader suffered
a heart attack, and he died at Rabat's Avicenna Hospital December 17. The body was removed to Ajdir in Beni Urriaguel, where
it was buried with full honors in the presence of various notables.

The Moroccan upheaval of the mid-1950's, which resulted in the
independence of the whole of Morocco, had its antecedents in the
Rif Rebellion. But though Abd el Krim wrote the most glowing
chapter in the saga of Moroccan resistance to European colonial-
ism, he had no part in forming the modern state. In the opinion
of Douglas Ashford, Abd el Krim was a symbol of freedom, but his
lack of monarchical connections—he was not a member of the ruling Alaouite or any other dynasty—and his lack of regard for Islam* alienated the nationalists.[5] Abd el Krim was old; however
memorable his struggle had been, it had failed; he was not only a
Berber in a predominantly Arab country, but a Rifian Berber at
that. A new school of Moroccan patriots had taken over. Men like
Mehdi ben Barka, the shrewd young Leftist, who some believed
would one day oust the royal family and become the real power in
Morocco, Allal el Fassi, and Ahmed Balafrej gradually organized
nationwide resentment against the European "protectors."

The European protectorates had been in their heyday from the
late 1920's through World War II as both the French and the
Spanish gained firm control of their respective areas of Morocco.
It was President Franklin D. Roosevelt's alleged promise to Sultan
Mohamed V at the time of the Casablanca Conference in 1943 that
the Americans would help Morocco obtain her independence that
stoked the fires of Moroccan patriotism. The new Moroccan leadership was focused on the clandestine Istiqlal (Independence) Party, founded at Rabat early in 1944. Urban terrorism, rioting, and

* Since Abd el Krim was a strong Muslim, perhaps Ashford means that the
Rifian was not an advocate of a pan-Islamic movement, and that he was too
willing to intrude Western concepts of government.

open rebellion followed in 1954–55, when the resistance spread to the Rif. In fact, the Geznaya were the center of the Moroccan "Army of Liberation." Today, Moroccans have that independence for which they fought, and for which thousands died. Abd el Krim, far ahead of his time and with only a small fraction of the Moroccan people behind him, could only point the way to national independence, not win it.

The hero of the new Morocco was Sultan Mohamed ben Yussef —King Mohamed V as he became officially in 1957—a meditative, intelligent, hardworking man whose stature grew with the weight of responsibility thrown upon him. Mohamed V was a link with Abd el Krim, since it was his own father who had nominally ruled Morocco during the entire course of the rebellion in the Rif. Mohamed V had been a distant but wholly fascinated observer of Abd el Krim's prodigious effort. Few people thought that the new king was more than just a nice young man until he began quietly opposing French plans for Morocco. Mohamed V became so firm in his public stand against France (for example, in a speech at Tangier in 1947) that the French decided to remove him. He was spirited out of Morocco and sent to exile on the Indian Ocean island of Madagascar on August 20, 1953. From that date onward, he personified the Moroccan struggle for freedom. After an ominous calm of a month or two, blood flowed freely in Morocco for the next two years. France did not have the strength to hold all of North Africa, and she apparently decided that Algeria was the place to take her stand. After a preliminary conference at Paris, which made French Morocco free, the king was brought back from his Madagascar exile in November 1955.* Hundreds of thousands of tribesmen swarmed into Rabat to acclaim him, including all the prominent Rifians. The same scene was repeated when King Mohamed made his first post-exile appearance in Tetuan in April, in Nador and the Rif in July, and in Tangier in September 1957, on which occasion the Tangerinos received him with the most riotous show of affection for a ruling monarch ever seen in northern Morocco.

Unfortunately, the government of the young Moroccan nation, controlled by the Istiqlal until the late 1950's, did not prove satisfactory to the tribesmen of the Rif. The Rifians felt that it was

---

* The French officially handed over their Protectorate on March 2, 1956.

their contribution to the guerrilla fighting in 1955 that swung the balance against France and won independence for Morocco. Strongly pro-monarchy, the Rifians made it clear that it was the Istiqlal Party they resented. With independence, the Istiqlal distributed most of the good jobs to its own members; no Rifians were represented at Rabat. Moreover, instead of fewer taxes, there were more—especially agricultural taxes, which hit hard in the Rif.

In 1957, Spain realized that with the French gone she could never hope to battle alone against the Moroccan nationalists; on April 7 of that year she surrendered the Spanish Protectorate to the Moroccan people. Ironically enough, this concession created new problems of administration. The tribesmen resented and were confused by the overturning of certain official usages to which they had grown accustomed throughout the years of Spanish domination. In place of Spanish bureaucracy, the Spanish language, and Spanish currency, with which they had been familiar for at least fifty years, the Rifians suddenly found that all official communications and all the administration's affairs were being conducted in the French language, and that currency, postage, and other items of everyday use were being printed in French or computed by French systems. Cooperation between government officials and tribal leaders was seriously weakened by this situation. Perhaps the most nettling factor was the presence of so many citizens of Fez, or Fasis, among the new Moroccan officials. The mountaineers disliked the Fasis, whom they accused of stealing governmental positions and mismanaging the country. The Rifians sneeringly refer to Fasis as "women with beards" and generally feel that they have been duped out of any benefits in the very government they fought so keenly to install. When the Rifians spoke out volubly, as they always have, they found the police methods of their own people every bit as brutal and sadistic as those of the Spanish and the French. Rifian victims, allegedly, were given enemas with wet cement, a "torture that even the French could not devise."[6] A uniformed Caid from the South told a French geographer in the Rif late in 1958: "Sure, you can go anywhere you like, as you are French, but I'm a Fasi, and the Rifians will kill me if I set foot outside this house!" Later on, the geographer met a group of Rifians armed with billhooks. After ascertaining that he was French, they told him that he was welcome in their country, and that they were hunting only for "Fasis."[7]

In October 1958, the tribesmen of Beni Urriaguel took the lead in open rebellion against the new Moroccan Government. Two parties rose in the Rif—one called the Popular Movement, and the other called the Rif Movement for Liberation and Liquidation. One of the new leaders of what was called the Central Region was a man named Mohamed Amzzyan, a former notary public of the Aith Bu Ayyash clan of Beni Urriaguel. Another prominent Rifian leader was Abd s-Saddek Sharrat Khattabi, a lawyer and a powerful orator, educated, like Mhamed Abd el Krim, in Madrid. Amzzyan claimed to have sent eighteen petitions to the King without receiving an answer. His most important demand was for the return from exile of the aging Abd el Krim; unless this particular request was fulfilled, all the others were as nothing. Here the situation became complicated, because Abd el Krim himself had reiterated that he would not return to Moroccan soil so long as foreign troops remained based there. In 1958 there were still thousands of French and Spanish soldiers, as well as American airmen, in Morocco.

If the King failed to reply to Amzzyan's plea, as alleged, he nevertheless acted promptly.[8] At the little port of Alhucemas (the former Villa Sanjurjo of the Spanish) the Moroccan Government ceremoniously restored forty-two farms confiscated by the Spanish in 1928 to the family of Abd el Krim. The deeds were handed over to Mohamed Bujibar, Inspector General of the 1920's Rifian Army, and Abd el Krim was officially declared a national hero who would receive a pension from the Moroccan Government for his past "inestimable services." Abd el Krim was even referred to on the Moroccan radio as "Amir," or prince. That was in December 1958. A few weeks later, the situation in the Rif had worsened to the point where the King sent a Royal Commission to the Alhucemas area to investigate complaints. The tribesmen said they resented being shut out of a place in the new government; they did not want to be treated like poor relations. Meanwhile, the new rebels in the Rif were in touch with Algerian guerrillas, and were evidently planning a large-scale uprising. The Rifian leaders said their quarrel was with the politicians and not with King Mohamed V, but the King failed to recognize this distinction. He saw the Rifian rebels as mutineers, and he broadcast a message to them in which he warned of cruel punishment if they did not come to terms within forty-eight hours. Moroccan Air Force planes

scattered reprints of the King's speech over the Rif, and a few of
the dissidents gave themselves up. But an unknown number of
Rifians decided to fight. They blocked the single road leading
from Tetuan eastward into the Rif, surrounded the Royal Army
barracks near Alhucemas, and took a small airport nearby. The
King sent two-thirds of the Royal Army—20,000 troops—into the
mountains under the command of Crown Prince Mulay Hassan,
but even this force, backed up by tanks, artillery, and six rocket-
firing planes, could not dislodge the Rifians. Checked in the mountains, Mulay Hassan decided to emulate the Spanish and land
from the sea at Alhucemas, a task made considerably easier by the
presence of a large contingent of the Spanish Tercio, who were at
least neutral, if not actually friendly to the Royal Army. The
Crown Prince appropriated all the smugglers' boats he could get
his hands on in Tangier Bay, rented a British-owned ferry, and
transported his troops 175 miles through the Mediterranean to
Alhucemas. Meanwhile, commercial aircraft of Royal Air Maroc
were commandeered to fly in supplies. This invasion was quickly
successful, and although the number of casualties on both sides
was considerable, the Rif reverted to the Blad l-Makhzen.

The situation in 1968 is somewhat better, although the Rif is
still considered to be the most unstable part of Morocco. The Government has succeeded in quartering troops at various strategic
points in the Rif, and an economic study of the entire area has
been made. Schools have been built, vineyards have been planted,
and mountain slopes have been terraced for crops. Perhaps the
greatest source of income for the whole area, from the Gomara
through to Alhucemas Bay, is tourism. Chaouen, Ketama, and Alhucemas all have great scenic beauty and pleasant little hotels, and
the rocky, sheer-walled cove at Cala Quemada, where General Goded's troops met such savage resistance during the 1925 Battle of
Alhucemas, today holds a resort complex. Eventually the Rifians
will have to be given a share in the Moroccan Government, although at present their opponents still fall back on the old imperi-
alist argument, insisting that these northern Berbers are altogether
too primitive and uneducated for the complicated task of running
a modern state. There have been rumors that today's Rifian leaders are pan-Arab in sympathy, and as such they have been accused
of receiving money and arms from Egypt, from Algeria, and even

from the Spanish, who now wish to appear as the Arab's friend. Other rumors suggest that a new and far more serious rebellion will get under way when the Rifian leaders and their foreign assistants are ready for it. Meanwhile the Beni Urriaguel have not directly engaged in politics since 1960, and they have solidly abstained from voting in any elections. David Hart says that one reason for this is their refusal to allow their women to vote.[9] The Rif remains a very poor land. The birthrate is high, and unemployment is widespread. But the Moroccan Government appears to be firmly in control—the techniques of control in the modern world heavily favor the government in Morocco—and it seems improbable that Rifian rebels will seriously disturb the Moroccan peace in the near future.

When King Mohamed visited Egypt in February 1960, he called on Abd el Krim and invited the old warrior to return home to the Rif. The newspapers reported that the Rifian leader had accepted the offer and that he would accompany the King back to Morocco. But the King arrived in Rabat in due course, while Abd el Krim remained in Cairo. In an interview granted on February 12, 1960, Abd el Krim said: "I am not concerned about the presence of Spanish and American forces in Morocco. The Americans have agreed to go (the American Air Forces in Morocco pulled out even before the agreed dates) and the Spaniards would follow the French." Revealing that he had experienced a complete change of heart since the 1920's, when he had claimed that his only enemy was Spain, the Rifian went on to explain: "My only fight is with France." And he capped this by stating: "If everything else fails, I shall go back and lead the fighting myself."

King Mohamed V died unexpectedly on February 26, 1961, following a minor operation—an immeasurable loss to Morocco. The Crown Prince, Mulay Hassan, an intelligent and attractive young man, has occupied the throne ever since. Struggling against tremendous problems, King Hassan has given Morocco stability and a degree of progress. In the forty-two years since Abd el Krim has been gone from the Rif, the general order of life among the tribesmen has changed little and Rifian social structure not at all. Labor migration, however, has developed greatly, and since the closing of the Algerian border in 1955, Rifian laborers have migrated in increasing numbers to the cities of Western Europe. In fact, as David Hart suggests, the values that underlay blood feuds have now been transmuted to labor migration. A man does not shoot his neighbor any more: both he and his neighbor go to a large Moroccan or Western European city and get jobs. But life in the Rif seems certain to change radically in the near future, especially in Beni Urriaguel, where the Moroccan Government is already planting the entire Plain of Alhucemas to sugarcane. The central Rif will thus support a new kind of agriculture, and its tribesmen seem destined to change roles from day laborers to a sort of rural proletariat.

Few Spaniards remain in northern Morocco. Tetuan is less bustling and prosperous than it was under Spanish administration. Its various *souks* and its rambling medina, the grand scenery of the valley of the Beni Hassan, and Chaouen, hidden in the mountains, are tourist magnets today. Few tourists know anything at all about the stirring battles fought here in the 1920's. In Tetuan, Chaouen, and Alhucemas, many Moroccan men wear Western dress, often used and shabby. A few of the wealthier men and many of the younger men, impeccably dressed in French or British styles, herald a new and very different order. The old, colorful Morocco is going. Still, as soon as one reaches the hills and mountains behind the cities, urban ways are forgotten; the jellaba, serwal, and turban remain the dress of the mountaineers. Nor have the Rifians lost their superb marksmanship, even though they have not had firearms, officially, since 1926. When a sharpshooting contest for three-month trainees was organized by the Moroccan Royal Army in December 1967, the Rifians proved to be far superior to their rivals from other parts of the country. And the trainees from Beni Urriguel were by far the best shots among the Rifians. These people have not forgotten Abd el Krim.

Until the end, Abd el Krim fulminated against his enemies. As old men will, he embellished the memory of his greatest victories with fanciful detail. In October 1956, W. R. Polk and J. T. Harris, Jr., published an interview with Abd el Krim in the *Atlantic Monthly* magazine supplement, "Perspectives of the Arab World." The Rifian hero gave them a synopsis of his own career. He said that at Anual he waited with a handful of men until the Spanish Army of 22,000, "handsomely dressed troops marching in perfect parade order," advanced right into his midst. He was much more accurate when he stated: "To people all over the Arab world, the Rif Rebellion became a symbol whose meaning can never die. To-day the war in the Rif is thirty-three years old and I am seventy-three. But neither of us, I am sure, has spent our force. The will to freedom does not die, and the determination of our people will outlast the strength of our oppressors."

Abd el Krim was almost certainly wrong in his prediction. The Rif lost its best chance for autonomy under his leadership. In view of the fact that Rifians number, at most, no more than 7 per cent of the population and that modern techniques of control more than ever favor the urban, more educated segment of a nation, it is unlikely that the Rif will ever achieve the freedom and inde-pendence for which Abd el Krim and his rebels fought. The non-Rifian establishment is firmly in command in Morocco. It is im-posing its will upon the Rif, probably for the general good.

But under the stars in the more remote valleys of the Rif, where deep-toned flutes wail and tambourines clash, hawk-faced gray-beards still tell entranced listeners around the flickering fires in the courtyards of Rifian houses about the magnificent years when Frenchmen and Spaniards quaked at the name of Abd el Krim, and the rebels of the Rif were the talk of the world.

NOTES

CHAPTER 1

1. Gibb, p. 13.
2. Le Tourneau, pp. 231–59; see also Barbour, *Morocco*, p. 47.
3. Harris, *France, Spain, and the Rif*, p. 19.
4. Weisgerber, p. 37.
5. Harris, *Morocco That Was*, pp. 40–41, 50.
6. Weisgerber, p. 130.
7. Harris, *France, Spain, and the Rif*, p. 3.
8. Madariaga, p. 265.
9. Landau, p. 71.
10. Harris, *France, Spain, and the Rif*, p. 4.
11. Stuart, p. 61. 12. *Ibid.*, p. 83.
13. Carr, p. 519. 14. Morel, p. 73.
15. Harris discusses the German position in Morocco in detail in *Modern Morocco*, pp. 151–60.
16. Morel, pp. 23–24.
17. Stuart, p. 9.
18. García Figueras, *Marruecos*, p. 106.
19. Stuart, pp. 70–74. 20. Hoffmann, p. 207.
21. McKenzie, p. 69. 22. Hoffmann, p. 202.
23. Weisgerber, p. 181. 24. Harris, *Modern Morocco*, p. 32.
25. Harris, *Morocco That Was*, pp. 298–300.
26. Morel, p. 44. 27. Monteil, p. 56.
28. Mellor, p. 43. 29. Monteil, p. 154.
30. García Figueras, *Marruecos*, p. 110.
31. Azpeitua, p. 31.
32. Marqués de Mulhacén, p. 186.

CHAPTER 2

1. Harris, *France, Spain, and the Rif*, p. 22.
2. David M. Hart, commentary on typescript, November 28, 1966. This chapter is based largely upon the work, published and unpublished, of David Hart and upon conversations with him. Mr. Hart is an American social anthropologist who lived and worked in the Rif in the Beni Urriaguel tribe from 1953 to 1955, and off and on from 1959 to 1965.

3. Hart, "Tribalism," p. 3.

4. Hart, commentary on typescript, November 28, 1966, Tangier.

5. Hart, "An Ethnographic Survey," p. 72.

6. Hart and Erola, "Arabization," p. 5.

7. O'Connor, p. 349.

8. Hart, "Rifian Morals," pp. 486–87.

9. *Ibid.*, pp. 481–90.

10. Hart, "Morocco's Saints and Jinns," pp. 46–53.

11. Gellner, p. 110.

12. Westermarck, p. 12.

13. Montagne, *Les Berbères et le Makhzen*, pp. 239–40. The account of this incident was verified and corrected by David Hart in 1953.

14. Harris, *France, Spain, and the Rif*, pp. 28–32.

15. Coon, *Caravan*, p. 312.

16. Coon, *Tribes of the Rif*, pp. 162–63. Professor Coon's work has been emended by David Hart, who has explained more exactly how the *liff* system works.

17. Hart, in "An Ethnographic Survey," p. 73.

18. Blanco Izaga, p. 80.

19. Biarnay, pp. 219–29.

20. Hart, "Tribalism," p. 5.

21. Harris, *France, Spain, and the Rif*, p. 88.

22. Coon, *Tribes of the Rif*, p. 111.

23. Brooks and Drummond-Hay, p. 164.

24. Monteil, p. 9.

CHAPTER 3

1. García Figueras, in *Marruecos*, pp. 75–96, presents the story of these early Spanish ventures in Morocco in some detail.

2. Ruiz Albéniz, *Ecce Homo*, p. 51.

3. Madariaga, p. 262.

4. Gallagher, p. 74.

5. Alfonso's early years are covered in detail in Graham, pp. 48–192.

6. Payne, pp. 92–93.   7. Carr, p. 475.

8. Fernández Almagro, p. 91.   9. Petrie, p. 235.

10. Payne, p. 106.

11. Eduardo Maldonado's *El Roghi* is an excellent source on this twentieth-century Moroccan Pretender.

12. Hart and Erola, "Arabization," p. 34.

13. García Figueras, *Marruecos*, p. 113.

14. Ruiz Albéniz, *España en el Rif*, p. 19.

15. Fernández Almagro, p. 240.

16. *Ibid.*

17. O'Connor, p. 348.

18. Harris, *Modern Morocco*, p. 74.

19. Maldonado, *El Roghi*, pp. 273–76.

20. Maldonado, *Miscelánea Marroquí*, p. 83.

21. Maldonado, *El Roghi*, pp. 497–504.

22. Fernández Almagro, p. 127.   23. Madariaga, p. 301.

24. Quoted in Payne, p. 109.   25. Brenan, p. 34.

26. Ruiz Albéniz, *España en el Rif*, pp. 120–21.
27. García Figueras, *Marruecos*, pp. 128, 132.
28. Herrera and García Figueras, p. 8.
29. Fernández Almagro, p. 193.
30. García Figueras, *Marruecos*, p. 122; Bastos Ansart, pp. 91, 107; Ruiz Albéniz, *Ecce Homo*, p. 105; Fernández Almagro, p. 385.
31. I. S. Allouche, who bases his statements upon Raisuli's own corresponhdence, is probably the best source on the controversial Raisuli. See also Forbes; Sheean, *An American Among the Riffi*, pp. 278–302; and Harris, *Morocco That Was*, pp. 179–263.
32. See Forbes, pp. xi, 44–47.
33. Allouche, pp. 4–29.
34. Azpeitua, p. 87.
35. Harris, *Morocco That Was*, pp. 185–98.
36. Barbara Tuchman's version of the Perdicaris kidnapping is reliable.
37. Forbes, p. 63.
38. Pryne, p. 40.
39. McKenzie, p. 12.
40. Harris, *France, Spain, and the Rif*, p. 94.
41. Hoffmann, p. 205.
42. Forbes, p. xi.
43. García Figueras, *Marruecos*, p. 124.
44. *Ibid.*, pp. 119–21.
45. Madariaga, p. 303.
46. García Figueras, *Marruecos*, pp. 122, 151–55.
47. Forbes, pp. 151–55.
48. Sanchez Pérez, *La Acción*, p. 48.

CHAPTER 4

1. Payne, p. 115.
2. Mulhacén, pp. 186–87.
3. García Figueras, *Marruecos*, p. 143.
4. Harris, *France, Spain, and the Riff*, p. 98; Payne, p. 155.
5. Vivero, pp. 30–31.
6. Bertrand and Petrie, p. 353.
7. Ruiz Albéniz, *Ecce Homo*, pp. 33–43.
8. Azpeitua, pp. 17–60.
9. Bastos Ansart, pp. 17–30, 200.
10. Aage, p. 19.
11. Barea, pp. 251, 285, 317.
12. García Figueras, *Marruecos*, pp. 143–46.
13. Herrera and García Figueras, p. 183.
14. García Figueras, *Marruecos*, p. 155.
15. Forbes, p. 175.
16. Herrera and García Figueras, p. 200.
17. García Figueras, *Marruecos*, p. 160.
18. Harris, *France, Spain, and the Riff*, p. 102.
19. Harris, *Morocco That Was*, p. 243.
20. García Figueras, *Marruecos*, p. 162.
21. Herrera and García Figueras, pp. 73, 232.
22. Harris, *France, Spain, and the Riff*, p. 106; Roger-Matthieu, p. 62.

23. García Figueras, *Marruecos,* p. 164.

24. Both Forbes (pp. 281–85) and Harris (*France, Spain, and the Riff,* p. 108) relate this incident. Harris adds that the Moroccans wore gas masks, used poison gas, and leisurely stabbed the Spaniards to death without firing a shot, but this is unsubstantiated.

25. Ruiz Albéniz, *Ecce Homo,* p. 84.

26. Herrera and García Figueras, p. 243.

27. *Enciclopedia Universal* (Apendice, Tomo 2), pp. 123–24.

28. García Figueras, *Marruecos,* p. 167.

29. Ruiz Albéniz, *Ecce Homo,* pp. 105–6.

30. Vivero, p. 44.

31. Fernández Almagro, p. 386.

32. Bastos Ansart, p. 92.

33. Ruiz Albéniz, *Ecce Homo,* p. 105.

34. Arrarás, *Historia de La Cruzada Española,* p. 97.

35. Silva, pp. 108–38.

36. Pryne, p. 119.

37. Thomas, p. 272.

38. Azpeitua, p. 60.

39. Thomas, p. 59.

40. Turnbull, p. 27.

41. Valdesoto, pp. 14–23.

42. Coles, pp. 117, 124.

43. Barea, pp. 365–66.

44. Pryne, p. 122.

45. Harris, *France, Spain, and the Riff,* p. 111.

46. Herrera and García Figueras, p. 283.

47. Barea, p. 284.

48. Azpeitua, pp. 23–42.

49. Herrera and García Figueras, pp. 291–97, 307–19.

50. Ruiz Albéniz, *España en el Rif,* p. 207.

51. Fernández Almagro, p. 385.

52. Carr, p. 520.

CHAPTER 5

1. The information given here is taken largely from the works of David Hart; Andrés Sánchez Pérez, one of the few men who knew the Rif and the Rifians well; Roger-Matthieu, who interviewed Abd el Krim after the rebellion; and Vincent Sheean, who interviewed both brothers in the Rif during the winter of 1924–25.

2. Sánchez Pérez, "Abd el Krim," p. 62.

3. Roger-Matthieu, p. 55.

4. Shinar, p. 160.

5. Hart, letter, August 27, 1966. Omar Ibn Nasser, p. 97, says that the Abd el Krims originally came from the Hejaz.

6. Furneaux, p. 44.

7. Roger-Matthieu, p. 69.

8. Shinar, p. 162.

9. Hart, quoting Blanco Izaga's files in a letter dated April 23, 1967.

10. Benoist-Méchin, p. 83.

11. Harris, *Modern Morocco,* p. 216.

12. Herrera and García Figueras, p. 311.

13. Sánchez Pérez, "Abd el Krim," pp. 67–68.

14. Payne, p. 162, quoting Ruiz Albéniz, in *Tánger y la colaboración franco-española en Marruecos* (Madrid, 1927).

15. Roger-Matthieu, p. 65.

16. Herrera and García Figueras, p. 311, quote a letter from the Duque de G. See also Sánchez Pérez, "Abd el Krim," p. 69.

17. Sánchez Pérez, "Abd el Krim," p. 68; Sánchez Pérez places the escape attempt in December 1915. The Payne–Ruiz Albéniz date of 1917 or 1918 seems more logical.

18. Roger-Matthieu, p. 65.

19. Benoist-Méchin, pp. 82–83.

20. Bastos Ansart, pp. 204–5.

21. Roger-Matthieu, p. 86.

22. Powell, p. 367.

23. Gómez Hidalgo, p. 153.

24. Hart, oral communication, December 13, 1966.

25. Eza, p. 132.

CHAPTER 6

1. Eza, pp. 227–32; Vivero, p. 131; Herrera and García Figueras, *Documentos*, p. 114.

2. Vivero, p. 76.

3. Ruiz Albéniz, *Ecce Homo*, p. 238; Berenguer, pp. 17–22.

4. Vivero, p. 100.

5. Eza, p. 212.

6. Maldonado, *Miscelánea Maroquí*, p. 72; Fernández Almagro, p. 407.

7. Gómez Hidalgo, p. 153.

8. Payne (p. 498), quoting San Martín Losada, *Sueldos* (1927), and San Martín Losada and San Martín, *Almanaque del Militar 1951*. Roughly calculated in American dollars, annual salaries for Spanish Army officers from 1920 to 1926 were as follows: Captain Generals, $4,300; Lieutenant Generals, $3,600; Major Generals, $3,000; Brigadiers, $2,140; Colonels, $1,430; Lieutenant Colonels, $1,140; Majors, $930; Captains, $643; 1st Lieutenants, $500; and 2d Lieutenants, $430.

9. Eza, pp. 173–92.

10. *Ibid.*, pp. 96–121.

11. Stuart, p. 232.

12. Gómez Hidalgo, pp. 153, 156.

13. Roger-Matthieu, p. 92.

14. Herrera and García Figueras, pp. 310–14.

15. Benoist-Méchin, p. 83.

16. Bertrand and Petrie, p. 353.

17. Berenguer, pp. 37–39.

18. Sencourt, p. 323.

19. Herrera and García Figueras, p. 319.

20. Cabello Alcaraz, p. 282.

21. Bastos Ansart, p. 137.

22. Usborne, p. 250.

23. Morel, p. 14.

24. Vivero, p. 125.

25. Berenguer, p. 74.

26. Bertrand and Petrie, p. 354.

27. Herrera and García Figueras, p. 327.

28. Bastos Ansart, pp. 141–44; Herrera and García Figueras, *Documentos*, p. 123.

29. Ortega y Gasset, p. 37.

30. Detailed incidents of the Anual disaster are found in a large number of references, among them Herrera and García Figueras; Bastos Ansart; Vivero; Ruiz Albéniz, *Ecce Homo;* Harris, *France, Spain, and the Riff;* and Fernández Almagro.

31. Sencourt, p. 325.

32. Conversation with Mohamed Azerkan, Hotel España, Villa Sanjurjo (Alhucemas), February 16, 1959.

33. Roger-Matthieu, p. 105.
34. Payne, p. 169.
35. Azpeitua, p. 83.
36. Silva, p. 24.
37. Herrera and García Figueras, p. 365.
38. *Ibid.*, p. 364; and *Documentos*, p. 125.
39. Pryne, p. 189.
40. Brenan, p. 61.
41. Barea, p. 352.
42. Harris, *France, Spain, and the Riff*, p. 83.
43. Vivero, p. 139.   44. Barea, p. 286.
45. Azpeitua, p. 175.   46. Pryne, p. 198.
47. Madariaga, p. 170.
48. Azpeitua, pp. 114–19; Barea, pp. 275–79.
49. Vivero, pp. 139–47.
50. Goded Llopis, p. 114.
51. Brenan, p. 75.
52. Sencourt (p. 325) reports two telegrams, but Fernández Almagro (p. 385), a much more reliable source, reports a single telegram reading: "Olé los hombres. El 25 te espero."
53. Fernández Almagro, p. 410; Barea, pp. 319–24.
54. Harris, *France, Spain, and the Riff*, p. 77.

CHAPTER 7

1. Berenguer, p. 109.
2. Barea, p. 306.
3. Harris, *France, Spain, and the Riff*, p. 72.
4. Arrarás, *Franco*, p. 72.   5. Berenguer, p. 111.
6. Arrarás, *Historia*, p. 117.   7. Pryne, p. 101.
8. Valdesoto, p. 34.
9. Herrera and García Figueras, p. 415.
10. *Ibid.*, pp. 433–35.   11. Pryne, p. 112.
12. Eza, p. 133.   13. Fernández Almagro, p. 411.
14. Payne includes a thorough discussion of the juntas de defensa, pp. 123–51, and pp. 182–83. Also see Carr, pp. 500, 560–61.
15. Silva, p. 175.
16. Carr, p. 521.
17. Pryne, p. 128.

CHAPTER 8

1. García Figueras, *Marruecos*, p. 189.
2. Letter from David Hart, April 18, 1967, Tangier. Roger-Matthieu, p. 107, erroneously places the Abd el Krim proclamation on February 1, 1922, but Hart gives the correct date—14 Jumada II on the Arabic lunar calendar, or February 1, 1923.
3. *Enciclopedia Universal Ilustrada*.

4. Madariaga, p. 337.
5. Valdesoto, p. 40.
6. Sheean, *An American Among the Riffi*, p. 164.
7. Bartels, p. 108.
8. Hart and Erola, pp. 46–47.
9. Payne, pp. 208–9.
10. Harris, *France, Spain, and the Riff*, pp. 249–52.
11. Stuart, p. 118.
12. Pryne, p. 140.
13. Fernández Almagro, p. 430.
14. Aunós, pp. 9–37.
15. Mulhacén, p. 188.
16. Payne, pp. 192–96.
17. Aunós, pp. 53–54.
18. Fernández Almagro, p. 441.
19. Brenan, p. 79.
20. Sencourt, p. 193.
21. Madariaga, p. 342.
22. Thomas, p. 37.
23. Brenan, p. 79.
24. García Figueras, *Marruecos*, p. 199.
25. Forbes, p. 68.
26. Mellor, pp. 85–86.
27. Roger-Matthieu, p. 182.
28. Hernández Mir, pp. 13–14.
29. Herrera and García Figueras, p. 476.

CHAPTER 9

1. Herrera and García Figueras, p. 467.
2. García Figueras, "Ahmed ben Mohamed el Hosmari," pp. 77, 99–102.
3. Herrera and García Figueras, p. 461.
4. Oral communication from Mohamed Azerkan, Hotel España, Villa San-jurjo (Alhucemas), February 16, 1959.
5. Arrarás, *Franco*, p. 99.
6. Miller, p. 159.
7. Barea, p. 416; Payne, pp. 211–12.
8. Arrarás, *Franco*, p. 100.
9. *Ibid.*, p. 104.
10. Fernández Almagro, p. 459.
11. *Ibid.*, p. 462.
12. Bertrand and Petrie, p. 356.
13. Fernández Almagro, p. 295.
14. Eza, p. 512.
15. Vivero, pp. 126, 131.
16. García Figueras, *Marruecos*, p. 203.
17. Montagne, *Révolution au Maroc*, p. 156.
18. Petrie, p. 226.
19. Barea, p. 317.
20. Payne, p. 199.
21. Herrera and García Figueras, p. 541.
22. Harris, *France, Spain, and the Riff*, p. 142.
23. Barea, p. 407.
24. Arrarás, *Franco*, p. 104.
25. Harris, *France, Spain, and the Riff*, p. 141.
26. Payne, pp. 213–14.
27. Sheean, *An American Among the Riffi*, pp. 309–29.
28. Goded Llopis, p. 109.
29. Pryne, p. 187.
30. Harris, *France, Spain, and the Riff*, p. 147; Fernández Almagro, p. 464; Barea, p. 407.

31. Herrera and García Figueras, p. 539.

32. Pryne, p. 195.

33. Sheean, *An American Among the Riffi*, pp. 173–86, 232–43, 283–88.

CHAPTER 10

1. Two excellent discussions of the Rifian wartime government and military organization appear in Goded Llopis, pp. 85–103, and Gabrielli, pp. 41–52. Together with David Hart's written and oral comments and his notes from Emilio Blanco Izaga's files, they form the basis of this chapter.

2. Sheean, *An American Among the Riffi*, p. 178.

3. *Ibid.*, p. 240.

4. Pryne, p. 143; Hart, letter, April 26, 1967.

5. Hart, commentary on typescript, November 28, 1966, Tangier.

6. Sánchez Pérez, "Abd el Krim," p. 75.

7. Hart, letter, April 21, 1967. This incident was noted in the files, dated 1928, of Emilio Blanco Izaga. He places the killings in 1920–21; but Hart's Rifian sources put them in the spring of 1925, just before Abd el Krim attacked the French. The Blanco files, which consist of information given him by various Rifians, include a report by Captain Santiago Mateo, dated September 5, 1927, claiming that these two chiefs and their men were shot, not stoned, to death. Hart, who now owns the files, suggests that if the men were stoned to death, it was in order to save ammunition.

8. Shinar, pp. 168–72.

9. Goded Llopis, p. 103; Monteil, p. 154; Brémond, pp. 141–42; Manuel and Armiñán, p. 125. Abd el Krim himself seems not to have given a definite figure.

10. Sheean, *An American Among the Riffi*, p. 146.

11. Vincent Sheean talked with Klemms on several occasions. See *An American Among the Riffi*, pp. 254–77; and P. C. Wren's short story, "Odo Klemmens" was based upon the German's career.

12. Roger-Matthieu, p. 114.

13. Hart, letter, September 19, 1966, Tangier.

14. Pryne, p. 152.

15. Prince Aage, p. 87.

16. Van Paassen, pp. 261–62.

17. Pryne, p. 186. Although there certainly was brisk smuggling of guns into the Rif, it seems unlikely that any *one* delivery would have consisted of 16,000 rifles. Perhaps Pryne means that the *total* number of rifles smuggled was 16,000.

18. Sheean, *An American Among the Riffi*, p. 183.

19. Goded Llopis, p. 82.

20. Gabrielli, p. 19.

21. Sheean, *An American Among the Riffi*, p. 174.

22. Hart, letter, September 19, 1966, Tangier.

23. Shinar, pp. 167, 173.

24. Pryne, p. 9.

25. Sheean, *An American Among the Riffi*, p. 184.

26. *Tangier Gazette*, May 2, 1924.

27. Roger-Matthieu, p. 184; the Harris version in *France, Spain, and the Rif*, for once, sounds more logical and accurate.

28. Sheean, *An American Among the Riffi*, p. 185.

CHAPTER 11

1. Harris, *France, Spain, and the Riff*, p. 151.
2. *Ibid.*, p. 150.
3. Hart, letter, April 26, 1967, quoting an interview held in 1932 between Emilio Blanco Izaga and Si Muhand n-Si Hmid nj-Mqaddim, of Temsaman.
4. Sheean, *An American Among the Riffi*, p. 297.
5. Fernández Almagro, p. 473.
6. Hart, letter, April 26, 1967; see note 3.
7. Harris, *France, Spain, and the Riff*, pp. 153–54.
8. Hoffmann, p. 214.
9. Harris, *France, Spain, and the Riff*, p. 188.
10. Gabrielli, pp. 3–4.
11. Harris, *France, Spain, and the Riff*, p. 208.
12. Sheean, *An American Among the Riffi*, p. xvii.
13. Maurois, p. 267.   14. Pryne, p. 17.
15. Landau, p. 92.   16. Harris, *Modern Morocco*, p. 35.
17. Knight, pp. 58–62.
18. Montagne, *Révolution au Maroc*, pp. 76–78, 134–35.
19. Jaques, p. 64.   20. López Rienda, p. 158.
21. Benoist-Méchin, pp. 86–87.   22. Pryne, p. 202.
23. Usborne, p. 268.   24. Pryne, p. 204.
25. Roger-Matthieu, p. 23.
26. Harris, *France, Spain, and the Riff*, pp. 153–54.
27. Hart, letter, April 18, 1967. Hart cites a communication he received from Kenneth Brown, who talked to Muhammed Hassan l-Wazzani in Fez in the spring of 1967. The statement is Wazzani's, Wazzani having lived in Cairo for five years, 1951–56, and having known Abd el Krim well there. He visited the Rifian hero often, was apparently the only man ever allowed to read Abd el Krim's autobiography, and reported that, for some obscure reason, Abd el Krim would not allow the autobiography to be published.
28. Shinar, p. 166.
29. Herrera and García Figueras, p. 549.

CHAPTER 12

1. Goded Llopis, p. 116.
2. Quoted by Furneaux, p. 162.
3. Harris, *France, Spain, and the Riff*, p. 214.
4. Hart, in letter of March 15, 1967, quoting André Adam of the Sociology Department of the University of Aix-en-Provence. In letter of April 18, 1967, Hart quotes Kenneth Brown as writing that his informant claimed a pro-Rifian group of young Fasis did much propagandizing for Abd el Krim in Fez in 1925.
5. Spillman, p. 36.   6. López Rienda, p. 143.
7. Furneaux, p. 185.   8. Jaques, p. 250.
9. López Rienda, p. 175.   10. Jaques, pp. 157–58.
11. López Rienda, p. 37.   12. Voinot, pp. 296–97.
13. Usborne, pp. 275–76.

14. García Figueras, *Marruecos*, pp. 205–6.
15. Gabrielli, pp. 81–91.
16. Harris, *France, Spain, and the Riff*, p. 235.
17. López Rienda, p. 25.
18. Usborne, p. 283.
19. Harris, *France, Spain, and the Riff*, p. 235.
20. Manuel and Armiñán, pp. 129–38.
21. Pryne, p. 216.   22. Tangier Gazette.
23. Van Paassen, p. 259.   24. Prince Aage, p. 85.
25. Voinot, p. 284.   26. Usborne, p. 277.
27. Pryne, p. 221.   28. Usborne, p. 281.
29. Jaques, pp. 291–95.   30. Pryne, p. 221.
31. Manuel and Armiñán, p. 146.   32. Laure, p. 84.
33. Manuel and Armiñán, pp. 174–82.
34. Herrera and García Figueras, pp. 573, 579–80.
35. Goded Llopis, p. 219.   36. Pryne, p. 227.
37. Coles, pp. 126–27.   38. *Enciclopedia Universal*.
39. Hart, letter, April 26, 1967, quoting an interview held in 1932 between Emilio Blanco Izaga and Si Muhand n-Si Hmid nj-Mqaddim, of Temsaman.
40. Herrera and García Figueras, p. 584.
41. Hoffmann, p. 221.   42. Knight, p. 62.
43. Usborne, p. 291.   44. Jaques, p. 312.
45. Selous, p. 210; Maurois, pp. 276–77.
46. Maurois, p. 239.
47. Knight, p. 62.
48. Laure, p. 103.
49. Herrera and García Figueras, p. 206.
50. Laure, p. 140.

CHAPTER 13

1. Herrera and García Figueras, p. 608.
2. Harris, *France, Spain, and the Riff*, p. 173.
3. Herrera and García Figueras, p. 611.
4. Harris, *France, Spain, and the Riff*, pp. 279–97.
5. Sánchez Pérez, "Abd el Krim," p. 62.
6. Prince Aage, p. 56.
7. Letter from David Hart, April 18, 1957, quoting Blanco Izaga's files.
8. Sheean, *An American Among the Riffi*, p. 171.
9. Azpeitua, p. 135; Harris, *France, Spain, and the Riff*, p. 165.
10. Turnbull, p. 28.
11. Maxwell, p. 99.
12. Roger-Matthieu, p. 80.
13. Harris, *France, Spain, and the Riff*, p. 300.
14. Miller, p. 162.
15. Letter from Curt Day, June 11, 1962, Tangier.
16. Harris, *France, Spain, and the Riff*, p. 300.
17. Hernández Mir, pp. 96–97.
18. Herrera and García Figueras, p. 618.
19. Shinar, p. 171.

20. Hernández Mir, pp. 208–14.
21. Montagne, *Les Berbères et Le Makhzen,* pp. 403–4.
22. Sánchez Pérez, "Abd el Krim," p. 74.
23. Brémond, pp. 126–29.
24. Montagne, *Révolution au Maroc,* p. 166.
25. Hernández Mir, pp. 194–201.
26. Goded Llopis, p. 104.
27. Hernández Mir, pp. 194–201.
28. Hart, April 18, 1967, letter quoting Blanco Izaga's files.
29. Herrera and García Figueras, p. 619.
30. Goded Llopis, pp. 330–36.   31. Fernández Almagro, p. 497.
32. Ballesteros, pp. 620–22.   33. Payne, pp. 237–40.
34. Goded Llopis, p. 345.
35. García Figueras, "Ahmed ben Mohamed el Hosmari el Jeriro," p. 107.
36. Herrera and García Figueras, p. 638.
37. Goded Llopis, pp. 369–88.
38. Fernández Almagro, p. 502.
39. Herrera and García Figueras, p. 632.

CHAPTER 14

1. Madariaga, p. 363.   2. López Rienda, p. 127.
3. Pryne, p. 220.   4. Ashford, pp. 27–29.
5. Shinar, pp. 172–73.
6. Hart, "Clan, Lineage, Local Community, and the Feud in a Rifian Tribe,"
p. 100. This whole paragraph derives largely from the investigations of David
Hart.
7. Hart and Erola, pp. 60–62.
8. Shinar, p. 174.

CHAPTER 15

1. Sencourt, pp. 230–31.
2. Goded Llopis, p. 89.
3. *The Times* (London), June 2, 1947.
4. Barbour, *A Survey of Northwest Africa,* p. 153.
5. Ashford, pp. 27–29.
6. *Time,* December 22, 1958, and January 26, 1959, discusses the 1958–59
Rifian troubles in some detail.
7. Hart, letter, March 15, 1967, quoting André Adam.
8. *Time,* December 22, 1958.
9. David Hart, personal communication to author, November 28, 1966.

BIBLIOGRAPHY

Aage, Prince of Denmark. My Life in the French Foreign Legion. London, 1928.

Allouche, I. S. Documents relatifs à Raisuni. Paris, 1951.

Arrarás, Joaquín. Franco. Burgos, 1938.

Arrarás, Joaquín, ed. Historia de la cruzada española. 8 vols. Vol. I, Madrid, 1940.

Ashford, D. E. Political Changes in Morocco. London, 1961.

Aunós [y Pérez], Eduardo. Primo de Rivera: soldado y gobernante. Madrid, 1944.

Azpeitua, Antonio. Marruecos, la mala semilla; ensayo de análisis objetivo de cómo fué sembrada la guerra en Africa. Madrid, 1921.

Ballesteros y Beretta, Antonio. Historia de España y su influencia en la historia universal. 9 vols. Vol. VIII, Barcelona, 1946.

Barbour, Nevill. A Survey of Northwest Africa. Oxford, 1959.

——— Morocco. London, 1962.

Barea, Arturo. The Forging of a Rebel. New York, 1946.

Bartels, Albert. Fighting the French in Morocco. London, 1932.

Bastos Ansart, Francisco. El desastre de Anual. Barcelona, 1922.

Beneitez Cantero, Valentín. Sociología Marroquí. Tetuan, 1952.

Benoist-Méchin, Baron Jacques G. P. M. "Lyautey et la guerre du Rif." Miroir de l'Histoire (April 1967), 82–91.

Berenguer, Dámaso. Campañas en el Rif y Yebala 1919–1920. Madrid, 1925.

Bermudo-Soriano, Eliseo. El Raisúni, caudillo de Yebala. Madrid, 1941.

Berque, Jacques. Le Maghreb entre deux guerres. Paris, 1962.

Bertrand, Louis, and Sir Charles Petrie. The History of Spain. London, 1934.

Biarnay, B. "Uncas de régression vers la coutume berbère chez une tribu arabisée. Archives Berbères, Vol. I, No. 4 (Paris, 1916), pp. 219–29.

Blanco Izaga, Emilio. El Rif. Ceuta, 1939.

Brémond, General Edouard. Berbères et Arabes: La Berbérie est un pays européen. Paris, 1950.

Brenan, Gerald. The Spanish Labyrinth: An Account of the Social and Political Background of the Civil War. Cambridge, England, 1934.

Brooks, L. A. E., and Miss Drummond-Hay. A Memoir of Sir John Drummond-Hay. London, 1896.

Bulletin de l'Enseignement Public du Maroc. "Rif et Jibala." No. 71 (January 1926).

Cabello Alcaraz, José. Historia de Marruecos. Tetuan, 1954.

Carr, Raymond. Spain: 1809–1939. Oxford, 1966.

Coles, S. F. A. Franco of Spain. London, 1925.

Cooley, John K. Baal, Christ, and Mohammed: Religion and Revolution in North Africa. New York, 1965.

Coon, Carleton. Caravan. London, 1952.

—— Flesh of the Wild Ox. London, 1932.

—— Tribes of the Rif. Cambridge, Massachusetts, 1931.

Damidaux, Captain Charles Joseph. Combats au Maroc, 1925–1926. Paris, 1928.

Drague, Georges. Esquisse d'histoire religieuse du Maroc. Cashiers de l'Afrique et de l'Asie, Vol. II. Paris, 1951.

Enciclopedia Universal Ilustrada. Madrid, 1932.

Eza, Vizconde de. Mis responsabilidades en el desastre de Melilla como Ministro de la Guerra. Madrid, 1923.

Fassi, Allal al. The Independence Movements in Arab North Africa. Washington, 1954.

Fernández Almagro, Melchor. Historia del reinado de Don Alfonso XIII. Barcelona, 1936.

Forbes, Rosita. The Sultan of the Mountains. New York, 1924.

Franco, Francisco. Diario de una Bandera. Madrid, 1922.

Furneaux, Rupert. Abdel Krim. London, 1967.

Gabrielli, Léon. Abd-el-Krim et les événements du Rif, 1924–1926. Casablanca, 1953.

Gallagher, Charles. The United States and North Africa. Cambridge, Massachusetts, 1963.

García Figueras, Tomás. "Ahmed ben Mohamed el Hosmari el Jeriro," in Misceláneo de estudios varios sobre Marruecos. Tetuan, 1933.

—— Marruecos: la acción de España en el norte de Africa. Madrid, 1944.

Garratt, G. T. Gibraltar and the Mediterranean. London, 1939.

Gellner, Ernest. "Tribalism and Social Change in North Africa," in W. H. Lewis, ed., French-Speaking Africa: The Search for Identity. New York, 1965.

Gibb, H. A. R. Mohammedanism. New York, 1958.

Goded Llopis, General Manuel. Marruecos: las etapas de la pacificación. Madrid, 1932.

Gómez Hidalgo, Francisco. Marruecos: la tragedia prevista. Madrid, 1921.

Graham, Evelyn. The Life Story of King Alfonso XIII. London, 1930.

Harris, Walter B. France, Spain, and the Riff. London, 1927.

—— Modern Morocco, Bank of British West Africa. Tangier, 1919.

—— Morocco That Was. Edinburgh, 1921.

Hart, David M. "Clan, Lineage, Local Community, and the Feud in a Rifian Tribe," in Louise Sweet, ed., A Reader in Middle Eastern Anthropology, New York, 1967.

—— "Emilio Blanco Izaga and the Berbers of the Central Rif." Revista de Investigaciones Marroqui, Vol. VI, No. 2 (Tamuda, 1958), pp. 171–237.

—— "An Ethnographic Survey of the Rifian Tribe of Aith Waryaghar, Tamuda." Revista de Estudios Marroqui, Año II, Semestre I (Tetuan, 1954), pp. 51–86.

—— "Morocco's Saints and Jinns." Tomorrow Magazine, Vol. VII, No. 1 (1959), pp. 45–54.

—— "Rifian Morals," in V. Ferm, ed., Encyclopedia of Morals, New York, 1956, pp. 481–90.

—— "Tribalism: The Skeleton in the Moroccan Closet." Unpublished paper. Marrakech, 1966.

Hart, David M., and José Erola. "The Arabization of a Berber Political System." Unpublished paper. Marrakech, 1967.

Hernández Mir, Francisco. Del desastre a la victoria. Madrid, 1926.

Herrera, Carlos, and Tomás García Figueras. Acción de España en Marruecos. Madrid, 1929. Also a second volume of Documentos.

Hoffmann, Eleanor. Realm of the Evening Star. Philadelphia, 1965.

Howe, Quincy. A World History of Our Times. New York, 1949.

Ibáñez de Ibero, Carlos, Marqués de Mulhacén. Política mediterránea de España, 1704–1951. Madrid, 1952.

Illustrated London News, 1921–26.

Jaques, Hubert. L'Aventure riffaine et ses dessous politiques. Paris, 1927.

Knight, Melvin. Morocco's French Economic Venture. New York, 1937.

The Koran, translated by J. M. Rodwell. Everyman's Library. London, 1948.

Lahbabi, Mohamed. Le Gouvernement marocain à l'aube du XXe siècle. Rabat, 1957.

Landau, Rom. Morocco Drama. London, 1956.

Laure, Lieutenant Colonel Auguste. La Victoire Franco-Espagnole dans le Rif. Paris, 1927.

Le Tourneau, Roger. "North African Rigorism and Bewilderment," in Gustave Von Grunebaum, ed., Unity and Variety in Muslim Civilization. Chicago, 1955.

López Rienda, Rafael. Abd-el-Krim contra Francia: impresiones de un cronista de guerra. Madrid, 1925.

McKenzie, Donald. The Khalifate of the West. London, 1911.

Madariaga, Salvador de. Spain: A Modern History. New York, 1958.

Maldonado, Eduardo. El Roghi. Tetuan, 1952.

—— Miscelánea Maroquí. Ceuta, 1953.

—— Retazos de historia marroquí. Tetuan, 1955.

Manuel, José, and Luis de Armiñán. Francia, el Dictador y el Moro: páginas históricos. Madrid, 1930.

Maurois, André. Lyautey. Paris, 1931.

Maxwell, Gavin. Lords of the Atlas. London, 1966.

Meakin, Budgett. The Moors. London, 1902.

Mellor, Frank. Morocco Awakes. London, 1939.

Miller, Webb. I Found No Peace. New York, 1936.

Montagne, Robert. Les Berbères et la Makhzen au sud du Maroc. Paris, 1930.

—— Révolution au Maroc. Paris, 1953.

Monteil, Victor. Morocco. London, 1964.

Morel, E. D. Morocco in Diplomacy. London, 1912.

Mulhacén, Marqués de. See Ibáñez de Ibero.

Muliéras, Auguste. Le Maroc inconnu. Vol. I, Exploration du Rif. Paris, 1895.

Nasser, Omar Ibn. Hero of the Rif. Beirut, 1944. (In Arabic; translated into Spanish for the author by Abdeslam Ben Thami, Tangier, 1967.)

O'Connor, Scott. A Vision of Morocco. London, 1923.

Ortega y Gasset, Eduardo. Annual. Madrid, 1922.

Payne, Stanley G. Politics and the Military in Modern Spain. Stanford, California, 1967.

Petrie, Sir Charles. The Spanish Royal House. London, 1955.

Polk, William R., et al. "Perspective of the Arab World." Atlantic Monthly, Vol. 198, No. 4 (October 1956), pp. 121–92.

Powell, Edward. In Barbary. New York, 1926.

Pryne, Rudyers. War in Morocco. Tangier, 1927.

Roger-Matthieu, J. Mémoires d'Abd-el-Krim. Paris, 1927.

Ruiz Albéniz, Victor. Ecce homo: las responsabilidades del desastre. Madrid, 1922.

—— España en el Rif: Estudios del indígena y del país. Madrid, 1921.

Sánchez Pérez, Andrés. "Abd el Krim," in Selección de conferencias y trabajos realizados por la Academia de Interventores durante el curso 1949–50. Tetuan, 1950.

—— La Acción decisiva contra Abd el Krim. Toledo, 1931.

Selous, G. H. Appointment to Fez. London, 1956.

Sencourt, Robert. Spain's Uncertain Crown. London, 1932.

Sheean, Vincent. An American Among the Riffi. New York, 1926.

—— Personal History. Garden City, New York, 1937.

Shinar, Pessah. "Abd al Qadir and Abd al Krim: Religious Influences On Their Thought and Action." Asian and African Studies, Vol. I, Annual of the Israeli Oriental Society. Jerusalem, 1965.

Silva, General Carlos de. General Millán Astray. Barcelona, 1956.

Spillmann, Georges. Du Protectorat à l'Indépendance, Maroc (1912–1955). Paris, 1967.

Stuart, Graham H. The International City of Tangier. 2d ed., Stanford, California, 1955.

Tangier Gazette, 1905–50.

Thomas, Hugh. The Spanish Civil War. London, 1961.

Tuchman, Barbara W. "Perdicaris Alive or Raisuli Dead." American Heritage, Vol. X, No. 5 (August 1959), pp. 18–21.

Turnbull, Patrick. The Hotter Winds. London, 1960.

Ullman, Joan Connelly. The Tragic Week: A Study of Anticlericalism in Spain, 1875–1912. Boston, 1968.

Ulloa Cisneros, Luis, et al. Historia de España. Vol. V, Barcelona, 1943.

Usborne, Vice Admiral C. V. The Conquest of Morocco. London, 1936.

Valdesoto, Fernando de. Francisco Franco. Madrid, 1943.

Van Paassen, Pierre. Days of Our Years. London, 1939.

Vivero, Augusto. El Derrumbamiento: la verdad sobre el desastre del Rif. Madrid, 1922.

Voinot, Colonel L. Sur les traces glorieuses des pacificateurs du Maroc. Paris, 1939.

Weisgerber, F. Au seuil du Maroc moderne. Rabat, 1947.

Welch, Galbraith. North African Interlude. New York, 1949.

Westermarck, Edward. Ritual and Belief in Morocco. 2 vols. Vol. II, London, 1928.

Wren, P. C. "The Life of Odo Klemmens," in Stories of the Foreign Legion. New York, 1929.

INDEX

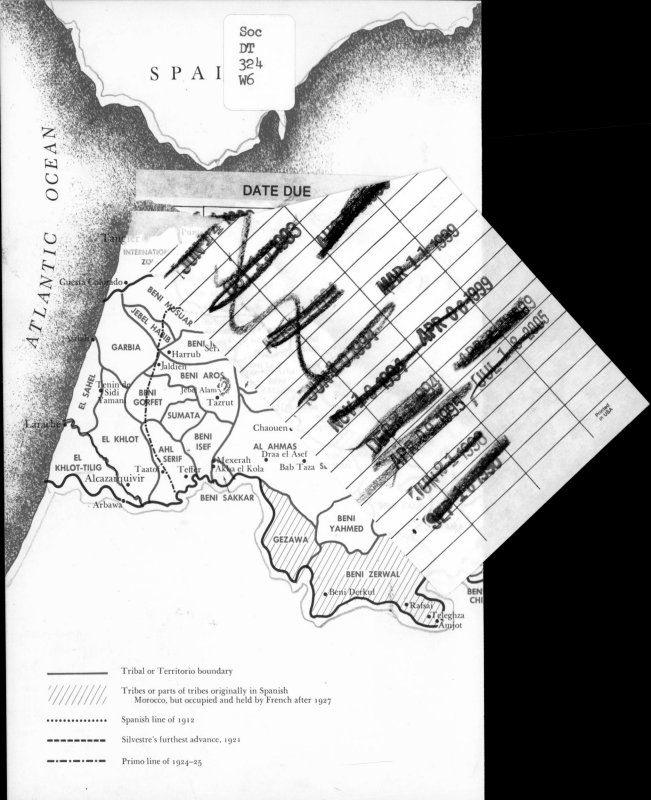

S P A I N

ATLANTIC OCEAN

Tangier
Cuesta Colorado
Asilah
INTERNATIONAL
ZONE
Punta

BENI MOSUAR

JEBEL HABIB

GARBIA

BENI
Harrub
Jaldien

Seri

BENI AROS
Jebel Alam
Tazrut

EL SAHEL

BENI
GORFET

SUMATA

Chaouen

Larache

EL KHLOT

BENI
ISEF

AL AHMAS
Draa el Asef

AHL
SERIF

EL
KHLOT-TILIG

Taatof
Alcazarquivir

Teffer

Mexerah
Akba el Kola

Bab Taza

Arbawa

BENI SAKKAR

GEZAWA

BENI
YAHMED

BENI ZERWAL

Beni Derkul

Rafsai
Teleghza
Amjot

BENI
CHI

——————— Tribal or Territorio boundary

///////// Tribes or parts of tribes originally in Spanish
           Morocco, but occupied and held by French after 1927

············· Spanish line of 1912

- - - - - - Silvestre's furthest advance, 1921

-·-·-·-·-· Primo line of 1924–25